A MEMOIR WITH RECIPES

STIRRING IT UP

with

MOLLY IVINS

Ellen Sweets

FOREWORD BY LOU DUBOSE

UNIVERSITY OF TEXAS PRESS ✦ AUSTIN

*This book was supported in part with
a gift from Lowell Lebermann, Jr.*

Requests for permission to reproduce material
from this work should be sent to:
Permissions
University of Texas Press
P.O. Box 7819
Austin, TX 78713-7819
http://utpress.utexas.edu/index.php/rp-form

The paper used in this book meets the minimum requirements
of ANSI/NISO Z39.48-1992 (R1997) (Permanence of Paper). ∞

LIBRARY OF CONGRESS CATALOGING-IN-PUBLICATION DATA

Sweets, Ellen, 1941–
Stirring it up with Molly Ivins : a memoir with recipes / Ellen Sweets ;
foreword by Lou Dubose. — 1st ed.
p. cm.
Includes indexes.
ISBN 978-0-292-72265-1 (cloth : alk. paper)
1. Ivins, Molly. 2. Women journalists—United States—Biography. 3. Cooking.
4. Cooking, American. 5. Sweets, Ellen, 1941– I. Dubose, Lou. II. Title.
PN4874.I92S84 2011
070.92—dc22
[B]
2011016693

FRONTISPIECE
People-watching and community chats were in order at the 2005 Sesquicentennial celebration in
Martindale, Texas. From left, David Butts and Mercedes Peña engage one another in conversation
while I watch the world go by and Molly holds her own tête-à-tête with an unidentified woman.
Photo courtesy of Joe Pinelli.

ISBN 978-0-292-75423-2 (pbk. : alk. paper)

doi:10.7560/722651

Stirring It Up with Molly Ivins

*Dedicated to
Hannah,
the* Texas Observer,
*and
ACLU families
everywhere*

Cooking is like love.
It should be entered into with
abandon or not at all.

HARRIET VAN HORNE
Vogue, October 15, 1956

Contents

Foreword

Lou Dubose

SOME YEARS BACK, MOLLY WAS HOLDING forth at the head of a long table at McCormick & Schmick's on Congress Avenue when I noticed that Adam Clymer's menu was on fire. Adam was midway down a table of twenty-one diners, just close enough to Molly to follow one of her long riffs on Texas politics and too close to a candle on the table.

Adam is the quintessential *Times*man—former editor of the *Harvard Crimson*, arid sense of humor on good days, hard facts, reasoned analysis, and all that. He's the *New York Times* reporter Dick Cheney called a "world-class asshole."

Molly adored him. Adam, that is.

Just in from Washington and travel-weary, Adam was the final arrival at a dinner party that had grown exponentially as waiters added tables—all on Molly's tab. (Molly would part ways with McCormick & Schmick after I told her its owners had tried to eliminate the minimum wage for waiters in Oregon and bankrolled Republican campaigns.) On this Friday night in December, however, she turned the restaurant's large dining room into her salon. Anyone lucky enough to be there—including Molly's "Chief of Stuff," Betsy Moon; Liz Carpenter, Lady Bird Johnson's former press secretary; omnivorous state representative Elliott Naishtat; *Texas Observer* publisher Charlotte McCann; Jane's Due Process founder Susan Hays; Fox newsgirl Ellen Fleysher—was, well, lucky to be there.

I tried to get Adam's attention, but he was not to be distracted. So I removed the menu from his hand and smothered the flames with a clean dinner plate. It was no surprise that Adam missed his own fire. Molly was a marvelous performer. She performed on paper, eight hundred words, three times a week for four hundred newspapers, until breast cancer ended it.

She also performed in the kitchen, where she could whip up a remarkable lobster bisque or a perfect steak au poivre. She performed at the table, where conversations were fueled by good wine and good food, or beer, burgers, and barbecue. She loved cuisine, haute and not-so-haute, served up with conversation, high- or lowbrow.

Regarding the not-so-haute, Molly and I once planned a magazine piece that would describe a white-linen dinner built exclusively on the recipes we found in *The Ron Paul Family Cookbooks*. That's Ron Paul, the Libertarian obstetrician Republican congressman adored by gold bugs, Ayn Randers, and conspiracy theorists (anyone who believes right-wing nuttiness isn't congenital might read up on the Kentucky Senate campaign of Dr. Paul's son Rand).

The cookbook has been filed away in my attic archives. But I recall ambrosia, a Spam recipe, Jell-O dishes, and green beans in cream of mushroom soup; it also had a Dream Whip dessert that I think required the crushing of Oreos. They embodied the congealed sixties-in-suburbia offerings that Johnny Depp's alien character found so utterly alien in the film *Edward Scissorhands*.

"We'll cook it. Alan Pogue will photograph it. Sweets will review it. And someone else will eat it," Molly said. Sometimes journalism requires sacrifices too great to bear.

I admit that I had misgivings about a book about cooking with Molly Ivins. It seemed that it was neither fish nor fowl, neither a cookbook nor a memoir. Yet the more I thought about it, the more the idea of a culinary memoir appealed to me.

Here's why: because she was a performer (she described herself as a professional Texan), Molly Ivins was a difficult person to know. Too often, even among large groups of friends, she was "in character" or "in voice." Molly's métier was that remarkable voice, appropriated from the gargoyles who pass for elected officials in Texas and from the decent elected officials who still speak in a genuine Texas idiom.

Yet there was much more to Molly than the public persona, as interesting and entertaining as it was. She was polyglot fluent, speaking Texan, Smith College English, and French. She was complex. She read broadly and deeply. She was loyal to a fault, often hiring a larger entourage of unemployed friends than did Elvis. She was an ardent Elvis fan and loved Jerry Lee Lewis enough to buy a piano she never learned to play in hopes of someday mastering "Great Balls of Fire."

It was in the kitchen and at the table with small groups of friends that Molly disarmed. It is Molly disarmed whom Ellen Sweets introduces to readers.

On the Sunday morning following the McCormick & Schmick dinner, Molly invited a group of about forty to brunch at Fonda San Miguel, an Austin Mexican restaurant that has cultivated a national following in the thirty-five years it's been in central Austin. The brunch at Fonda, an elaborate buffet of dishes you would have to travel to Oaxaca or Mexico City to find, was the end of a weekend celebrating the fiftieth anniversary of Molly's beloved *Texas Observer*, which continues kicking ass and taking names in a state where a substantial number of asses need kicking.

At one end of a long table, my wife and I sat with Adam Clymer. Adam wore a sport coat, a freshly laundered white shirt, and dress slacks. Because it was Sunday, he had forgone the tie and was wearing a Washington Nationals baseball cap.

At the other end of the table sat Molly, in a *Texas Observer* shirt and dark velour pants so worn they were weirdly iridescent. (I always considered her something of a sartorial felon.)

Adam was magisterial, quoting polls and attitudinal surveys that defined the insurmountable challenge that lay between then-Senator Barack Obama and the presidency, when the other end of the table erupted in laughter as Molly wrapped up a story.

"You know," Adam said with a smile, "she never fit in at the *Times*."

She didn't. But she found a home in four hundred smaller newspapers in smaller markets, where hundreds of thousands of readers isolated by geography and political beliefs devoured her columns. Those readers, who knew Molly on paper, will now get to know her in the kitchen.

Acknowledgments

I'M ETERNALLY INDEBTED TO MY PARENTS, Melba and Nathaniel Sweets. Before my mother died at the age of ninety-seven, I grudgingly but sincerely thanked her for all those red-pencil corrections she applied to everything I wrote, even after stuff had been published. She was often right, damn it all.

I'm grateful to my father for teaching me that the power of the printed word is something to be treasured and never taken lightly; that respect is earned, not conferred; and that if you drive into the back of another car it's always your fault.

When I said I was going to write a book, my brothers, Fred and Nathaniel Jr., shrugged and said, "Hey—cool; do we get free books?"

Committing to paper kitchen tales from Molly's big love—after family and journalism—would have been difficult, if not impossible, without assistance from friends who ate and/or cooked with and/or for her. I am one of the luckiest people ever to know such good people, not one of whom ever said, "Are you nuts? What do you know about writing a book?!" I said it to myself instead.

Thank you, Stu Wilk, who, as *Dallas Morning News* assistant managing editor, hired me. If I hadn't come to Dallas, I might never have met Molly, let alone become her friend.

The *Denver Post* deserves an appreciative mention, especially editor Greg Moore, who not only understood my sense of loss when Molly died but in 2009, for two and a half months, provided me with space to write a substantial portion of this book.

Reference librarians are almost always unsung heroes, but not here. I'm indebted to Cleora Hughes at the *St. Louis Post-Dispatch*, Darlean Spangenberger and Angelo Cortez at the *Dallas Morning News*, and Barb Hudson, Jan Torpy, and Vickie Makings at the *Denver Post* for their research assistance.

I owe a debt of gratitude to folks in Boulder, including Tracy and Michael Ehlers, who were Molly's Colorado hosts for several years, and Maura Clare, communications director for the University of Colorado's Conference on World Affairs. Molly loved the CWA, and it loved her right back, as evidenced by invitations returning her again and again and again.

A big fat *muchas gracias* goes to a supportive hometown posse in St. Louis— Harper Barnes and his wife, Rosanne Weiss; my other "sister," Rose Jonas, and her husband, Ed Finkelstein; Art and Gayla Hoffman; and former *Post-Dispatch* colleague Christine Bertelson, who, when I told her about the book, exclaimed, "Holy shit!" That's when I got scared.

I met Lewis and Phyllis Sank and Beth and Ravenel Curry when I moved to New Jersey in 1981. Both couples were generous with moral support, shelter, and dinner on several varying occasions. (My daughter and I moved around so much that once, when a classmate asked Hannah why we lived in so many different places, she told them we were in the witness protection program. Not bad for a ten-year-old! She made me proud.)

I must thank Austin friends who gave of their time, especially eagle-eyed copy editors Charlotte McCann and Kaye Northcott. Malcolm Greenstein and I went to dinner one night and reviewed pages of notes on flaws he extracted from the original manuscript.

What a mensch.

Without help from librarians at the Dolph Briscoe Center for American History at the University of Texas at Austin, where Molly's papers reside, this book would have serious holes. It might anyway, but it's not their fault. Andy and Carla Ivins saved many of Molly's cookbooks and shared them along with their collection of family photographs and food memories.

Finally a truly appreciative nod to the folks at UT Press: Allison Faust, my editor, who took a chance on me; copy editor Jan McInroy, who caught stuff, fixed it, and all the while made me feel good about my words; in-house manuscript editor Lynne Chapman, who pulled it all together; and expert proofreader Regina Fuentes.

To all I've mentioned and to those who might have been shortchanged, thank you, thank you, thank you.

Hillary Clinton was on the right track: it takes a village to write a book.

Stirring It Up with Molly Ivins

1

Meeting Molly

PEOPLE OFTEN ASK HOW I MET MOLLY and how we became friends. And I always say the same thing: our meeting was an indirect consequence of missing the newsroom.

I'm a Midwesterner who grew up in a newspaper family. My father owned the *St. Louis American*, a black weekly in Missouri, and my mother was an editor and columnist. Ink in the blood and all that.

It's also altogether possible I became a reporter in part because I was born nosy. Reporting is one of the few jobs where you get to ask people all sorts of personal stuff and more often than not, by God, they'll tell you. Maybe I could have done that as a cop or a federal agent, but neither of those professions would have had me. Trust me.

Unfortunately, as a single parent I needed to earn enough to put my kid through college. When it transpired that she was seriously smarter than I, I went in search of a more substantial salary to subsidize whatever college she got into. Through a friend I learned of job openings for ex-reporters at Bell Laboratories, AT&T's former research and development arm. Equally unfortunately, I later learned that in corporate America, when you do a good job at something, you probably will be promoted. And when you get promoted, you get new bosses. Some are good and you want to work with them forever. When you get to the other ones, it's perfectly acceptable to look elsewhere.

If you're really dumb, you take a job someplace you've never been, earning a whole lot less, redeemed only by the fact that your kid is out and on her own and you're having a good time being paid to be nosy. I sailed from a cushy corporate port in a Fortune 100 company back into the turbulent waters of the Fourth Estate. I missed newsroom insanity, so in 1989 I hired on as an editor at the *Dallas Morning News.*

Loved my work at the paper. Dallas? Not so much. It just didn't feel like a good match. Endowed with a job I liked in a town I didn't, and locked into a contract that said moving expenses had to be repaid if a new employee departed within a year of hire, I embarked on a quest for kindred spirits. The search ended several months later, in November 1990, when, thanks to the transfer of my ACLU membership, I got invited to a Jefferson Day dinner honoring Ken Gjemre, founder of Half Price Books. It was to be moderated by a spunky woman reporter whose work I had admired over the years. Her name was Molly Ivins.

I sent a check and marked my calendar. As a reporter, and therefore theoretically a neutral purveyor of information, I wasn't supposed to belong to the ACLU at all, but hey, the membership had been paid in full in my former corporate life. Finally, in the interest of full disclosure, I must here confess that as an intrepid reporter I am fearless; but walking cold into a social situation where I know no one, oh dear.

If it hadn't been for the movie *The Princess Bride,* I might never have met Molly up close and personal. What, you might reasonably ask, does that have to do with anything? Well, this: near the end of the movie, Mandy Patinkin's Spanish character, Inigo Montoya, has long been searching for the six-fingered man who murdered his father. Montoya finally finds the homicidal villain and at last is able to speak the mantra that has sustained him through the long, circuitous journey to this, his adversary's final swashbuckle. As hero faces down dastardly bad guy, Montoya repeats the phrase that has guided him lo these many years: "Hello; my name is Inigo Montoya. You keel my father. Prepare to die."

Borrowing from the first part of the mantra and modifying the rest, I sallied forth. En route to the entrance to where the ACLU shindig was to be held, I kept repeating to myself, "Hello; my name is Ellen Sweets. I just moved here and I don't know a soul." Seated on a stone bench outside the entry door was a rather substantial woman extracting a few final drags from a Marlboro Light. As she picked up the pack, I launched into my spiel. She looked up, nodded and smiled as she shook my proffered hand, and replied in that unmistakably resonant voice of hers: "Well, hello thay-uh, Ellen Sweets," she intoned. "Mah name is Molly Ivins." Just like that, the woman I had hoped to at least speak with after the dinner was speaking to me. Her columns had been generating serious buzz for a quite a while; a book based on them was due out any minute. And there she was, seated outside, waiting to meet me. *The Princess Bride* had worked its magic.

She squished her cigarette in the adjacent sand-filled stone ashtray, took my arm, and escorted me in to the dinner, allowing as how, although she couldn't invite me to join her table because she was seated with the honoree, she would park me with friends. After dinner and some lighthearted speechifying, Molly, her friends John and Susan Albach, and I adjourned to a nearby piano bar for drinks. Midway through my second vodka martini, I learned that Susan was from Short Hills, New Jersey, and a graduate of Kent Place School in Summit. I had lived in Summit, and my daughter graduated from Kent Place exactly twenty years after Susan.

So far, not bad.

It was my first internally uttered "thank you" to Miz Ivins. I had met two of her friends and found common ground. More introductions were to come. If it hadn't been for Molly, who knows if I'd have met the Albachs, who introduced me to Betsy Julian and Ed Cloutman, a husband-wife tag team of extraordinary legal talent—having been the minds behind almost all of Dallas's significant voting rights, housing, and school desegregation cases starting in the 1970s and continuing through the 1980s and well into the 1990s. It's worth noting that their son, Edward IV, a graduate of Baylor University Law School, is following in their footsteps with a plaintiff's litigation practice, including civil rights. Such are the people Molly called "friends."

With those initial introductions, more followed. Through the Cloutmans I met Linda and Steve Anderson, who could always be counted on to have fine food and fabulous gatherings at their Dallas home. In addition to being an attorney, Steve was an excellent cook and Linda was an exuberant hostess. Steve and Linda have since gone their separate ways, but Molly spoke often and fondly of Steve's paella and Linda's hospitality. Steve's sister, Austin artist Courtney Anderson, became a confidante and one of Molly's closest friends.

When Molly and I weren't railing against some aspect of social injustice, we talked about food, from farming and ranching to organics and free trade to the joys of foie gras, vichyssoise, and red beans and rice, prompting a detour to discussing foods that provoke flatulent responses from the average digestive system and thereby providing irrefutable proof that Molly was as capable of lowbrow conversation as the next ten-year-old. She could hold forth on almost anything, and it seemed that the more obtuse the subject matter, the more she relished it, although there was nothing obtuse about her love of pork—be it ribs, chops, roast, or tenderloin.

We talked about food as memory, authoritatively and with no scientific data whatsoever, placing the blame for family breakdowns squarely on the fact that so few families sit down and eat together anymore. We shared remembrances of little details, like when we learned how to set the table, how brothers and sisters took turns screwing up the placement of knife on the right and fork on the left, and how nobody ever wanted to load or empty the dishwasher despite the fact that it relieved us of having to wash dishes by hand.

She called me a liar when I told her about *The White Trash Cookbook* and how I owned both volumes and had actually found a recipe for an onion sandwich that I made and loved. My father loved them too: thin-sliced Bermuda onion, Miracle Whip (*not* mayonnaise), and lots of black pepper between two slices of Wonder Bread constitute heaven on a plate. You could gussy it up with a slice or two of tomato, but the basics worked just fine, thank you very much. For some reason this prompted a segue into why Americans ate so much bad food. In the mid-1990s she saw food issues as a neglected component of a serious social narrative. By then I had moved from editing to reporting to being a food writer. I began to focus more on food beyond its value as joy and sustenance, trends and recipes. I thought more about how corporate marketing foisted food-like substances on us, how we fell for it, and how the more we fell for it and the more sedentary we were, the fatter and sicker we got. If you wanted to elicit one of those wonderful Molly sneers, all you had to do was mention Archer Daniels Midland, Cargill, or Monsanto—especially insanely litigious Monsanto.

How I wished she could have lived to meet Robyn O'Brien, the feisty writer, born in Texas but living in Colorado. She wrote a remarkable book called *Unhealthy Truths*, about how additives and chemicals and hormones in livestock have combined to promulgate allergies and mysterious ailments in children. Like Molly, she came from well-heeled Houston social stock; like Molly, she could rattle off the ironic ways in which corporate agriculture is not necessarily food-friendly and how Frankenfoods are making us fat and sick.

Molly, who stood an inch or so over six feet, fought an often losing battle with her weight. I had long since abandoned my struggle, along with the amphetamines that were supposed to curb my appetite but made me crazy instead. On food-filled Austin weekends we pretty much settled for just eating good stuff—food free of pesticides, additives, preservatives, artificial colors, nitrates, and nitrites. Well, except for red velvet cake, bacon, and smoked sausage. Hebrew National made the hot dog cut.

Once Molly's health became fragile she paid even more attention to what we ate, almost always buying organic or at least preservative-, hormone-, and additive-free foods. (To enhance the value of appreciating this newfound commitment, you might want to read at least a couple of chapters of *Bushwhacked*, the book Molly and Lou Dubose published in 2001. He and Molly coauthored three books altogether. Revisit how Bush dismantled proposed Clinton-era safeguards that would have expanded food inspection and tightened USDA regulations. Pay particular attention to the word *listeria*, and hope this particular food-borne bacterial infection never gets close to you or anyone you care about.

Mercifully, First Lady Michelle Obama has taken up the healthy-food sword and has led a national charge into battle against bad food, moving many communities to take a long, hard look at what they feed themselves.

By the time Molly's health took its worst turn, neither she nor I was counting calories. Instead of trying to lose weight, it was important for her to gain as that hateful duo of cancer and chemo took its toll. We took great pride, however, in knowing that almost every pound we carried was free of high-fructose corn syrup, monosodium glutamate, red dye #5, and yellow dye #3. In truth, most of the time we spent a lot more time eating than we did intellectualizing and deconstructing food's sociopolitical underpinnings. Relentless examination of American food flaws can really wear you out. Eating is much more fun. Better to just get on with it.

It never occurred to either of us that we wouldn't have all the time in the world to get on with it, including a mountain of silly conversations.

2

Dining In, Dining Out

ALTHOUGH SECURE IN HER INTELLECTUAL ABILITIES, Molly was in fact quite shy—an aspect of her persona that few knew. With close friends she was able to privately be goofy to the point of convulsive laughter over the kind of stuff that, when conveyed to others, elicits a pained, stone-faced response as listeners seek to divine a kernel of anything approximating hilarity.

Some of us have experienced such a visage: midway through relating what seemed like a rip-roaringly funny event at the time, we see a perplexed look envelop the listener's face, a look that suggests it's best to wind down immediately. With a feeble, "Well, you had to have been there," your voice trails off in the hope that someone will pick up the conversational non-thread. We shared those too. For the longest time, Molly's favorite "Ellen is a doo-doo brain" story dated to the time she invited me to a Texas Book Festival gala, held the night before the festival's official opening. It was an impressive gathering of prominent writers and authors. I loved going to those things despite feeling like a fish out of water.

"Um, I'm a food writer," sounds so feeble when you're making small talk with the likes of, say, James K. Galbraith. So when I realized I had been pontificating about the glories of how bacon, sausage, and salt pork complemented various dried beans in a way smoked turkey never could, it was too late. I had no idea I was rattling on to a noted economist who was also the son of John Kenneth Galbraith—one of the twentieth century's foremost economists. I'm sure he was enthralled by my monologue about culinary relativism, and how

Boston baked beans were probably related to the Southern combination of ham hocks and navy beans. Bet he couldn't wait to get home and test both recipes.

There was an even better encounter before we were seated. Molly had been invited to the VIP cocktail party that preceded the seated dinner. Shortly after arriving at Austin's downtown Marriott Hotel, I released Molly from the responsibility of introducing me around. I knew our table number and we agreed to meet there. So there I was, having staked out a strategic spot to do what I love to do anywhere: watch people. After a while, I noticed a familiar face looking as though he might be people-watching too. So I summoned up the courage to engage him under the guise of going to the bar. He smiled. I smiled. I secured liquid fortification and headed toward the smiling man. I introduced myself and said he looked really familiar.

He nodded and smiled some more. I asked him if he lived in Austin. No, he said. He asked me if I lived in Austin, I told him no, I live in Denver, but I'm visiting a friend. He smiled. I smiled. I reiterated my feeling that I'd seen him before. Maybe, he said. So being as I'm from St. Louis I thought maybe I knew him from there. And as I asked him if he was from the Gateway to the West, Molly saw me and walked in our direction. He perked up and greeted her by name.

"Ah, Sweetsie," she said, invoking the nickname she conferred on me from time to time, "I see you've met my friend Salman Rushdie." At that point I prayed for a hole to swallow me and to do so quickly. Molly dined out on that story for weeks. I mean, shoot, it's not like I didn't say I knew his face from *somewhere*. . . . It certainly broke me of ever again suggesting that I might recognize people because I thought they were from St. Louis.

I liked that I could make Molly laugh. Through alternating waves of internal smiles gleaned from silly and somber moments and bone-deep sadness, I kept returning to food memories and decided they are a good way to remember people you care about.

The notion of creating a chronicle of cooking with Molly probably began percolating when Bonnie Tamres-Moore and her husband, Gary Moore, approached me during the 2007 Texas Book Festival. I was part of a panel discussion about Molly, which had been held in the same church where her memorial service had drawn standing-room-only mourners only ten months earlier.

Fellow panelists held forth with all manner of erudite observations. I was sandwiched between Lou Dubose and author and humorist Roy Blount Jr., and award-winning documentary filmmaker Paul Stekler was the fourth panelist.

They addressed the hows and wherefores of research; engaging an audience through the deft use of humor; and the importance of historical accuracy. All I could talk about was cooking with Molly. I realized after the session that hardly anyone knew she was an outstanding cook and as clever in the kitchen as she was on the page. Only a small band knew. Food stories slid into conversation sideways if at all.

I had found a parking space just in front of the church, and the Moores and I stood talking for a while. They insisted that people would be interested in knowing more about Molly's kitchen skills. I thanked them for their kind comments. They gave me a cooking game they had just bought called Food Fight. I thanked them again and went back to Denver. A year later I realized they were onto something I hadn't considered.

Anthony Zurcher, who for nine years was Molly's editor at Creators Syndicate (the outfit that made it possible for readers across the country to read her), was frequently in touch with Molly and shared intermittent lunches. Her destination of choice was almost always the Eastside Cafe.

"Whenever we went there someone always knew her," he said. "Molly was great at holding court, being warm and generous with her time. After I moved to California I returned to Austin periodically and usually took her to lunch. Once she asked me if lunch was coming out of my pocket or Creators'. When I said it was on the company, she laughed and said, 'Well, in that case let's have dinner at Jeffrey's [a high-dollar, white-linen Austin restaurant popular with local powerbrokers]!'"

Like others, Zurcher attended many end-of-the-month gatherings held for years at Molly's house. Known as Final Friday, it was a catchall, salon-hootenanny-ribald-poetry-laced kind of evening generously endowed with beer and food, sometimes in that order. "Mostly I remember casseroles and tamales and salsa and queso and chips on award plaques she used as trivets," he added.

Donna Shalala, former US secretary of Health and Human Services who is now president of University of Miami, tells of the time she and Molly were on a fishing trip. No one was catching anything.

"Suddenly we saw a big dead fish and Molly got the idea to hook it on the line, pull it out of the water, and pretend we'd caught it," she said. "Immediately someone suggested we cook it that night. We looked at one another and it promptly 'fell' off the hook and back into the water. Later, at a going-away party for her, we actually brought a great big *live* fish and put it in her bathtub. She hooked it, pulled it out of the water, and killed it—but this time we did cook and eat it."

As I offered recollections of playing in the kitchen, Keystone Kops grocery-shopping expeditions, zany epicurean escapades, and Molly's impressive culinary skills, friends offered their stories or told me about someone else with a story to tell. As word of the book spread, food dominoes began to fall.

3

Who, Me? No Way!

WRITING A BOOK ABOUT COOKING WITH MOLLY was nowhere on my horizon. I was still mourning her death. It felt unseemly. Writing a book felt too much like capitalizing on a friendship, not to mention way too much work. Plus, I've always been suspicious of tell-all tomes that pop up within femtoseconds of a famous person's demise. She wasn't "famous" to me; she was my friend. I was still dealing with the fact that, as in years past, I had planned to be with her on my birthday. She died on the afternoon of January 31, 2007. On February 1 I would turn sixty-six, sharing double digits with my favorite highway.

Clearly, since you're reading this, you can tell that the Moores planted the seed of an idea. Over a two-year germination period the idea grew, blooming in a clichéd movie moment. In late winter 2009 I sat bolt upright in bed in the middle of the night and thought: of course—a Molly cookbook.

Not a cookbook kind of cookbook, but one built around memories from people who knew her and her fondness for good food; people who, like me, had cooked with her, eaten with her, shared stories and told tales around a dinner table of comestibles consumed during somber discourse, raucous laughter, big fat Texas lies, or some permutation thereof. Such stories were legion, moving many of her fans to echo one another: "Wouldn't Molly have a field day with Sarah Palin's particular brand of nuttiness? or Glenn Beck's? or Michele Bachmann's?"

Never mind John Edwards's; there's a child involved there, so it's anybody's guess how she would have handled that—but she would have written a nice eulogy for Elizabeth Edwards, who died of breast cancer in 2010. I truly believe she'd have had a field day with the bombshell dropped on Mark Souder, the eight-term family-values Indiana Republican whose television "interview" on sexual restraint was conducted by a woman who just happened to be his mistress. He stepped down shortly after that dark matter came to light. As Molly often said, you can't make this stuff up.

Closer to home, she for sure would gleefully have pounced a couple of years ago on the Associated Press revelation that anti-tax conservative state representative Joe Driver, a Republican from the Dallas suburb of Garland, thought it was "perfectly appropriate" to double-bill the state *and* his campaign coffers for more than $17,000 in personal expenses incurred on high-dollar travel. She for sure would have toasted Gary Cobb, the lead attorney who successfully prosecuted former Texas representative Tom DeLay, who was convicted in 2010 for money laundering and conspiracy to commit money laundering.

Molly's Austin universe was such that I decided to limit my focus almost exclusively to her local cadre, who, for the most part, were within a thirty-mile radius of her Travis Heights home. It only made sense that, given her progressive, populist proclivities, feisty Julia Child—another Smith "girl" and a classmate of Molly's mother, Margot—would be one of Molly's heroes. Molly didn't rattle easily, but she came as close as she needed to when Julia Child turned up at one of Molly's book signings in San Francisco. It lent a new definition to a smile lighting up one's face.

Molly's sister, Sara Maley, remembers Molly's Julia Child cookbooks as treasures. "Mother had given us the usual Rombauer and Becker books [*The Joy of Cooking*] and we used them, but the last summer I lived at home, our parents were in Europe and Molly and I cooked together. I must have been twenty-two and she was twenty that summer. Ordinarily Mom did all the cooking, but Molly had spent a year in France and learned a lot. She was cooking out of Julia Child's books before anybody else we knew. She had all these recipes underlined, with comments in the margins. I just remember lots of butter and lots of pastry."

Patricia Wells's *Simply French* was another of Molly's favorites. It is dog-eared, grease-spattered, well-marked, and in several places just plain falling apart. From these pages came her fabulous cheese and bacon potato cake, a perfectly herb-roasted chicken, a luscious veal stew with spring vegetables, sea scallops with fresh ginger sauce, and a cool summer gazpacho.

Molly's lifelong love affair with Paris began with this 1961 visit to France as part of her high school junior year abroad, where her class at the Ecole du Montcel visited the Supreme Headquarters Allied Powers Europe (SHAPE). She is in the first row, third from left. Official SHAPE photograph by SP-4 L. Harmon, SHAPE Pictorial Section.

4

Meeting Multiple Mollies

ALMOST EVERYONE KNEW A SIDE OF MOLLY, but it wasn't until a bunch of us were sitting around a dinner table (of course) that we began to deconstruct the many facets of Mary Tyler Ivins: writer, loyal and loving sister, devoted aunt, raconteur, rugged outdoors aficionado, accomplished cook and skilled baker, and music lover, as long as it didn't include too much grand opera, except for a few warhorse choruses and Luciano Pavarotti's "Nessun Dorma." She said opera beyond Gilbert and Sullivan made her flesh crawl and her toenails grow inward.

Molly's love affair with French gastronomy had its origins in her multiple visits to Paris (France, not Texas), including living there for a year as a student. French is scattered throughout these pages, primarily because when she described something she planned to cook, it was often in French, which she spoke fluently. It might have been "trout with almonds" to you, but it was *truite amandine* to her. The intersection of Molly and food is but one aspect of a multifaceted, complicated, kind, and very stubborn woman.

There was Pet Lover Molly, who lavished love and attention on her badly behaved dogs, showering them with the kind of forbearance and affection that she doubtless would have shown children had she had them. Even if you don't like dogs, you can't help but be impressed with the cunning of Athena, Molly's too-smart standard poodle, as the number of dressed ducks, destined for a dinner-party conversion to *canard a l'orange*, diminished proportional to each successive trip Athena made from the kitchen counter to her secret place at the bottom of Molly's heavily wooded backyard.

After a respectful mourning period following Athena's heartbreaking death due to cancer, Molly acquired Fanny Brice, another standard poodle every bit as pampered as Athena and almost as badly behaved.

Fondly remembered is Persistent Molly, who finally decided to treat herself to a month-long vacation in Paris. She left in mid-August 2001 and was due home in mid-September. On September 11 she experienced the day's horror from the European side of the Atlantic. Instead of accepting an embassy offer to fly her back to Texas, she did what good reporters do: she stayed and wrote about it, refusing to be cowed by one of this country's worst catastrophes.

Solitary Molly frequented the locally owned Austin Land & Cattle Company restaurant, often quietly accompanied by only a book. ALC is an old-school kind of family-owned steak house with superb food and outstanding service. She always sat at the same table and had the same server. Owner and general manager Theresa Mertens expressed the same sentiments voiced by restaurateurs and servers at Molly's other favorite haunts: they recognized her, but out of respect for her privacy, they left her alone.

She earned the family nickname "Mole" for being Voracious Reader Molly, who devoured books from all genres throughout her abbreviated life.

At her most relaxed was Chef Molly, who could reduce a kitchen to shambles in the course of assembling an exquisite clafouti—the fresh cherries having been first addressed by her handy-dandy cherry pitter. She loved kitchen gadgets.

If you've never been camping on one of the scenic rivers of Texas, grab a longneck and float along with Outdoors Molly and the guys—and there were almost always more men than women on these sojourns. Join the unofficial camp cookout at Bob Armstrong's ranch in the Texas Hill Country.

It would be disingenuous to ignore Tippler Molly, whose affinity for wine and beer is not classified information. Eddie Wilson, founder of the late, great Armadillo World Headquarters, and now proprietor of Threadgill's World Headquarters, doesn't remember meals with Molly, but in his inimitable curmudgeonly way, recounts "knocking back a whole buncha beers" with her. When friends suggested naming a library for her as a long-lasting memorial tribute, he suggested instead a mobile library and bar that served beer on tap.

Most people knew Molly only as a keen observer of the sociopolitical scene, highly ranked in a hierarchy populated by similarly astute observers of the human condition—H. L. Mencken, Mark Twain, and Will Rogers, or, more recently, writers Calvin Trillin and Garrison Keillor, and political cartoonists Ben Sargent and Garry Trudeau, who once paid homage to Molly by reiterating her characterization of former president George W. Bush as "all hat and no cattle."

Author and columnist Jim Hightower was a friend and confidant whose unwavering commitment to populist causes forged a strong bond with Molly's progressive politics. Both trained watchful eyes on corporate and political shenanigans. He continues to do so through books, columns, and lectures.

Hightower, like Molly, was a veteran of the *Texas Observer*. Unlike Molly, though, he did hard time in government service, most notably as a legislative aide to the late senator Ralph Yarborough, an endangered species known as a Texas liberal. Hightower also served as state agriculture commissioner, advocating for sustainable farming, organic foods, and small farms long before it was fashionable. He is unsparing in his denunciation of independents, observing that "there's nothing in the middle of the road but yellow stripes and dead armadillos"—a bromide that became the title of one of his books.

Left to right: Paul Krugman, Jim Hightower, and Molly. Photo by Alan Pogue.

Hightower also has his own way with catchphrases, as demonstrated in an interview with Bill Moyers during Moyers's farewell PBS program in 2010. Over a fifteen-minute time span Hightower characterized wavering Democrats as "weaker than Canadian hot sauce"; credited Republican Texas governor Rick Perry with having "put the goober in gubernatorial"; and, citing corporate arrogance coupled with influential lobbying efforts, said, "They think they're the top dogs and we're the fire hydrants."

It was this facility for uniting pithy commentary with razor-sharp wit that forged a bond between Molly and Hightower. It's a fitting tribute to her that when Sarah Palin silliness bubbled to the surface during the 2008 Republican presidential campaign, a frequently heard refrain was, "God, wouldn't Molly have had a field day covering *this* convention."

When Houston swindler Allen Stanford's billion-dollar scam imploded—following the collapse of Bernard Madoff's multibillion-dollar Ponzi scheme—the lament became, "God, if only Molly were here to write about this."

And what about that panoply of philandering goody two-shoes who surfaced after Molly slipped the surly bonds of earth—not to mention the bizarre 2010 Supreme Court decision that essentially established a corporation as a person, thereby freeing each greedy, power-hungry company with deep pockets to buy even more elections than its lobbyists had already purchased? Molly would have gleefully pounced on George Rekers, the homophobic founder of an organization that, among other efforts, seeks to "cure" homosexuality. He was caught on a European vacation with a male companion secured through rentboy.com, a gay website.

Or with John Ensign, the not-so-honorable senator from Nevada and once-upon-a-time presidential hopeful who was banging his friend's wife? And Lordy, let's not forget South Carolina governor and presidential wannabe Mark Sanford, whose peccadilloes with an Argentinean woman not his wife introduced the term "hiking the Appalachian trail" to every late-night comedian's shtick in 2009? And, no, stupid behavior is not the exclusive purview of the Dems: Eliot Spitzer's dalliance with a hooker cost him his job too. The Repubs are just better at theological hypocrisy.

The heart aches for that too-soon-silenced Ivins raillery.

The more I considered the prospect of writing a book, the more I thought maybe a peek at another side of Molly would provide a momentary distraction from how much we still miss her singular political voice—a little lagniappe, as they say in Cajun country, to smooth the rough edges of loss.

Just maybe, I reckoned, it could be fun to share Molly stories from myriad friends, almost none of them household names but nonetheless an integral part of her substantial Rolodex. She never could remember anyone's address or telephone number, so well-worn cards detailing digits for friends and acquaintances were interspersed with names and numbers for cabinet members, governors, members of Congress, musicians, cabinetmakers, mechanics, and plumbers.

Molly, in her favorite purple plaid velour shirt, makes a serious political point while tackling the pasta special at Magnolia Cafe, a frequent South Congress dining destination.

5

The Molly Too Few Knew

LOTS OF FAMOUS FOLKS KNEW MOLLY, but not in the way her Austin crew did—the ones who gathered Saturday mornings at Polvo's, a South Austin Mexican restaurant where the food was decent, the prices were right, and from time to time folks actually got what they ordered more or less at the same time.

Gal pals were a solid component of the Molly menagerie. They were the ones who participated in potluck lunches, brunches, and dinners. Meals might be built around a recipe theme as arch as a Julia Child all-vegetable brunch or as lame as a repast of all-red foods. Some were camping compadres on trips that invariably included a canoe whose sole purpose was to haul beer.

At the other end of the spectrum were meticulously planned dinner parties for notables she rarely discussed and certainly never bragged about knowing. Even less well known were the aspiring writers she encouraged; the sons and daughters she counseled without ever tattling to their parents; the myriad friends who drove her to chemo treatments, overfilled her refrigerator with food, and sat with her when failing health laid her low.

These then are remembrances from the people Molly knew and who knew her best; who shared Sunday brunch at grandiose Fonda San Miguel; who protected her privacy when she stopped for breakfast at the considerably less-than-grandiose but much-favored Magnolia Cafe South (to distinguish it from its sister restaurant on the *other* side of town); or who chowed down with her at Hoover's, long Austin's only soul-food hash house.

Molly was equally at home fracturing Spanish at a taqueria, knocking back a snort on the Trio terrace at the Four Seasons Hotel, or using the proper utensils to deal with escargots at Jeffrey's, the upscale restaurant credited with introducing fine dining to Austin.

One of her favorite movie scenes in *Pretty Woman* occurs when Julia Roberts's character, unfamiliar with the technique for extracting a snail from its butter-and-garlic-laced shell, sends one flying across a room full of diners. The ever-astute maître d' catches and pockets the airborne escargot in midflight. It was the kind of deft maneuver that longtime Jeffrey's waiter Johnny Guffey could have easily accomplished.

He has taken orders and delivered meals to Jeffrey's tables for more than a quarter century. Over that time he's also served meals to his share of notables, but Molly was a favorite. "Being a Yellow Dog Democrat myself, she was always an idol," he says. "Her quips and quotes were always entertaining. Waiting on her was great fun because she always came in with interesting people, especially strong women.

"One time she walked in with Donna Shalala. There was a bunch of redneck Texas Republicans in that night and I could see that just Molly being there made them nervous. They were seated near her table and they all stood up and exchanged pleasantries. I kept thinking, 'Look at them; she has bigger balls than any of 'em.'"

Guffey frequently saw Molly as she dined solo at the Austin Land & Cattle Company, accompanied by her book of the moment. One evening she arrived as he was midway through his meal. As she sat alone at her favorite table, rather than run the risk of intruding, he quietly instructed her waiter to bring her tab to him. Guffey finished his meal, paid both tabs, and asked the waiter to simply tell her that her dinner had been a gift from an admirer. It's not known whether Molly ever determined his identity, but it was a measure of how she affected people around her. ALC owner and general manager Theresa Mertens says diners often did that for Molly. They knew who she was; they just chose to respect her privacy and leave her alone.

For some, a Molly-and-food book almost feels too small for her until you consider the kick-ass job she could do on a quiche Lorraine, creamy chilled cucumber soup, a robust coq au vin, or ratatouille. She bypassed chains to patronize local restaurants, large and small. She frequented the Magnolia, clad in jeans and her favorite purple plaid velour shirt, with a book or a friend, her mom or a group. I came to view that velour shirt as her version of a blankie. Utterly unconcerned with anything remotely resembling fashion sense, she wore it everywhere in cool weather.

Molly enjoyed a fat, juicy hamburger as much as she enjoyed properly prepared foie gras. On column days, after she finished writing she frequently headed to nearby Hill's Cafe for a medium rare Hickory Burger—a mound of nicely seared meat on a kolache roll, finished off with green leaf lettuce and sliced tomato.

Betsy Moon, Molly's right hand for the last six years of her life, steered clear on days when Molly had to write, but when she did appear, she usually arrived with food.

"On non-column days when I was heading her way I'd sometimes call ahead and ask if she wanted lunch," she says. One of her favorites was a sandwich called La Nicoise—what else?—from Texas French Bread. It was just white albacore tuna tossed with homemade vinaigrette and capers and served on focaccia with lettuce and tomatoes, but she loved it. If she took a fancy to you she would spring for a meal at McCormick & Schmick's Seafood Restaurant, at least until she found out they were big Republican donors; then she switched to Ruth's Chris Steakhouse."

Molly (center) at one of her (in)famous chili parties at her home in Denver, Colorado, during her tenure as Rocky Mountain bureau chief for the *New York Times*. She is flanked by Senator Tim Wirth (left) and a correspondent for *U.S. News & World Report*. Zeik Saidman photo.

6

Are You Feeling Chili?

MOLLY LOVED FOIE GRAS, RACK OF LAMB, tournedos, and roasted duck breast as much as the next food freak, but she was just as much at home whipping up a pan of jalapeño cornbread as accompaniment to a spicy bowl o' red. She served her chili in heavy, oversized blue-and-white bowls emblazoned with images of broncos, cowboys, and lassos.

A sincere chili aficionado, she clipped all manner of recipes for it, and even organized chili parties during her stint in Colorado as the *New York Times*'s Rocky Mountain bureau chief. *Denver Post* reporter Jack Cox, a longtime friend, still remembers the 1979 "First Annual Rocky Mountain Correspondents' Chili Cookoff," organized by Molly and Oklahoman Gaylord Shaw, who, the year before, had won a Pulitzer Prize for the *Los Angeles Times*. Her wry wit is again evident even in the flyer she mailed out to friends:

> Chili is a variety of nutriment invented by Canary Islanders and perfected by Texans, Oklahomans, and, some claim, others as well, for over a century. Its virtues include, but are not limited to curing trombonophobia, preoperative lobotomy complications, decreased mental alertness, antropomania, peptic ulcers, falling hair, fallen arches, ingrown toenails, in-law troubles, recession, apathy, frostbite, cynicism, pollution and acute sobriety.

As was often the case with Molly events, families and children were welcome. Jack brought his daughters, who are now adults. "[Molly] had a rent house in Denver, and we actually dug a pit and built a fire in the backyard," Jack recalled. "People were bustling around in the kitchen and Molly was giving orders. It was a kind of organized chaos." Chaos is a recurring theme where Molly and cooking are mentioned.

Her archives include dozens of recipes for one kind of chili or another—a festival version of Frank X. Tolbert's Chili, Neiman Marcus Chili, Senator Barry Goldwater's Fine Chili, Mrs. Lyndon Baines Johnson's Pedernales River Chili, and Louisiana Bayou Chili from US representative Lindy Boggs. There is also a recipe for Joe Cooper's Chili, whoever Joe Cooper might have been, with a note from Molly's mother informing Molly that it had taken her father two days to make it.

The invitation to "Ze Beeg Chili Cookoff" of '79 featured a guest list that could easily have been plucked from a "Who's Who" of Colorado Democrats, give or take a governor or two—John Echohawk, executive director of the Boulder-based Native American Rights Fund; Howard Higman, founder of the Conference on World Affairs at the University of Colorado (more about that later); Pat Schroeder, the first woman elected to the US House of Representatives from Colorado; and to affirm her egalitarian sensibilities, *Denver Post* reporter and noted contrarian Joe Sinisi was also part of the crowd.

"I have one of those memories where I remember stuff like Mickey Mantle's batting average in 1955, and a really good chili party," Sinisi said. "And she had a really good one when she had that little house down in Englewood [a close-in Denver suburb]. There were about thirty-five to forty people and the chili was good and spicy. It was a Saturday afternoon and there was a good mix of people, not just a bunch of media types but people who tended to be more interesting than a bunch of reporters. There was a table full of snacks and stuff. Nobody was gonna go home hungry.

"What really impressed was the fact that she had done all the cooking. Molly wasn't the type to have anything catered. And I remember thinking how cooking isn't something that people would ordinarily associate with her but there she was, being the gracious hostess."

She and I once had a chili cookoff of our own where she pitted her bowl o' red against mine, but, she insisted, the competition was nullified by the presence of beans in my version. As if that weren't bad enough, I intensified her horror by boiling spaghetti to create what was lovingly known in my hometown as "chili mac," made in most Midwestern places by piling chili onto a mound of macaroni or spaghetti and topping the whole mess with chopped onion and Cheddar cheese. Mind you, the St. Louis version isn't to be confused with Cincinnati chili, which is laced with cinnamon, for cryin' out loud. St. Louisans do have *some* standards.

There was no such nonsense as beans in the Ivins iteration. Barely tolerant of my ground pork and beef mixture, she had the butcher chop hers into little chunks. I was not permitted to see how much of what seasonings she put in hers, but at least we agreed that our respective pots needed to simmer for hours and rest overnight before they could be deemed fit for consumption. Of course, by the time mine was done she had already decided that, what with beans and spaghetti, the Sweets version was absolutely not ready for prime time. At least we agreed that the only acceptable beverage for the occasion was beer—as both an ingredient and a libation.

I knew how to make only three things in my post-college life, and I took them with me when I moved to New York City: chicken noodle soup, spaghetti with meat sauce (or semi-decent meatballs), and chili. I'd already made soup once and spaghetti twice for my newfound boyfriend, so it was time to feed him my other masterpiece. Somewhere down the line I learned that if you wanted to use black beans instead of red, it kinda spruced it up.

Black bean chili still triggers a retrospectively amusing moment in my culinary career, such as it is. It dates to my life in New York City. I lived on the sixth floor of an ancient apartment building in Harlem. As in any self-respecting old Manhattan high-rise, there were roaches. I lived on the seventh floor. The closer you were to the ground floor, the more of them there were—hateful little ovals on stumpy legs that scampered with remarkable speed up walls and across ceilings, especially ceilings in a tiny closed–up kitchen with a steaming pot of chili simmering below. Sometimes, steam makes cockroaches fall. The results can be unpleasant if the pot doesn't have a lid.

In a stockpot, without their legs clearly visible, they look a lot like black beans. Once alien ingredients impose themselves on a dish prepared on a severely restricted budget and under equally severe time constraints, starting over is not an option. Should you make the chili too soupy and need to reduce it by leaving the lid off for a protracted period of time, it is possible that scampering Norwegian cockroaches might fall into the steaming open pot. This can easily result in the addition of black beans with legs, a presence that lends a whole new meaning to "bon appetit."

Molly approached the making of chili with the same intensity she invested in snapper *en papillote*—and she was just as likely to serve the fancy fish to her gal pals as, say, to Pulitzer Prize–winning economist Paul Krugman. Now and then she would share a tidbit about a particular meal she prepared—but it was not because she had prepared it for a prominent federal judge; it was because she had dared to try it for the first time *and* serve it to a prominent federal judge. What I called her "show-off" meals were invariably from either *Simply French* or *Mastering the Art of French Cooking*.

MOLLY'S CHUNKY TEXAS CHILI

All this needs is beer and a hunk of jalapeño-Cheddar cornbread. Molly made her cornbread from scratch, but darned if I could find the recipe. I strongly recommend southernfood.com for ideas.

INGREDIENTS

1 tablespoon bacon drippings
3 yellow onions, chopped
1 large green bell pepper, chopped
2 celery stalks, chopped
4 garlic cloves, minced
3 pounds coarsely ground chuck
1 can beer
1 small can tomato sauce

4 tablespoons chili powder
1 tablespoon ground cumin
1 tablespoon dried oregano
1 large bay leaf
1 teaspoon dry mustard
2 cups beef stock
Salt and pepper to taste

DIRECTIONS

Heat bacon drippings in a heavy-bottomed stockpot and sauté onions, pepper, and celery until vegetables soften. Add chuck and stir until it browns. Add beer, tomato sauce, chili powder, cumin, oregano, bay leaf, mustard, and beef stock and bring to a boil. Lower heat and simmer, covered, about 2 hours. Check periodically to see if more liquid is needed. If so, add water. Check for seasoning. Just before serving, remove bay leaf. Serves 4 to 6.

★ ★ ★

ELLEN'S ST. LOUIS CHILI MAC

Like most soups and stews, this should be made the day before it is to be consumed, or at least 4 to 6 hours in advance. I make a mean jalapeño cornbread too, only mine is made by adding buttermilk instead of plain milk, 2 tablespoons grated Cheddar cheese, and chopped jalapeños to a package of Jiffy corn muffin mix. And if your arteries can take it, heat ¼ cup of bacon drippings to smoking in a cast-iron skillet before adding the cornbread mixture.

INGREDIENTS

3 tablespoons bacon grease
2½ pounds ground chuck
1½ pounds ground pork
3 large white onions, chopped
1 bell pepper, chopped
5 to 6 garlic cloves, chopped fine
   or put through a press
4 tablespoons chili powder
1 tablespoon paprika
1 teaspoon oregano
3 tablespoons ground cumin
1 8-ounce can tomato sauce

1 tablespoon Lea & Perrins
   Worcestershire Sauce
3 cups beef stock
1 12-ounce bottle of beer
2 15-ounce cans red (or black)
   beans, rinsed and drained
1 pound spaghetti, cooked
   according to package directions
   and drained
3 cups grated Cheddar cheese
2 cups finely chopped white onion
Sliced jalapeños (optional)

DIRECTIONS

In a heavy-bottomed stockpot, brown beef and pork in bacon grease. Add onions, bell pepper, and garlic and sauté until vegetables are soft. Add chili powder, paprika, oregano, and cumin and sauté for about 5 minutes. Add tomato sauce, Worcestershire sauce, beef stock, and beer. Cover and simmer for 45 minutes. Add beans and continue simmering for another 30 minutes. Remove lid and simmer for an additional 20 minutes or until reduced to desired consistency.

To serve, place some spaghetti in a shallow bowl, ladle chili on top, and finish with a heaping spoonful of cheese and a teaspoon or so of raw onions. Garnish with jalapeños if desired. Serves 6 to 8.

★ ★ ★

7

Julia Child Meets
Chicken-Fried Steak

I THOUGHT ABOUT MOLLY WHEN THE MOVIE *Julie & Julia* was released in 2009. When I told her about interviews I had done with Julia Child during my time as a food writer with the *Dallas Morning News*, she hung on every word. Mol loved it that Mrs. Child, while a guest at Dallas's Mansion on Turtle Creek, visited the kitchen where my daughter cooked and did so because she had heard there was a female chef in the kitchen. Molly got an even bigger laugh when I told of how I once encountered Mrs. Child in No Place, a local East Dallas neighborhood favorite that reflected the quirkiness of its owner, the late Matt Martinez.

No Place had an unlisted number. No window sign announced its existence, and nothing indicated that it served superb steaks in addition to the only one-pound smoked baked potato in town.

The point here is that early in the 1990s Matt arranged for No Place to serve chicken-fried steak, smoked mashed potatoes, and sautéed spinach to Julia Child. When she walked in, I was already there with my houseguest Catherine Sabbah, a French reporter visiting from Paris.

France.

Not Texas.

"My God, that's Julia Child," I said to Matt, trying to contain my childlike glee. He had known she was coming. "Yeah," he whispered back. "I can't introduce you because she already has an interview set up with another publication. I don't want her to think I tipped you off."

"That's okay," I replied. "If you can, tell her my guest is from France and I would like to introduce her." As he pondered the possibility, Catherine piped up and asked—a little louder than I would have liked—"But oo ees thees Zhu-lia?" Of course I was the one dying to say hello, and I had no shame about using Catherine as an excuse. Suddenly we were in a parallel universe: an American icon famous for introducing French food to the US was about to meet a French reporter who didn't know who Julia Child was. Julia recognized the accent, smiled and nodded. Matt, Catherine, and I smiled and nodded. The human bobbleheads of No Place.

Before Matt or I could say anything, Catherine moved to Mrs. Child's table and introduced herself. The two of them commenced nattering away in French. Julia, as she insisted on being called, was in Texas to promote the companion volume to her PBS series about master chefs cooking at home. Matt remembered the meal in detail because he introduced her to regional dishes. I talked to him before he died in 2009, and he shared his memories of the evening.

"Julia had never had chile con queso or chicken-fried steak," Matt said. "I did stuffed prawns with smoked garlic over my Indian rice—brown rice cooked with corn, broccoli, cauliflower, onions, and mushrooms. She also had a taste of our wild-boar sausage with smoked mashed potatoes. I'll always remember her response when I told her the sausage was low in fat. She said, 'Doesn't that defeat the whole point of eating sausage?'"

Today, Matt is gone and No Place is no more. Catherine is back in France, married with children and living in suburban Paris. If there is an afterlife and we're all reunited in it, I'd like to believe that by now Matt, Julia, and Molly have encountered one another.

Somewhere in the mysterious mind meld that not even neurosurgeons fully comprehend, dinner tables and home-cooked meals and groceries merge in that part of the cerebrum that unites the love of food with the love of friends and family. Our cooking together cemented a friendship in life, and here's hoping it moves all who read this to do more cooking for those they love.

MATT MARTINEZ'S CHICKEN-FRIED STEAK

I didn't grasp the concept of chicken-fried steak until I first had it, at Matt's restaurant. I became a hopeless fan: chicken-fried steak with cream gravy and mashed potatoes; with chili, cheese, onions, and jalapeños; with green chile sauce, Jack cheese, refried beans, and rice. By the way, you can use vegetable oil to make the cream gravy, but it won't taste the same.

INGREDIENTS

2 to 3 cups soft plain bread crumbs (1 cup all-purpose flour or ¼ of a 15-ounce box of saltine crackers—about 40 crackers—coarsely crushed, may be substituted for bread crumbs)

1 teaspoon salt

½ teaspoon pepper

1½ pounds ½-inch-thick sirloin, or flank steak, fat trimmed and cut into 6 portions, then flattened to about ¼ inch (ask your butcher to do this, or do it yourself by placing each piece between two pieces of heavy plastic wrap and pounding it with a meat mallet)

¾ to 1 cup buttermilk (½ cup milk and 2 large eggs whisked together may be substituted for buttermilk)

⅓ cup vegetable oil

6 (6-inch) corn tortillas (optional)

1½ cups shredded Monterey Jack cheese (optional)

Cherry tomato wedges, avocado slices, fresh cilantro, or sliced red jalapeño for garnish

Cream gravy (recipe follows)

DIRECTIONS

Combine bread crumbs, salt, and pepper in a large, shallow dish. Dredge steak pieces in bread-crumb mixture. Dip into buttermilk, and dip again in bread-crumb mixture.

Heat oil in a large skillet over medium-high heat until hot. If desired, add corn tortillas, one at a time, and cook until crisp. Drain, pressing between layers of paper towels.

Add steak patties to hot oil; cook 3 to 5 minutes on each side or until crisp. Remove from heat, reserving 3 tablespoons drippings if making cream gravy. Drain steak patties on paper towels.

Place steak patties on tortillas, if desired. Top with sauce of your choice and sprinkle with cheese, if desired. Broil 5 inches from heat (with oven door partially open) until cheese melts. Garnish, if desired. Serves 6.

★ ★ ★

CREAM GRAVY

INGREDIENTS

3 tablespoons reserved chicken-
fried steak pan drippings

3 tablespoons all-purpose flour

1½ cups milk

½ teaspoon salt

¼ teaspoon pepper

DIRECTIONS

Cook drippings in a heavy-bottomed skillet over medium heat until hot; add flour, stirring until smooth. Stir continuously until light golden brown. Gradually stir in milk; cook, stirring constantly, until thickened and bubbly. Stir in salt and pepper.

★ ★ ★

Molly at the iconic Threadgill's, an Austin eatery that was another of her favorites. Here she chats up Roy Stanley of Tyler, who "won" lunch with Molly at a *Texas Observer* fund-raiser. Photo by Alan Pogue.

8

Mise en Place

(MISE EN PLACE: A FRENCH TERM THAT MEANS "everything in its place." As in having ingredients ready for use in meal preparation.)

Before one can cook, one must shop. With Molly, grocery shopping was as much an expedition or excursion as it was a utilitarian exercise.

In advance of rattling pots and pans, we would plan a menu and reconnoiter the pantry and refrigerator. Molly rarely kept frozen food other than ice cream, preferring to buy and prepare foods fresh—and this was several years before Michael Pollan, Eric Schlosser, and Marion Nestle admonished us to do so on a national stage.

We'd make a grocery list, divide it in half, leave for the store, and forget the list. Before we boarded Bob, her well-dented forest-green pickup truck, the conversation tended to go something like this:

Molly: "You got the list?"

Ellen: "No, you put it in your purse."

M: "No, I handed it to you because I had to lock the door/let the dog out/let the dog in/pee/answer the phone/find my wallet."

E: "No, I'm telling you, I don't have it. You must have put it down somewhere."

M: "Would you please just look in your goddamn purse and see if it's there?"

E (producing the list): "Oh."

M (shaking her head): "Jesus Christ."

With luck running right, this conversation occurred in the driveway or just a few blocks from the house. For whatever reason, the longer the list, the more likely it was to be left. Even more probable was the likelihood of returning without some singularly crucial ingredient—usually the one that had triggered the need to shop in the first place. Take, for example, the time we decided to do a menu that concluded with a Key lime pie. Back from one of those extended shopping excursions that had been undertaken primarily to buy Key limes, there followed a brief conversation along the lines of:

E: "Where are the limes?"

M: "They must be in that bag."

E: "They're not here. It's gonna be problematic, making a Key lime pie with no Key limes."

M: "Sheesh. They were on your part of the list."

E: "Nope. You had produce, protein, and wine. I had canned goods, spices, nuts, and chips. I remember."

M: "Shit."

This consistently favored exclamation applied to minor irritations. Strong expletives were assigned to the major stuff, usually reactionary Republicans, most Fox "news" commentators, or knuckleheads in the state legislature.

Molly and I loved supermarkets, especially the inner aisles. Any seasoned shopper will tell you this is such a bad idea, especially for those given to impulse buying. She liked to see what was new on the shelves. Never mind whether it was on the list, belonged on the list, or was even on the menu. Molly and me shopping for food was like what shopping for shoes must have been for Imelda Marcos.

We once counted how many different brands of Dijon mustard occupied a shelf. Another time we set out to do a meal of grilled asparagus, chicken, and ribs, with potato salad, but ended up buying hot dogs, bratwurst, hot links, relish, pickles, buns, and sauerkraut because there were so many mustards that we decided to try as many of them as we deemed worthy. Dijon dominated. Next came Jack Daniel's horseradish. How wrong can you go with anything from Black Jack?

I once gave Molly a gift pack of mustards from the Mount Horeb Mustard Museum just because she called me a liar when I told her there really was such a thing. She still had some of the jars left a few months later. So out came the green peppercorn-, garlic-, vodka-, champagne- and beer-flavored mustards. The Walla Walla onion mustard with bacon was all gone, as was the Stonewall Kitchen version with blue cheese and herbs, which she said was great with celery and carrot sticks.

How I'd love for her to see today's mustard invasion: honey-balsamic, brown sugar and pecan, horseradish and maple, Merlot and chocolate, orange-espresso, wasabi-sake. This is not to mention such concoctions as Dijon with black truffle, Tulocay's Tomato Vodka Mustard with Celery Seed, or root beer mustard. I am not making these up. If you don't believe me, Google the Mount Horeb Mustard Museum and see for yourself. It's in Wisconsin. And it's okay to doubt. Remember—she did too until she got her gift pack.

We also had great fun in the fresh meat section, although Molly demurred, especially after the Case of the Uncontrollable Giggles.

We were in the oversized Whole Foods Market on Sixth Street. I couldn't find smoked andouille, a Cajun sausage critical to gumbo. (Yes, you can use other smoked sausages, but they really aren't the same and probably don't have the same ingredients, but you probably don't want to know anyway. Really.) I made the mistake of telling a "store associate" that I wanted the real deal, the kind of andouille that comes out of Louisiana, a garlicky, spicy, smoked pork sausage. (Whole Foods doesn't have stackers or sales clerks; it has "associates.") I was willing to temporarily sacrifice health to maintain the integrity of this Louisiana classic.

Lordy, what was I thinking, here in the shrine to all things natural, organic, and frighteningly expensive, that there should be a smoked sausage, loaded with nitrates, nitrites, and heaven only knows what else? I wanted to defend myself against this heartfelt homily, to let him know it was only this one time, truly, and that I absolutely didn't—did *not*—make a habit of ingesting processed foods with additives like nitrites and nitrates. Truly. By the time he completed his tutorial on why I wouldn't find *smoked* andouille sausage polluting this temple of food purity, I felt giggles welling up from that part of me that is still ten years old. He was so sincere, so earnest, so, so, right.

As any Cajun worth his boudin (a popular Cajun sausage) can tell you, there are times when calories, cholesterol, and nitrate calculations can just go to hell; andouille is andouille, and it's not like it's gonna be a three-times-a-day staple in my diet and, and, and suddenly I was feeling a little too defensive.

As anyone who has ever succumbed to giggles can attest, once they start, they cascade. Ask any high school sophomore—it's called sophomoric behavior for a reason. Regaining marginal control, I thanked him, made for the meat counter, and bought the made-on-the-premises, boring-assed *unsmoked* andouille. Meanwhile, Molly had vanished into another aisle and was beyond view, presumably so I would embarrass only myself.

From then on, when I shopped for gumbo ingredients, which was easily every third Austin visit, I went to Central Market, partly because I knew exactly where to find *smoked* andouille and partly because I wanted to give the young man at Whole Foods a chance to forget me.

Both the upscale Central Market—the haute cuisine echelon of the Texas-based, family-owned H-E-B grocery chain—and the Austin-based Whole Foods engage in a kind of guerrilla food warfare, each determined to lure the lion's share of the well-heeled, the health-conscious, the semi-conscious, locavores, food snobs, vegans, food freaks, carnivores, and vegetarian shoppers.

Whenever we'd hit Central Market, people almost always recognized Molly and smiled or nodded. Sometimes they'd nudge a companion as they smiled and nodded not always subtly in her direction. You didn't have to be a skilled lip reader to discern the nature of their query.

Shopper A: "Isn't that Molly Ivins?"

Shopper B: "Looks like her."

Hello? Looks like her? There was no missing or mistaking Molly's six-foot presence, especially when she had that head of burnt-orange hair found nowhere in nature—a dye job some publicist talked her into and one that, thank goodness, didn't last long.

But the stubby black woman with her? Who's she? The cook?

Well, come to think of it, yes.

Every now and again someone made a point of speaking to her. Molly never put on airs about her ever-ascending popularity in the People's Republic of Austin. It was my job as a friend to stand patiently aside, maybe even saunter into an aisle of my own while she responded to admirers. Thereby I could avoid the temptation to engage in impatient shifting from one foot to the other; no rolling eyes upward when flattery spilled over the top; no smirks or flippant responses to comments not directed to me in the first place.

And for damned sure, no giggles.

One woman really pushed the envelope. We were standing amid bins of shallots and red, white, and Texas 1015 onions, picking through the garlic heads, looking for perfect ones with big cloves. A woman nudged me and asked if the tall person standing nearby was actually Molly Ivins. She wanted to know if I cooked for her. With a perfectly straight face, and, with a conspiratorial lean-in, as though sharing a secret, I confessed that, well, yes. I told her we were shopping for a dinner party that would feature a member of the state legislature; a civil rights lawyer and his partner, Stan; a reporter from the

Dallas Morning News; and a Cuban refugee and her partner. I leaned closer and intoned, "I hear the Cuban is a communist."

She loved it. How was this poor woman to know that Stan, partner to civil rights attorney Malcolm Greenstein, was a woman whose real name is Kirsten; I was the reporter; and the Cuban was artist Mercedes Peña, who was no more a communist than I was, or that her partner, Ed Wendler, was a man, not another woman?

Clearly afflicted by an advanced case of arrested development, I was unable to restrain myself. All was accomplished with a straight face. Molly made earnest eye contact with her admirer while I looked away. She later swore it was the last time she would allow me in the store without a muzzle.

The experience triggered a flashback. It was conversation fodder for Molly at several dinner party discussions about race and class in America. Specifically, race and class in Texas. Okay, race and class in Dallas, where I was a reporter for twelve years—plus two years at Neiman Marcus, where my fashion sense left a lot to be desired. A lot.

Anyway, at the *DMN*, I was assigned to cover writer John Berendt's visit to Dallas. His novel *Midnight in the Garden of Good and Evil* was flying off bookshelves at a rate that stunned him and delighted his publishers. In 1994, the Wellesley Club of Dallas invited John to participate in its thirtieth annual book and author luncheon. My job was to shadow him morning to night, from his first talk show to the evening cocktail party honoring him at a chichi Highland Park home. I was to do a feature story on John and "The Book," as it came to be known.

Not wanting to embarrass my subject or my employer with my lack of fashion sense, I detoured home, showered, spritzed, donned a smart black dress, polished almost-new sensible shoes, arrived at my appointed destination, and walked briskly up the perfectly landscaped stone walk to the front door.

As I approached, our hostess opened the inner door. I announced that I was there for the reception for John Berendt, and she responded by pointing through the storm door that separated us—to a walkway that led to the side of the house. "They're in the kitchen," she said. "You can go around the back." In a nanosecond, arrested development once again snapped into play, moving me to do as instructed, knowing that I would be waiting in the kitchen when John and the photographer arrived. How interesting it would be, I thought, to see how this weirdness would play out.

The caterer, whom I knew, was pleasantly surprised to see me. I knew her food to be really good, so I nibbled. I didn't want the catering crew to be uncomfortable, so I just said I was hanging out until the hostess was ready to receive guests.

An increased decibel level signaled the punctual arrival of guests, and I was able to recognize John's resonant voice when he said to the hostess, "That's strange; I've been with her all day, and she said she would be here early. Let's ask the photo editor."

This was before everyone had cell phones, so once it was determined that the photo editor hadn't heard from me either, the hostess suggested the photo editor use the kitchen's wall phone in an effort to determine my whereabouts.

As she entered through the swinging door that led from dining room to kitchen, there I sat under the wall phone the photo editor was already reaching for.

"What are you doing in here?" he asked. "Hanging out with the catering crew," I replied with a smile. He looked at me quizzically. Our hostess's face was by now the hue of a vine-ripened Brandywine tomato. The rest of the evening was uneventful unless you want to count the guy who asked me for a martini refill. What he said was, "Excuse me, I need another martini." To which I replied, "God, so do I—vodka, up, three olives. Thank you *so* much."

I left him holding two glasses, as discombobulated as our hostess had been earlier. Neither the dress, the nicely polished shoes, makeup, notebook, nor the pen suggested I could be anything other than the Help. Molly dined out on this story for a while too, usually as a lead-in to some rant on the sorry state of race relations in Dallas/Texas/America/the world in the 1990s.

Once, when my brother Fred, then a photographer with the *Los Angeles Times*, was interviewing with the *New York Times* for a job as a photo editor, some newsroom muckety-muck took him to one of those high-dollar restaurants where editors take prospective employees they want to woo. Brother Fred was tricked out in a black cashmere turtleneck with a polished pair of my father's cuff links, a dark charcoal heather tweed jacket, and wool slacks. Italian loafers completed the look, tassels and all.

While Fred was waiting for a cab after dinner, a Jaguar pulled up. As the occupants emerged, the driver pressed the keys into Fred's hand and said, "Keep it safe and there's a big tip in it for you." Fred smiled and replied, "I'll keep them right here in my pocket." And he did, until the next day, when he returned the keys, by courier, to the restaurant. He can't remember the name of the restaurant, or the name of the editor who took him out, but he remembers the magical moment when he realized he had the potential to be a felon.

My reverie dissipated as I realized we were still surrounded by onions and garlic and the woman was still talking.

That was Molly, always willing to stop, listen, smile, thank you for speaking to her, ask your name and thank you again, this time addressing you personally. And she meant it. She refused to see herself as a celebrity. She certainly never behaved like one, and God knows she never dressed like one until she reluctantly yielded to a personal shopper. As often happened on these supermarket junkets, despite the fact that we'd take different carts, our paths would overlap.

On one such occasion, I saw from a distance that Molly was in deep attentive mode, looking into the speaker's face, nodding but not really smiling—engaged, but not in a good way.

The woman was taking Mol to task for something she had written about then-president George W. Bush, whom we had come to know in Molly parlance as "Shrub."

Quelle surprise.

The woman was jibberjabbing away, as some people do when making a point, reiterating and, not getting the desired response, saying the same thing again. She droned on, a sclerotic passive-aggressive smile fixed in place.

I didn't know how to intervene, but I now stood behind the woman, facing Molly, spasmodically shifting from left to right and regressing to somewhere around sixth grade. I was twitching, doing a bit of furtive glancing here and there, and scrunching my face into strange contortions.

I knew Molly wanted an out, but I just didn't know what to do. So there she was, listening, nodding, and waiting for this scold to wind down. Suddenly Molly interrupted, apologized, and excused us, leaning in and conspiratorially whispering that she had to get me home for my medication, which was almost overdue.

We concluded our foray up and down the aisles—intermingling impulse purchases with stuff actually on the list. We arrived at the checkout counter shocked—shocked!—to learn we'd spent almost three times as much as we had anticipated.

E: "I thought we were using artichoke hearts in the salad."

M: "I thought we were doing hearts of palm."

E: "Why don't we do both?"

Problem solved.

After the drive home in Bob the Pickup, much slicing and dicing, chopping and pureeing, ensued in Molly's not-so-spacious kitchen.

A sip of Chardonnay for her, a sassy Shiraz for me.

Hellman's in the potato salad? *Mais non.* Out came the blender, eggs, lemons, oil. Hellman's might be the mayo of choice when I flew solo in the Ivins kitchen, but when I was sous chef, it was homemade or not at all.

Hope Reyna, Molly's housekeeper extraordinaire, insisted the kitchen was never as much a mess as it was when I visited. She was kinda right, which is why I hid from her on the morning after a particularly enthusiastic meal. Leftovers went to Athena the poodle, who devoured them voraciously.

So, yes, anyone who ever ate at Molly's house has most likely eaten from a plate touched by Athena's big, long, pink poodle tongue.

9

Food in the 'Hood

MOLLY'S FOUR-PERSON KITCHEN often felt like some kind of architectural afterthought, but there was actually great order about it. Nevertheless, four people would be hard-pressed to maneuver in it in any meaningful way.

Built-in floor-to-ceiling cabinets housed odds and ends of dishes on the three bottom shelves of one side, while upper shelves and door shelves were stocked with herbs, spices, and all manner of oils—safflower, olive, extra-virgin olive, peanut, grapeseed, canola.

There were salts—sea, kosher, smoked, pink (from Hawaii), *fleur de sel* from France—not to be confused with gray salt, also from France but indigenous to the coast. Oh, and let's not forget sauces—Worcestershire, A1, tamari, light soy, dark soy, Chinese soy, Japanese soy, and Thai fish sauce, for the one time we decided to cook a Thai meal. She didn't love it. Actually, she didn't even *like* it. The photograph in the magazine looked appetizing enough, and Molly was never above trying new flavors. Although Thai remains one of my favorite ethnic cuisines, it was not Molly's—then or ever. She never liked collard greens either, although she could lay into their cousins, Swiss chard and kale. I filed that under "go figure."

The other side of the cabinet housed wheat flour, white flour, rice flour, organic raw sugar, light brown sugar, dark brown sugar, turbinado sugar, and honey—orange blossom, raw, and wild. Canned goods consisted mainly of artichoke hearts, hearts of palm, anchovies, large capers, small capers, capers rolled in anchovies, Italian tuna packed in olive oil, and those remarkable San Marzano tomatoes.

Until I met Molly I had never heard of San Marzano tomatoes or, for that matter, of Campania, Italy—which, I learned, is in southern Italy and was for the longest time the only place these exquisite tomatoes grew. Flourishing there had something to do with a perfect confluence of sun, soil, and precipitation.

By the time we finished talking about tomatoes I was ready to dust off my passport and head for the Amalfi coast. Call it a food-pantry-as-geography lesson. The kitchen cabinet's odds and ends of canned goods also reflected her propensity for impulse shopping, such as an escargot kit replete with snails packaged with shells and a recipe for assembly. Maybe she made them, but not with me.

Increasingly frequent forays to Austin assured respite in Molly's kitchen. Whether we barbecued shrimp, roasted hot dogs, or baked meat loaf, the therapeutic value of cooking was immeasurable, especially when I could sit at the kitchen counter and look out over a stone patio surrounded by live oaks and see the sky change color at sunset—all the while squishing together ingredients that anchored one of my favorite birthday meals.

February 1, 2003. The date and year are, as they say, indelibly etched in the old memory bank. I had only recently left the *Dallas Morning News* to join the *Denver Post*, but I returned to Texas on January 31. John and Susan Albach had organized a birthday dinner for me the next day, my real birthday. We were going to rendezvous at Javier's, a lovely Mexican restaurant. It was not to be.

Early on the morning of February 1 NASA's Columbia shuttle exploded minutes after reentering the atmosphere, and the resulting debris field covered parts of Central Texas. The *Denver Post* found me and I was dispatched to Amarillo to assist with coverage. I had been at the paper barely five months, so I answered duty's call, flew to Amarillo, covered my piece of the story, attended the church service where shuttle commander Rick Husband was eulogized, and returned to Dallas thirty-six hours later.

I had known that my daughter, the chef, wouldn't be able to attend the dinner, but her husband at the time assured me he would go in her stead, convey apologies, and explain on my behalf. At the last minute, for reasons unknown to this day, he decided not to go. I had no idea that they never knew what had happened until I returned from Amarillo to find a series of telephone messages trying to find me, escalating from concern to annoyance to alarm. Molly had not felt able to make the drive to Dallas, which was just as well. The party proceeded without either of us, much to my everlasting chagrin.

With many apologies and considerable embarrassment behind me, I now headed to Austin and the house in Travis Heights to continue my birthday celebration—or more accurately, to begin it. When I arrived, Molly was scrubbing big fat Idahos. One of her favorite vegetables, haricot verts—what the rest of us call baby green beans—were rinsed and ready to go. At the last minute they would be steamed and buttered and Molly would make the dressing for the Caesar salad.

I settled into my favorite perch at the kitchen window, smushing together milk-soaked bread, beef, pork, veal, onions, herbs, bell pepper, celery, garlic, ketchup, and Worcestershire sauce. The remaining vestiges of guilt over my dinner party absence earlier the week before vaporized concurrent with aromas of a baking meat loaf.

As the meat loaf rested, Molly whisked together lemon juice, garlic, and vinegar, incorporating a raw egg yolk and chopped anchovies into the olive oil.

It was a perfect birthday dinner: Caesar salad, meat loaf, mashed potatoes, mushroom gravy, baby green beans, and a red velvet cake with cream cheese frosting. As a special Molly treat I even had those candles that always relight no matter how hard you blow.

The year 2003 was memorable for another reason, though: Molly's cancer was back. Thank goodness for her Travis Heights friends and neighbors.

Say "Travis Heights" to locals today and they know you're talking high-dollar real estate. Nice lawns. Nice landscaping. Hybrid cars. Taxes through the roof. At least one chocolate Lab, standard poodle, golden retriever, or some designer or rescue dog on every third porch.

Not so in the early '90s. Hookers trolled the intersection of Live Oak and Congress Avenue, almost right around the corner from Molly's house. The only neighborhood theater was on South Congress, and it showed triple-X movies all day and half the night.

South by Southwest, now one of the world's premier music events, was in its early gestational stage. Nothing much legal happened south of Riverside Drive, save for thrift shops, an occasional restaurant, the iconic Austin Motel, the old Hotel San Jose and the equally iconic Continental Club, whose musical attractions worked their way from '50s supper club status to '60s burlesque (remember Candy Barr?) through the blues, swing, rock, and rockabilly sounds of the '70s and '80s.

In short, the area in those early days had a quasi-seedy, kinda cool, funky, edgy look and feel. Artists and musicians sought out the neighborhood because it was affordable. Prescient entrepreneurs knew, to quote '60s R&B singer Sam Cooke, a change was gonna come. The area now has a quasi-edgy, faux-funky, expensive look and feel. Molly moved into her house in the 1980s when it was a compact little bungalow on a spacious corner lot. Financing was made possible by the enormous success of *Molly Ivins Can't Say That, Can She?*

Nothing like having a runaway hit spend a year on the *New York Times* bestseller list to underwrite a first-time home purchase.

As successive books followed suit, Molly had to do something with her money besides shell it out in taxes or give it away, more often than not without benefit of tax breaks. She decided one way to get relief was to buy a bigger house.

By the time she made the decision, however, she discovered that housing values and their attendant prices had escalated beyond her proletarian sensibilities. Besides, she liked her neighborhood. She'd become accustomed to the house where she had written the columns that catapulted her to even greater fame through syndication.

For what she would have paid for a newer, bigger house in a "nicer" neighborhood, she could add on, expand to her specifications, and stay right where she was—especially since her neighborhood was getting nicer anyway.

Before the Great Renovation, a curvy stone walkway led to an entrance set back some twenty yards from the street. The addition featured a semi-secluded driveway leading to a front door that opened onto a garden room.

A pond to the immediate left was stocked with koi. Among the plants thriving in the humid atrium were dill, thyme, basil, and chives. A skylight allowed just enough filtered sun to keep the plants happy. An automated watering system maintained proper humidity for trees, shrubs, and bromeliads.

Just when there seemed to be nothing else to add, Molly installed a five-foot-tall birdcage that housed four pairs of lovebirds. Every now and again she would open the cage door and let the pretty little critters soar across the atrium. When they got hungry, they'd fly back in.

For the most part.

(If you already see where this is going, you're right; just know that somewhere in Travis Heights there are bound to be beautiful descendants of, oh, finches and a few of Molly's lovebirds. When the birds were flying free, the ceiling fans were always turned off. Well, almost always. 'Nuff said.)

A walkway through the atrium brought visitors to a second front door that opened onto a large living/dining room. The dining area was immediately to the right, and a large glass wall was straight ahead, opposite the entry. For reasons that were never clear to those who tripped up it, a step led to a twenty-by-fifteen-foot master bedroom that included a large walk-in closet, a wall of shelves filled with novels, histories, thrillers, crossword puzzles, books of poetry, and works ranging from William Makepeace Thackeray, Carl Hiaasen, and Elmore Leonard to J. K. Rowling, Sue Grafton, and Madeleine Albright.

Floor-to-ceiling bookshelves in Molly's office—which had once been the living room—housed histories, political treatises, art books, and dozens of cookbooks. Molly even had an entry in the 1990 *Austin Hill Country Celebrity Cookbook* for her Hungarian Paprika Mushrooms recipe. (Proceeds went to the Austin Parks Foundation.)

A working fireplace tucked into one corner of the living room warmed the room when the outside temperature dropped below forty degrees.

The cramped New York apartment–style kitchen angled off to the right of the entryway. A sharp right just before the kitchen took you past the dining table and down a short, narrow hall. Photographs of family and friends completely filled the wall. Opposite the wall was a bathroom with a spa-type tub. At the end of the hall was the guest room.

The kitchen, as noted earlier, was reminiscent of a truncated railway car—big enough to comfortably accommodate the simultaneous occupation of four, maybe five people as long as no one moved around too much. Okay, six, as long as two remained stationary at all times. A Jenn-Air cooktop, set into a well-ventilated alcove, begged for, and received, frequent use.

Molly eventually replaced the rectangular dining table that seated six—and would have seated eight or ten if she had ever found the extensions. To facilitate dinnertime conversation she commissioned woodworker Louis Fry to build a round table. Fry, noted for his handcrafted furniture, created a stunner. The table, six feet in diameter, was made from curly maple with an inlaid circle of rare African bubinga wood about eight inches inside the perimeter. She finally broke down and told me how much she paid for the table and chairs, but my pledge of secrecy survives her.

The eight matching chairs, whose seats consisted of latticed leather strips that covered overstuffed cushions, made for ridiculously comfortable seating. The end product encouraged many long, comfy post-dinner conversations.

Meals were taken under the watchful eye of John Henry Faulk, whose large framed photograph hung in the center of an alcove opposite the table.

Faulk, arguably Texas's finest folklorist and raconteur, fell victim to the witch-hunting demagoguery of Wisconsin senator Joseph McCarthy and the House Un-American Activities Committee. For anyone who thinks the foaming-at-the-mouth pronouncements of modern-day pundits are bizarre, it's worthwhile to revisit the senator's April 16, 1954, response to a criticism leveled by Edward R. Murrow.

Molly offers a toast following a Saturday night supper in 1999 at the spacious round table that she commissioned from a local craftsman; it comfortably seats eight. Ellen Sweets collection.

In his rambling diatribe, McCarthy suggests an American government penetrated by communists at every level, but he stops short of accusing Murrow and his employer, CBS, of being communist sympathizers. The allegations were eventually proved to be without merit, but it was an ugly, divisive time, and if the word "venal" had a photographic depiction in the dictionary, McCarthy's face would be there.

The House Un-American Activities Committee and fellow traveler McCarthy wreaked havoc with many in the nation's creative community at the time—a whole battalion of artists, musicians, and writers who refused either to testify or to accuse others were cited for contempt of Congress. Some got off with fines and suspended sentences, while others went to prison—some for as long as a year. Once released, they were placed on what came to be known as a "blacklist," which rendered them unable to find work. Reputations were destroyed. Some left the country, some wrote under pseudonyms, some killed themselves. Like broken Indian treaties and the internment of Japanese Americans during World War II, the HUAC witch hunts were not shining moments in America's history.

John Henry Faulk was one of those who fought back, ultimately winning a libel suit against AWARE, Inc., a red-baiting newsletter that had engaged in a cavalier campaign against scores of artists, labeling them as communists. His lawsuit ultimately brought the blacklist to an end—not, however, before his career was in tatters. His book *Fear on Trial* chronicles the unsettling experience.

By the time John Henry cleared his name, he was virtually penniless and one of Molly's true heroes. He died in 1990, but not before Molly promised him that in tribute to him she would champion free speech whenever and wherever she could. She made good on that promise, crisscrossing the country for years, from big cities to rural hamlets, often speaking to ACLU chapters for no fee beyond a warm place to sleep, a good meal, and the opportunity to talk progressive politics to those otherwise without access to fellow travelers.

Up to her death Molly kept a well-read copy of John Henry's book on a table between two comfy wingback chairs in her living room.

Progressives who lived through that era thought it was over and done with—until the socially conservative, Republican-dominated Texas State Board of Education successfully sought to rewrite history to soften McCarthy's image in its 2010 textbook revisions—and succeeded in the effort.

Don't be shocked: this is the same body that tried to remove Thomas Jefferson from the list of political philosophers who shaped world history. And don't blame Texas students if they are undereducated and ill-informed. They had help. As Molly was oft wont to say—you can't make this stuff up.

MOLLY'S HUNGARIAN PAPRIKA MUSHROOMS

From the 1996 *Austin Hill Country Celebrity Cookbook*, edited by Sheila Liermann and Nancy Reid. In it Molly notes: "Paprika sprinkled on a dish as a garnish really doesn't do justice to the great flavor of paprika from Hungary. To get the full flavor of the spice, use several teaspoons and be sure to cook it a few minutes, just as curry powder needs to be cooked to develop its true flavor. Hungarian paprika is the world's finest. Paprika harvests are graded for quality like wine vintages—with good and better years! Sweet paprika really just means less hot."

INGREDIENTS

1 tablespoon unsalted butter

2 tablespoons finely minced shallots or green onions

¾ pound mushrooms, rinsed, trimmed, stems on and sliced into quarters

½ teaspoon kosher salt

¼ teaspoon freshly ground black pepper

2 teaspoons finely chopped fresh marjoram or ½ teaspoon dried marjoram

2 teaspoons hot or sweet Hungarian paprika, or 1 teaspoon of each

¼ teaspoon all-purpose flour (don't be tempted to use more)

⅓ cup light sour cream, or crème fraîche

DIRECTIONS

In a large skillet, melt butter. Add shallots or onions and mushrooms and sauté over medium heat for 5 minutes, stirring occasionally, and then lower heat. In a small bowl, combine salt and pepper, marjoram, paprika, and flour, and mix together well. Stir paprika mixture into mushrooms and sauté for an additional 2 to 3 minutes to develop the flavor of the paprika. Just before serving, stir in the sour cream or crème fraîche and heat through. Do not boil. Serves 4.

★ ★ ★

CHEF PAUL'S LOAF

This is the original recipe from Louisiana food god Paul Prudhomme for my favorite birthday dinner. It is one of the few recipes Molly and I never tinkered with. It is what I hope meat loaf will taste like when I get to heaven, and I have to believe in heaven because in *Defending Your Life*, Meryl Streep got to eat as much as she wanted of anything she wanted. (If you ask ahead and say "please," the butcher might grind the beef and pork together for you.) Reproduced with permission.

INGREDIENTS

4 tablespoons unsalted butter
¾ cup finely chopped onion
½ cup finely chopped celery
½ cup finely chopped green bell pepper
¼ cup finely chopped green onion
1 tablespoon plus 2 teaspoons Chef Paul Prudhomme's Meat Magic *or* Chef Paul Prudhomme's Pork and Veal Magic *or* Magic Seasoning Salt
2 teaspoons minced garlic

1 tablespoon Chef Paul Prudhomme's Magic Pepper Sauce
1 tablespoon Worcestershire sauce
2 whole bay leaves
½ cup evaporated milk
½ cup ketchup
1½ pounds ground beef
½ pound ground pork
2 eggs, lightly beaten
1 cup very fine dry bread crumbs

DIRECTIONS

Melt butter in a 1-quart saucepan over medium heat. Add onion, celery, bell pepper, green onion, Magic seasoning blend, garlic, Magic Pepper Sauce, Worcestershire sauce, and bay leaves. Cook, stirring occasionally and scraping the bottom of the pan, until the mixture starts sticking excessively, about 6 minutes. Stir in milk and ketchup. Continue cooking for about 2 minutes, stirring occasionally. Remove from heat and allow to cool at room temperature.

Preheat oven to 350°F.

Place beef and pork in a large mixing bowl. Add eggs, cooked vegetable mixture (remove bay leaves), and bread crumbs. Mix by hand, being careful not to overmix, since overmixing will release the protein in the meat and make it mushy. Blend no longer than necessary to distribute ingredients. Place mixture in an ungreased 13-inch-by-9-inch baking pan. Shape into a loaf about 12 by 6 by 1½ inches—it will not touch the sides of the pan—and bake uncovered for 25 minutes. Raise heat to 400°F and continue cooking until done, approximately 35 minutes. Serves 6.

Copyright © 1984 by Paul Prudhomme

★ ★ ★

MOLLY'S CAESAR SALAD

Because raw eggs are a component, prepare this just before serving and warn anyone who has a compromised immune system to seek an alternative dressing. Discard leftovers.

INGREDIENTS

1½ teaspoons coarsely ground black pepper

4 garlic cloves, forced through a press or minced

3 anchovies

1 tablespoon Dijon mustard

2 tablespoons freshly squeezed lemon juice

1 teaspoon Worcestershire sauce

½ cup extra-virgin olive oil

2 tablespoons red wine vinegar

2 egg yolks

2 heads Romaine lettuce, rinsed, dried, deribbed, and torn—not cut—into bite-size pieces

½ cup shredded Parmesan cheese

DIRECTIONS

In a bowl combine pepper, garlic, and anchovies, smooshing them into a paste. Whisk in mustard, lemon juice, Worcestershire sauce, olive oil, vinegar, and egg yolks. Add lettuce to the dressing. Immediately toss gently, gradually adding cheese. Serves 6 to 8.

★ ★ ★

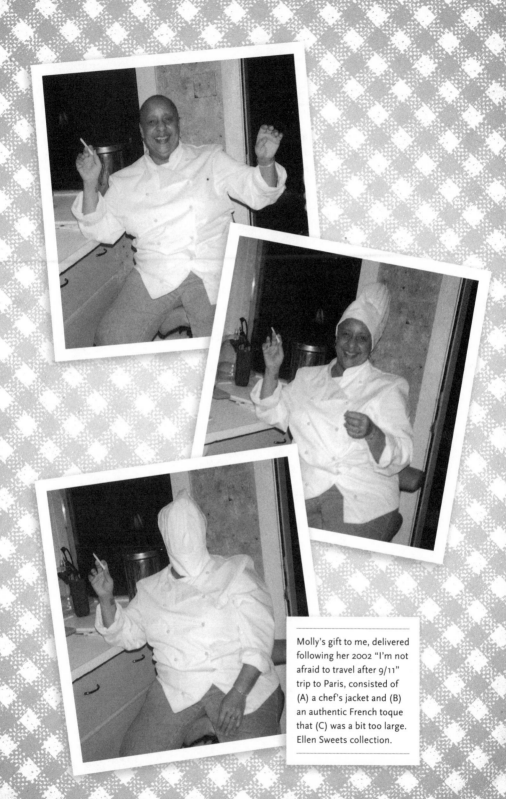

Molly's gift to me, delivered following her 2002 "I'm not afraid to travel after 9/11" trip to Paris, consisted of (A) a chef's jacket and (B) an authentic French toque that (C) was a bit too large. Ellen Sweets collection.

10

Vive la France!

UNDAUNTED BY THE HORROR OF SEPTEMBER 11, 2001, Molly returned to the City of Light in November 2002, breaking a long-standing tradition of family Thanksgiving at home.

She was determined to see Paris again, to make up for all those times she was too busy to go where she really wanted to go. Friends who joined her from as far away as New York and New Orleans still talk about it.

John Pope and his wife, Diana Pinckley, flew in from New Orleans. He is a reporter with the *Times-Picayune,* and she is a widely respected communications consultant. Pope, as he is generally called, had known Molly since his university days at UT and had shared many a meal at her home and in local eateries. It was my good fortune that John keeps meticulous notes on his travels, so rather than paraphrasing his chronicle of events, I've selected excerpts from his Paris diary, below.

Molly somehow managed to score three eight-pound turkeys—not bad in a country where the fourth Thursday in November is just another day—unless you're dining in an elegant St. Louis flat lent by San Antonio millionaire and Molly fan Bernard Lifschutz.

Thanksgiving Day began with Molly and Eden Lipson, a former *New York Times* editor and Molly's surrogate mother at the *Times,* removing quills from the birds with their eyebrow tweezers, while Pope and Pinckley assembled crudités and adorned each place setting with a little chocolate turkey that they had carefully brought from New Orleans. Guests began arriving around 6 p.m. The guest list included a foreign correspondent who had known Molly and his wife; a pianist from Plano, Texas; Molly's goddaughter, Nicole, an architect, and her beau, Philippe, an editor at *Liberation*, a progressive publication started by French philosopher Jean-Paul Sartre; journalist and author Charles Kaiser and his partner, Joe Stouter, who contributed Molly's much-loved haricots verts and a sublime Roquefort; and Joe and Charles's friend Mark Trilling, a nephew of Lionel and Diana Trilling, two of the twentieth century's most prominent authors and intellectuals. Other friends, including Tamara Kreinin, who now works with health programs for women and children at the United Nations Foundation, Rosalind Hinton, who teaches at Tulane University, and Roz's niece Nora, brought wine and Veuve Clicquot. Pope was bartender.

Of the experience, he wrote:

> Charles, Eden, and I carved. Before we dined, we stood in a big circle—that flat had plenty of room—and Molly reminded us all of the importance of the day—to give thanks for our blessings and remember those who aren't so well off.
>
> Dinner was at the dining table and the massive coffee table. In addition to the aforementioned beans, we feasted on baked sweet potatoes, creamed onions, two types of dressing and three styles of cranberry sauce from Neal and one from us, which we had found in Harrods Food Halls earlier in the week. Wine flowed.
>
> Sometime during the evening, Molly decreed that, in honor of the apartment owner's hometown, we all should do something called the San Antonio Shuffle. We were waving napkins and doing a second line à la New Orleans.
>
> Because we ate so much, Eden decreed that we take a good walk before tucking into dessert. So off we went into the brisk night to stroll the Ile St.-Louis. . . . We all marveled at our good fortune to be at that dinner in that city. All because of Molly. . . . Neal [Johnston; Eden's husband] had made four pies with precisely measured spices he brought over in medicine bottles. The pies: lemon, chocolate chess, pumpkin Cointreau, and a cranberry concoction. The last guests left around midnight. Pinckley cleaned up until about 12:30, when Molly ordered her to stop.

Susan Concordet, one of the Smith classmates Molly stayed in touch with over the years, couldn't join her because Susan's husband, Jean, was dying of cancer. Nicole, the Concordets' daughter, represented the family. Molly and Susan had formed a strong bond during their time together at Smith. Both were somewhat estranged from their families, and Molly kept her counsel about her family's wealth.

"She was very discreet about her family," Susan said during a telephone interview from France. "I never knew Molly was rich. She never talked about it, except when her brother was sick. She just said her father was a lawyer, not that he was the president of an oil company. Once, she made chili con carne for me and we talked all night. She told me stories; I was impressed by that easy, free, storytelling tradition. But I never knew she was famous until she came to Paris and spoke to the Democratic party here, and when she had that Thanksgiving party at the Ile St.-Louis. I knew she knew impressive friends, but I didn't know *how* famous. But then, that was Molly."

MOLLY'S FAMOUS "ORPHANS AND STRAYS" Christmas dinners were legendary. Give friends half a chance and anyone who participated will tell you a tale from one of them. One year she decided to make *caneton à l'orange*, known to the rest of us as roasted duck with orange sauce or, by its more familiar name, duck *à l'orange*.

The way these dinners worked, Molly provided the main event and everyone else brought a side dish, salad, bread, dessert, or something to drink. As always, the guest list might range from ten to twenty. One never knew. Courtney Anderson still gets a giggle out of recalling the orange duck evening.

"So Molly bought all these ducks and had them lying out on the counter to come to room temperature. She had rubbed them with butter and herbs and more butter and who knows what-all inside. Anyway, she counted out the ducks, and counted to herself the approximate number of dinner guests. She made periodic visits to the living room to survey the celebrants, refill wineglasses, and pour more eggnog, only to return to the kitchen and notice what seemed to be an empty space where she was sure a duck had been.

"Figuring she had miscounted, she ran the numbers again, this time certain she was one duck short. Failing to associate a vanished poodle with a missing duck, Molly rejoined her guests momentarily, only to return just as Athena bolted with duck number two locked in her perfectly groomed aquiline jaws."

Molly quickly contemplated the probability of rescuing the duck and possibly quietly assigning it to her plate—it would be instantly recognizable as the duck with the canine tooth marks—if she could catch Athena.

Which, of course, she couldn't.

The bad news was the purloined ducks were never to be seen again; the good news was Athena was strangely subdued throughout the remainder of the evening.

Molly's house sat on a quarter-acre corner lot with lines of demarcation intersecting at the bottom of a steep slope. Somewhere down there, in addition to duck bones, is a purple Birkenstock sandal that vanished several years ago during one of those visits when I brought only one pair of shoes—the ones I wore. Fortunately Austin's only Birky store at the time had another pair.

Athena's secret hiding place area was so overgrown that no one save the surveyor was ever known to have set foot at the bottom. In fact, it was so over-grown that it was a year or two before Molly knew it was also home to a lovely fox family. Apparently Mr. and Mrs. Fox lived in one section and Athena's stash occupied another.

It was here that the ebony purebred standard poodle sequestered shoes, bones, rubber balls, and as of that Christmas, butter-rubbed ducks.

Molly's response was predictable: "*Caneton à l'orange*," she intoned, in her best French accent. "What did you expect? She's a French poodle."

DUCK À L'ORANGE

If I were roasting this duck, I'd save the skimmed fat and freeze it for fu-ture use in a cassoulet. This recipe, another Molly fave, first appeared in 1943 and was reprinted in *Gourmet* in 2006.

INGREDIENTS

1 tablespoon kosher salt	2 fresh flat-leaf parsley sprigs
1 teaspoon ground coriander	1 small onion, cut into 8 wedges
½ teaspoon ground cumin	½ cup dry white wine
1 teaspoon black pepper	½ cup duck stock, duck and
1 (5- to 6-pound) Long Island duck	veal stock, chicken stock, or
1 juice orange, halved	reduced-sodium chicken broth
4 fresh thyme sprigs	½ carrot
4 fresh marjoram sprigs	½ celery rib

⅓ cup sugar

⅓ cup fresh orange juice (from 1 to 2 oranges)

2 tablespoons white-wine vinegar

⅛ teaspoon salt

2 to 4 tablespoons duck or chicken stock or reduced-sodium chicken broth

1 tablespoon unsalted butter, softened

1 tablespoon all-purpose flour

1 tablespoon finely julienned fresh orange zest, removed with a vegetable peeler

DIRECTIONS

Place oven rack in middle position and preheat oven to 475°F.

Stir together salt, coriander, cumin, and pepper. Pat duck dry and sprinkle inside and out with spice mixture.

Cut 1 half of orange into quarters and put in duck cavity with thyme, marjoram, parsley, and 4 onion wedges.

Squeeze juice from remaining orange half and stir together with wine and stock. Set aside.

Spread remaining 4 onion wedges in roasting pan with carrot and celery, then place duck on top of vegetables and roast for 30 minutes.

Pour wine mixture into roasting pan and reduce oven temperature to 350°F. Continue to roast duck until thermometer inserted into a thigh (close to but not touching bone) registers 170°F, 1 to 1¼ hours more. Turn on broiler and broil duck 3 to 4 inches from heat until top is golden brown, about 3 minutes.

Tilt duck to drain juices from cavity into pan and transfer duck to a cutting board, reserving juices in pan. Let duck rest for 15 minutes.

While the duck rests, cook sugar in a dry 1-quart heavy saucepan over moderate heat, undisturbed until it begins to melt. Continue to cook, stirring occasionally with a fork, until it melts into a deep golden caramel. Add orange juice, vinegar, and salt (use caution; mixture will bubble and steam vigorously) and simmer over low heat, stirring occasionally, until caramel is dissolved. Remove syrup from heat.

Discard vegetables from roasting pan and pour pan juices through a fine-mesh sieve into a 1-quart glass measure or bowl, then skim off fat and discard it. Add enough stock to pan juices to total 1 cup liquid.

Stir together butter and flour to form a beurre manié (a paste made to thicken sauce). Bring pan juices to a simmer in a 1- or 2-quart heavy saucepan, then add the beurre manié, whisking constantly to prevent lumps. Add orange syrup and zest and simmer, whisking occasionally, until sauce is thickened slightly and zest is tender, about 5 minutes. Serve with duck. Serves 4.

★ ★ ★

11

Gumbo Daze

MOLLY AND I HAD COOKING DATES, which probably sounds just as weird as "play dates" for kids, but those escape-from-Dallas cooking weekends produced rollicking good times, except for the occasional mishap, like the time a heavy container of gumbo destined for a dinner party tumbled out of the fridge and onto Molly's right foot, breaking her big toe.

We should have used something rectangular instead of an oversized cylindrical blender bowl to fit into her already overstuffed fridge. Even I, the D-in-math-and-physics-forget-about-it student, knew that. Molly was tired and cranky and insisted that the giant cylindrical container would do just fine. The reconstructed conversation went something like this:

Me, regarding overstocked shelves: "Mol, I don't think this is gonna work."

Molly: "Of course it will. I'll just give it a good shove" (jamming the container into place). "There" (with a triumphant crow—the container is precariously balanced but stationary).

Me: "Jesus, I hope one of us remembers to open the door carefully tomorrow."

Molly: "Sweets, sometimes you're a real pain in the ass. It's too heavy to fall out."

I shrugged, acquiescing. It was rarely a good idea to argue with her once she set her mind to something.

The next day, with the previous night's exchange about potentially hazardous refrigerator door openings a distant memory, I yanked open the door to surf for breakfast food, hoping to find remnants from the hearty beef stew served two nights before. I love leftovers. I'll eat almost anything for breakfast if it has an over-easy egg on top.

Molly stood by, seeking jam for a rapidly cooling croissant.

First to fly out was a package of cream cheese, easily intercepted with a midair catch. Next came the six-quart gumbo-laden bowl, the one containing a meticulously browned roux blended with homemade shrimp stock chock-full of chopped onions, green bell peppers, chopped celery, paper-thin hand-sliced discs of fresh okra, bay leaves and thyme, and generously endowed with crab claws, andouille sausage, and big fat shrimp.

A slo-mo camera should have been there to capture me going "Nooooooo!!!" and Molly going "I got it!" and neither of us reacting in any meaningful way to halt the no-slo-mo, 100-mile-a-minute trajectory from mid-fridge to tile floor. The resounding *thunk!* was in fact the sound of heavy glass breaking into three perfectly cleaved chunks.

On Molly's foot.

I looked at her, stunned. She shot me an "I dare you to open your mouth" look heavily weighted with a combination of frustration, annoyance, and, as I later learned, pain. We instantaneously directed our attention to the mess slowly radiating outward from the point of impact. It could have been a scene from a bleeding body on a *CSI* television episodes, except that the corpse in this instance was our Saturday-night supper.

Without uttering a word, we each grabbed a pot from the nearby stove and began retrieving shrimp, crab legs, crab claws, and sausage slices. Making another roux was no problem. Buying more shrimp, crab, and sausage at that point was. Mercifully, the oysters had not been added. We exchanged knowing glances that sealed an unvoiced pact that we would never again speak of recycled ingredients.

She did not argue when my grocery run included Knorr shrimp bouillon cubes, chicken stock—albeit organic—and frozen okra for the new roux. Time was now of the essence. No quibbling over onion-chopping techniques, though. Molly refused to use the food processor to chop onions, bell pepper, and celery. If you're persnickety, skip the following account of how Molly further injured herself while stubbornly re-chopping the onions by hand. It is a morality tale, and as good a reason as any for not rushing while cooking and, truth be told, for avoiding beverages stronger than water while using sharp knives.

Let's just say the edge of the onion pile was showing a curiously pinkish tinge of undetermined origin until it was revealed that the razor-sharp blade of Molly's eight-inch chef's knife had seriously nicked the end of her left middle fingertip.

We once again exchanged meaningful glances. We looked first at one another, then at the pile of onions—three pounds of them—that she had carefully, painstakingly, chopped. In unspoken agreement we trotted out a big colander, rinsed the onions with lots and lots of running water, and added them to the roux along with bell peppers, celery, garlic, and okra.

As the vegetable mix was added to the roux, followed by the requisite seasonings, a neighbor, out on an exercise walk, popped in to ask what we were cooking. Actually her comment was, "Whatever y'all er fixin' shure smells good!"

To speak proper Texan you must internalize certain grammatical constructs: one doesn't cook or prepare a meal; one "fixes" it. One is never "about to leave." You're "fixin' to leave." And if you're running behind schedule, you're "fixin' to be late." Fluency in Texan is achieved when you instinctively understand that a qualifying commentary is superfluous when the phrase "Bless her/his heart" is employed. The person so objectified is doomed.

Texas aphorisms have leaked out as far as Los Angeles—I once heard a guy who has one of those self-help, pop psychology shows inform a participant, "This ain't my first rodeo, y'know." He and the quip came from Texas.

Disagree with an argument? "You can put your boots in the oven, but that don't make 'em biscuits."

Hit a stumbling block? No. You've got a "hitch in your getalong."

Looking tired? "You look like you been rode hard and put up wet."

Our accelerated cooking activity had alerted the neighborhood to the fact that we were *fixin'* something good and garlicky. Thanks to the open door that led from kitchen to patio, the area immediately surrounding Molly's house was redolent with aromas rising from that sizzling sauté. Following an hour-long slow simmer, we added sausage, chicken, and crabmeat just prior to reintroducing salvaged shrimp and crab claws. It was all done by early afternoon, leaving plenty of time for the flavors to marry—or at least live in sin for a while.

At dinner even Molly had to laugh at the inevitable commentary on the tiny condom-like cover on her bandaged middle finger. In keeping with the general tenor of the moment, she raised the injured finger in the direction of successive speakers.

As for the saga of hastily reassembled gumbo ingredients and blood-free onions, both remained a Molly-Sweetsie secret.

That was a long time ago, and with any luck all anyone remembers from that particular gumbo supper—if they remember anything about it at all, inasmuch as Jamaican, Dutch, and Louisiana beers were involved—there was enough for seconds and even some for our friend Elliott to take some home. Remember that name. State Representative Elliott Naishtat views food through a prism not unlike that of a lion spotting antelope in the savannah: see, stalk, seize, savor.

Anyway, dinner was salvaged, the reconstructed gumbo was cheerfully consumed, nobody got sick, and the secret was secure. Until now.

I later recounted the broken-toe, sliced-finger gumbo saga in New Orleans during dinner at one of Molly's favorite restaurants, Commander's Palace. Situated in the heart of the Garden District, the sprawling turquoise and white Victorian structure represents the confluence of good food and good fun. Originally founded in the 1880s, Commander's is generally recognized as the grand dame of Crescent City restaurants, and a member of the Brennan family has presided over its Victorian grandeur since 1969. This might well be part of the reason Molly loved it so: not only did she love good food, she loved the idea of family-owned businesses. Ti Adelaide Martin—daughter of matriarch Ella Brennan Martin—is, like her mother, a staunch Molly fan.

Ti, as she is called, recalls in particular how, despite suggestions that she try something different from a constantly evolving menu, Molly returned time and again to the restaurant's Pecan Crusted Catfish, which gives the lie to the notion that catfish is somehow less deserving of elegant treatment than snapper, trout, or flounder.

Here our bottom-feeding, whiskered finny friend gets a Cinderella makeover with Creole seasoning, a light egg wash, and a dusting of pecan flour before being finished with lemon, Worcestershire sauce, thyme, and our dear friend, butter. It is worth buying the cookbook for this recipe alone, but for a full-fledged at-home Commander's experience, start with an oyster chowder, segue to a green salad tossed with avocado and a light vinaigrette, then dig into the pecan catfish, maybe with sides of garlic-wilted spinach and Creole mashed new potatoes.

When Molly's nephew Drew graduated from Tulane University, the family celebrated the event as Molly's guests at Commander's, joined by Carlton Carl, whose niece, Rebecca, was completing rabbinical studies. Drew now lives and works in South America, and Rebecca is a cantor in Philadelphia. So, yes, you come here for the magical Creole cuisine for which New Orleans is famous, but you come here for a good time too.

ELLEN AND MOLLY'S GARBAGE GUMBO

This inelegant moniker owes its genesis to the fact that purists tend to make gumbo with standard combinations—chicken and sausage, sea-food, seafood and sausage, and for Lent, greens. We threw it all together—okra, chicken, andouille, shrimp, crab, and oysters. You can make your own shrimp stock by buying large shrimp with the heads on, then use the shells and heads to make a stock—just cover well with water, add a garlic clove, half a lemon, a bay leaf, and a smidge of salt. Let it reduce, simmering low for 1 hour. Use the stock as part of the liquid added to the roux.

Make the base with chicken and sausage the day before. Then add shrimp and crabmeat once the pot has been brought to a high simmer on the day you serve it. Offer Tabasco and filé powder for guests who want it. Some say you don't need filé powder when you've included okra. I say so what? If you want it, add it. But don't use a hot sauce other than Tabasco. Not for gumbo.

INGREDIENTS

1 small chicken (cleaned and rinsed, giblets removed)
1 medium white onion, chopped
4 bay leaves, divided use
8 large garlic cloves, divided use
1 teaspoon celery seed
Salt
Freshly ground black pepper
2 quarts shrimp or fish stock (Knorr makes shrimp bouillon cubes, which will work if you're not of a mind to make your own fish stock)
¾ cup canola or grapeseed oil
¼ cup bacon grease
1 cup flour
3 to 4 large yellow onions, diced
1 large green bell pepper, diced
4 to 5 ribs celery, diced
½ pound fresh okra, sliced thin (tops and tips removed)

2 tablespoons Old Bay, Zatarain, or Paul Prudhomme seasoning, divided use
2 tablespoons dried thyme leaves (or 4 tablespoons fresh)
1 teaspoon oregano
1 teaspoon basil
1 pound andouille sausage, sliced
3 pounds large shrimp, peeled and deveined, tail removed
½ pound fresh crabmeat, picked for cartilage and shell and rinsed
2 dozen small oysters, with liquor
3 tablespoons Lea & Perrins Worcestershire sauce
Juice from 2 lemons
1 tablespoon Tabasco (or to taste)
Salt and pepper to taste
8 to 10 cups cooked long-grain white rice
Filé powder

In a large stockpot, combine chicken, water to cover, onion, 2 bay leaves, 3 garlic cloves, celery seed, salt, and pepper. Cover and simmer low, covered, for 25 minutes.

Remove chicken to a platter to cool and reduce stock to approximately 2 quarts. Add fish/shrimp stock.

Mince the remaining 5 garlic cloves, put them in a small bowl, and set aside.

In a second large, heavy-bottomed stockpot, heat oil and bacon grease over medium heat and stir in flour to make the roux. Stir continually until dark brown. Take care not to let the mixture scorch (wear an apron in case the oil/flour mixture splashes, which is No Fun). This should take about 4 to 5 minutes. When it is dark brown, carefully add onions, bell pepper, celery, and remaining garlic. Sauté until vegetables soften. Add okra, seasoning, thyme, oregano, and basil. Stir until okra wilts. Ignore the slime; it'll go away. Stir continually to make sure nothing sticks, about 10 to 15 minutes. Bring stock to a low boil and stir in the vegetable/roux mixture, a large spoonful at a time. Return to a boil, then immediately reduce heat and simmer, covered, for 30 minutes, checking periodically to make sure it isn't sticking (add water or stock as necessary). Add sausage and simmer, low, for another 15 to 20 minutes.

When chicken is cool enough to handle, pull it into bite-size pieces. Pull away wings and throw them back into the pot with the chicken pieces. If you can't make the stock the day before serving, try to let it rest at least several hours. Be frugal like me and freeze the chicken bones for soup or for making more stock, or be like Molly and throw them away.

When you're ready to serve, reheat gumbo to a strong simmer. Add shrimp and crabmeat. Simmer until shrimp curl and turn pink. Stir in Worcestershire sauce, lemon juice, and Tabasco. Season with salt and pepper. Just before serving, stir in oysters and their liquid. Heat until the edges of the oysters curl. Serve over rice. Pass filé powder for those who want it. Serves 8 to 10.

★ ★ ★

CATFISH PECAN WITH
LEMON THYME BUTTER

This is one of Molly's favorite fish dishes from Commander's Palace in New Orleans. When making browned butter with pecans, don't let the butter brown too much; if you do, it becomes bitter. Finally, the thickness of the fish you use determines the actual sauté time. If fillets are especially thick, finish cooking them in the oven to avoid burning the crust. This recipe is reproduced with the restaurant's permission.

INGREDIENTS

3 cups pecan halves
1½ cups all-purpose flour
Creole seafood seasoning to taste
1 medium egg
1 cup milk
6 catfish fillets, 5 to 7 ounces each
 (or flounder, trout, or bass, free
 of bones and scales)

12 tablespoons (1½ sticks)
 unsalted butter
3 lemons, halved
1 tablespoon Worcestershire sauce
6 large sprigs fresh thyme
Kosher salt and freshly ground
 pepper to taste

DIRECTIONS

Place half the pecans, flour, and Creole seasoning in the bowl of a food processor and process until finely ground. Transfer to a large bowl.

Whisk egg in a large mixing bowl and add milk. Season both sides of the fish fillets with Creole seasoning. One at a time, place the fillets in the egg wash.

Remove one fillet from the egg wash, letting any excess fluid drain back into the bowl. Dredge the fillet in the pecan flour and coat both sides, shaking off any excess. Transfer to a dry sheet pan and repeat with the remaining fillets.

Place a large sauté pan over high heat and add 2 tablespoons of the butter. Heat for about 2 minutes, or until the butter is completely melted and starts to bubble. Place three fish fillets in the pan, skin side up, and cook for 30 seconds. Reduce heat to medium and cook for another 1½ to 2 minutes or until fillets are evenly brown and crisp. Turn fish over and cook on the second side for 2 to 2½ minutes, or until fish is firm to the touch and evenly browned. The most important factor in determining the ideal cooking time is the thickness of the fillets.

Remove the fish, place it on a baking rack, wipe the pan clean with a paper towel, add another 2 tablespoons of butter, and repeat with the three remaining pieces of fish. When all the fish fillets are cooked, wipe the pan clean and return the heat to high. Melt the remaining 8 tablespoons of butter and, just as the butter turns brown, add the remaining 1½ cups of pecans and sauté for 2 to 3 minutes or until the nuts are toasted, stirring occasionally. Put lemons facedown in the pan, first squeezing a little juice from each half. Add Worcestershire sauce and fresh thyme. Season with salt and pepper and cook for 30 seconds more, or until thyme starts to wilt and becomes aromatic.

Place one fish fillet and a lemon piece on each of six dinner plates, spoon some pecan butter around each piece of fish, and use the wilted thyme to garnish each plate. Serves 6.

12

We Get By with a Little Help from Our Friends

OVER THE YEARS MOLLY REALIZED she needed help managing her schedule, which, with the success of her first book, became ridiculously demanding. Riding to her rescue was a series of steady assistants. One was Nadine Eckhardt, to this day a bit of an Austin legend.

Think steel magnolia wrapped in C4. Or just let her tell it, which she pretty much does in her book, *The Duchess of Palms*. The title is taken from her reign as a high school beauty queen. She married Billy Lee Brammer, a talented but troubled soul who died of a drug overdose and with whom she had three children, Sidney, Shelby, and Willie. Brammer was best known for *The Gay Place*, a trilogy that has been described as one of the great political novels of all time.

Nadine then married Texas congressman Bob Eckhardt, with whom she had a daughter, Sarah, a lawyer who sits on the Travis County Commissioners Court. Bob, a labor lawyer who died in 2001, was another one of those hard-driving, hard-drinking, larger-than-life Texas mavericks Molly gravitated toward. A seven-term representative from Houston, he was known as a staunch proponent of civil liberties in general and civil rights in particular. Molly spoke at his funeral.

Nadine met Molly when Molly and Kaye Northcott were coediting the *Observer*. During periodic visits to the nation's capital, the two of them would drop into Bob's office, where the women would embark on an old-fashioned gabfest. Nadine would regale Molly and Kaye with the gossip that was currently circulating in the nation's capital, and in return Nadine would get the latest 4-1-1 from Austin. She eventually took over from Liz Faulk and was Molly's "mail mistress," as she called herself, from 1992 to 2002. Her principal duties consisted of

opening, sorting, and assigning letters according to the columns they responded to, and holding her nose when the semiliterate vitriol rolled in.

The granddaughter of a farmer and a child of the Depression, Nadine Eckhardt came from a family that milked its own cows, made its own cheese and
butter, and in general lived off the land. The Depression drove the family from
Oklahoma to the Rio Grande Valley, where she grew up in an extended family
of nine.

In the early 1980s, after two marriages and four children, she and her son,
Willie, invested her life savings of $60,000 and opened a Sixth Street storefront
restaurant in East Austin that promptly attracted Austin's political, creative,
and intellectual renegades. Its booths and mismatched tables and chairs seated
about thirty-five.

The eatery attracted a predominantly left-of-center clientele (and those who
were just hungry and wanted a good, cheap meal). Because it was not a popular destination for most well-heeled white folks, the lefties had it pretty much
to themselves. There was a food distributor down the street, so there were no
transportation costs, and Eckhardt's hardscrabble upbringing kept her focused
on fresh foods and away from processed stuff.

Nadine's was open from 11 a.m. to 10 p.m. Monday through Saturday. A
mimeographed menu on plain white paper offered a limited menu that featured
a $2.50 bowl of Nadine's beans—pintos with ground chuck, tomatoes, onions,
celery, and chiles—with cornbread; your choice of a BLT or chicken sandwich
for $3.25 or a club sandwich for $4.25; a pan-broiled fish and two sides for $6.50;
or a veggie plate at 95 cents a pop. Beer was $1.25 and wine was $1.75.

Austin painter and sculptor Malou Flato had a salad named for her because
it was all she ever ate. She's married to author and former *Newsweek* senior editor
John Taliaferro, who also was a senior editor at *Texas Monthly* and was the founder of *Third Coast*. Malou's studio was on the East Side. She became a regular.

"Originally it was called 'Missy's Salad,' named for Willie's girlfriend at the
time," she says. "Then they broke up and Missy left. Nadine was trying to think
of a new name for it so I said, 'Since I'm here all the time and this is all I eat, why
not call it Malou's Salad?' And she did."

Sure enough, an old yellowed mimeograph sheet lists "Melissa's Salad,"
with green leaf lettuce, cabbage, carrots, Jack cheese, avocado, and chicken. For
$3.95. A later, spiffier version of the menu lists "Malou's Salad" at $4.95. A bowl
of Nadine's beans is $3.50 on the newer menu and the sandwich board had a
vegetarian addition: a $3 avocado number with cheese and a homemade salsa.

"I tried to keep prices affordable and produce fresh," Nadine said. "It helped to have a food distributor down the street. I would just walk down, see what was fresh, and buy it. Sometimes we got the same fish and meat much fancier restaurants got, but they didn't have to deliver to me; Willie and I would go get it ourselves."

Guests sometimes bussed the tables, and the restaurant was cooled by a window unit. Decor came courtesy of deliberately spray-painted walls. Nobody was going to confuse this joint with Jeffrey's.

Nadine's staff consisted of Willie in the kitchen, with Nadine between the kitchen and meet 'n' greets. Ann Richards, who would go on to be governor, ate at Nadine's, as did workmen, politicians, lawyers, lobbyists, and their secretaries. Deals were struck; gossip was shared. Friends contributed recipes. Molly provided a recipe for garlic potatoes and spinach that became a restaurant favorite.

Malou Flato had a smile in her voice as she remembered her "salad" days, only with her it's a literal recollection. "What's really funny is for years after Nadine's was gone I'd run into people and when I'd tell them my name they'd say, 'Are you the one that salad was named for?!'"

MOLLY'S GARLIC POTATOES AND SPINACH

Mercifully, prewashed baby spinach is easy to find these days.

INGREDIENTS

2 tablespoons extra-virgin olive oil
2 pounds small new potatoes,
  unpeeled, cut into quarters
3 large garlic cloves, crushed
1 cup water

Juice of 1 lemon
1 pound fresh spinach or Swiss
  chard (no stems)
Kosher salt
Freshly ground black pepper

DIRECTIONS

Heat olive oil in a 9-inch nonstick skillet (with a lid) until very hot. Add potatoes and cook over high heat, uncovered, shaking often to redistribute potatoes so they'll brown evenly.

Lower heat and stir-fry for 5 more minutes or until tender. Add garlic and stir-fry for 2 minutes. Add water, cover, and simmer for 5 minutes. Squeeze lemon on potatoes and cook longer if needed. Add spinach and toss until spinach wilts. Add salt and pepper to taste. Serve immediately. Serves 4 to 6 as a side dish.

★ ★ ★

Molly and Sandy Richards wring the final notes from the chorus of Bonnie Raitt's "Sweet and Shiny Eyes": "Your sweet and shiny eyes are like the stars above Laredo / like meat and potatoes to me." Photo courtesy of Sandy Richards.

=== 13 ===

Wine, Women, and Song

MUSIC FREQUENTLY ACCOMPANIED MOLLY and me when we worked in the kitchen. My tastes ran to classic folk, traditional jazz, '60s/'70s rock, Bach, Beethoven, Brahms, and, until she changed the station, whatever was on the Metropolitan Opera broadcast on Saturdays.

Molly was seriously into bluegrass, ethnic music, rockabilly, a few classics, and whatever was local. To her credit, she never lost patience with the fact that I consistently confused the Melancholy Ramblers, a popular Austin musical ensemble, with the New Lost City Ramblers, a folksy string band that periodically appeared on campus at my alma mater, Antioch College.

I once gave her a CD of the NLCR just for the heck of it. She pronounced them okay, smiled, and decided to "listen to the rest of it later," which I interpreted to be roughly somewhere between never and never ever, although she was willing to cut them some slack on account of how cofounder Mike Seeger was a half brother to Pete Seeger. Thematic music often accompanied meal prep, although not even *Aida* made it past the Act I Triumphal March. She tolerated *La Bohème*. Ever the romantic, she said it had a good storyline.

One Saturday Molly consented to listen to that Puccini favorite and we listened to Marcello sing his heart out to Mimi as we discussed plans for a turducken Thanksgiving. It was one in an endless series of dinners, lunches, and brunches we concocted. Many were themed—an Academy Award evening of food from various nominated movies; a brunch of only seasonal vegetables; a potluck dinner made from authentic Julia Child recipes (no cheating); a gourmet Super Bowl party; a brunch of only green food—or was it red?

The real fun started when "Chef Ellen" had to divine a way to stretch food for four into a meal for six—or sometimes eight or ten—by the time Miz Molly extended spontaneous invites at a quarter past the last minute.

Numbers became more controlled once Molly commissioned that round table, because it worked as long as seatings were kept to eight, Thanksgiving and Christmas dinners excepted.

Mood and the guest list determined the menu. It might be beef tenderloin with leeks and pureed potatoes or a bowl o' red topped with chopped onion, cheese, and Molly's jalapeño cornbread. Depending on the season it might be standard summer fare—ribs, hot dogs, chicken, potato salad, and her perennial favorite, asparagus. Christmas dinner might yield a standing rib roast with mushrooms, Yorkshire pudding, fingerling potatoes, and baby vegetables.

Although she favored salmon in later years, Molly was a dedicated carnivore early on. She especially loved old-fashioned dishes, so a frosty winter's Saturday dinner might demand pot roast, potatoes, carrots, and peas as the main attraction. Until illness laid her low, as you probably guess by now, Molly was a certified meat-and-potatoes girl.

Seasonal music was de rigueur. Voices emanating from her boom box might be anything—Donna Summer, Bing Crosby, Aaron Neville, the Chipmunks, or Elvis. One year Molly managed to find something called *Yodeling the Classics*. If there was ever anything with the power to make gums itch, this CD was it. She couldn't stop playing the damned thing. With each successive yodeling of Mozart's "Eine Kleine Nachtmusik" she'd dissolve in laughter. God help us if three or four people arrived solo instead of together. We'd have to hear it again and again and again with each successive arrival. She couldn't even stop reading the liner notes aloud: "Not since Spike Jones gargled the 'William Tell Overture' has there been a recording to compare with this."

Amen.

Smothered pork chops were another favorite, as was *poulet* Dijon, actually nothing more than a gussied-up variation on that chicken recipe calling for forty cloves of garlic.

Although we couldn't always agree on what constituted good music, we were in sync on the value of good food—two of life's more satisfying components. So it was not unusual from time to time to have the Melancholy Ramblers—Frances Barton, Brady Coleman, Marco Perella, and Blackie White—

jamming away in Molly's living room, on her patio, or on her CD player.

All are accomplished in their own right, but Frances represents the kind of woman Molly liked to have around. Frances, of the rich contralto voice, was the lone distaff member of the Melancholy Ramblers. She met Molly in the 1970s, through Ronnie Dugger, founding editor of the *Texas Observer*, and business manager Cliff Olofson.

(As will become increasingly obvious, Molly stories can't be told without recurring mention of the *Texas Observer*, where she wrote for six years before heading off to the big time in New York City.)

Just knowing Molly's friends helps you know the real Molly, and Frances lends insight to those whom Molly viewed with trust and respect. Frances's husband, physician and sculptor Richard Leverich, was among Austin's comparatively few physicians in private practice who accepted Medicare patients, before he retired in 2010.

Molly and Frances didn't know each other well at first, but they had many mutual friends. Frances started working at the *Observer* as business manager in 1981, when Olofson, who retired continually right up to the day he really did once and for all, asked Frances to work with him with a view toward replacing him. She lasted only a couple of years but had a great time in those twenty-four months. Olofson never left the *Observer* until he died in 1995.

At the time the *Observer* shared space on the second floor of a two-story house that Dave Richards had bought when he and Ann were still married. Although he bought the building to house the law firm he and Sam Houston Clinton shared, the *Observer* shared the second floor with the Texas Civil Liberties Union. Dorothy Browne, who was the TCLU assistant director, remembers those wild and woolly days. She went on to become administrative assistant to Elliott Naishtat, arguably the most liberal member of the Texas Legislature, who keeps getting reelected in spite of his progressive politics.

"It was quite an assembly," Dorothy said. "It was so completely crazy. Molly had that raggedy dog called Shit, the place looked like it was falling down, and the toilet was on the back porch. Heaven help you if you wanted to use it in cold weather—I remember one time Hazel Clinton came and poured antifreeze in it because the water had frozen solid."

Minor inconveniences aside, the building's second-floor veranda was a perfect place to unwind after a long day of trying to publish a political journal, defend civil rights, and seek justice for the downtrodden. Design appointments for the veranda featured a tattered overstuffed sofa, mismatched chairs, and a small refrigerator perpetually filled with beer.

If you're beginning to sense a pattern related to the role of hops and barley in sustaining Austin's progressives, well, nicely done. There was a decidedly *laissez les bon temps rouler* air about it all. When this crew worked, they worked; and when they didn't, stand back. It was a heady time, especially for Frances, who grew up cradled in the arms of the church.

"Molly was a huge celebrity in my eyes, and I was a little intimidated, although I felt closer to her later on," Frances said, recalling a family photo of a different kind. "My niece Lisa had come to stay with me. She was sixteen or seventeen at the time and I took her to one of the parties Dave Richards used to throw at the office. This was a Halloween party, held in the back parking lot. Lisa and I went dressed as hookers. She knew all kind of tricks with makeup and managed to give us a pretty believable look for our roles. Somebody snapped a photo and gave it to me later. Dick scanned it, cleaned it up, and I have it hanging on the wall in my bathroom. Reminds me of those good times."

Like several of Molly's friends, Frances came to the city of Austin from somewhere else. In this instance, Nelsonville, a small Czech and German community in Austin County. (When she was twelve, her family moved to Taylor.)

Her ancestors emigrated from Moravia, one of the provinces of what is now the Czech Republic. Her grandfather and father were both ministers in the old Hussite church, called the Unitas Fratrum (Unity of the Brethren). It has a long religious as well as political history in Bohemia and Moravia and was one of the inspirations for the democratic uprisings there, including the Velvet Revolution of 1989.

Her parents both attended the University of Texas in the 1930s, where they belonged to a club called the Hot Czechs. Her mother, who didn't speak English until Frances was five, went on to become a high school English teacher. Her father, who received his theological degree from Oberlin College, was a passionate FDR Democrat.

"He preached in Czech and English," Frances said. "He had a beautiful bass voice. When my brother and I were old enough, we formed a family quartet: Mother sang soprano, I sang alto, my brother sang tenor, and my father sang bass. I loved it and count it as one of the joys of my life."

The family sang together at churches, funerals, revivals, rest homes, and hospitals. Her father was eventually drummed out of the church for his anti–Vietnam War sermons and for supporting VISTA volunteers working in the Taylor area. Working for VISTA was a legal alternative to participating in the Vietnam conflict for some, but not for others, and that included lots of folk in Taylor.

"I held a grudge against Taylor for a long time but have made my peace with the place. After all, the Ramblers do get paid [when performing there]."

Thank goodness for that; Taylor has some of the best barbecue in Texas.

Like many old-school Austinites rotating through Molly's vast circle of contacts, Frances has led an eclectic life—choir and Sunday school pianist, waitress, Volkswagen mechanic, VISTA trainer, library clerk, substitute funeral home organist, legal secretary, proofreader, writer, campaign manager, fundraiser, and accomplished gardener.

The Barton-Leverich duo have a daughter, Jubilee Rose, completing a fellowship in pediatric intensive care, and a son, Jacob Barton Leverich, born on the bathroom floor of the family home. He has risen above that inglorious start to earn a PhD in computer science from Stanford. Friends thought they should commemorate the physical place of his birth and name him John. Mercifully his parents thought otherwise.

So now we have Dorothy Browne's progressive politics and invaluable organizational skills paired with Elliott Naishtat's populist politics, Frances on the board of the *Texas Observer*, and Dave Richards practicing law on behalf of the downtrodden. If a chorus of "Will the Circle Be Unbroken" is starting to reverberate as background music for identifying the cast of characters in Molly's life, there's a reason for that.

═══ 14 ═══

Steel Magnolias, Texas Style

ANCILLARY TO SPEAKING TEXAN is learning to understand the language of the steel magnolia, and almost all of Molly's female friends in Texas could qualify for magnoliadom.

Since I was an outsider it took me a while to learn how to interpret magnolia-speak, as when you encounter a house where no expense has been spared and good taste has not been allowed to intervene. The appropriate observation is "My goodness, I don't think I've ever seen anything quite like this," or "My, my, my, this is *really* something!"

Said with a beatific smile and breathless sigh, its true import comes into focus much later, if ever. Marilyn Schwartz, who met Molly when both were on the same Memphis assignment, hails from Mobile, Alabama. An authentic Southern belle, she documented steel magnolias and Southern politesse in her book *A Southern Belle Primer: Or Why Princess Margaret Will Never Be a Kappa Kappa Gamma*.

When this gentle spoof on gentility first appeared in 1991, Molly had great fun with it. She would read passages after dinner as she pointed out the use of authentic sterling silver, as prescribed in the *Primer*; or as we were sitting down to dinner and she would call attention to the asparagus tongs; or after dinner, as she would note the appropriate configuration of spoon and fork as we prepared to enjoy dessert.

Marilyn's book was a droll, stiletto-sharp send-up of protocols drawn from Atlanta, Charleston, Vicksburg, and, of course, her beloved Mobile. In the South of then and, in some places, now, almost the worst thing you could be called was "tacky."

The very worst was "*tacky* tacky."

The *Primer* reveals that Southern belles don't put dark meat in their chicken salad; do take pride in the fact that they have never hired anyone who chews gum; never substitute Miracle Whip for mayonnaise; and always serve deviled eggs on a deviled-egg plate. While they would never, ever participate in a lawsuit of any kind, they would most assuredly know the right person to make a point on their behalf.

Molly, by the way, had her mother's china, sterling silver tea service, a cut-glass iced tea pitcher, *and* a deviled-egg plate. She once had an afternoon tea with perfect cut-out rounds of cucumber, tomato, and egg salad sandwiches on equally perfect cut-out rounds of white bread. Just as I blamed the undue influence of Martha Stewart for Molly's taking to fancy glass bottles to hold dishwashing detergent, I blame Maryln Schwartz for Molly's infatuation with tea sandwiches.

Maryln, an excellent cook whose silver also matched and whose china was well chosen, is possibly among a select few who ever taught Molly how to cook anything, and that's saying something. You see, Southern belles rarely share their recipes. Even more rarely do they tell you *all* of the ingredients—even though they truly cannot give precise measurements.

Maryln and Molly met in Memphis in 1977. Both were among the minuscule number of women covering Elvis's funeral. The female population in the newsroom in those days was relatively small.

(It should be noted that by 1985 an organization called JAWS—the Journalism and Women Symposium—had come into being. Launched at a gathering of fifteen women from varied news backgrounds, it grew over the years to include hundreds of women in media who invited a range of influential women to speak and meet with them. Speakers included women such as Congresswoman Pat Schroeder, children's advocate Marian Wright Edelman, artist Judy Chicago, USAF Brigadier General Wilma Vaught, Pulitzer Prize–winning *New York Times* reporter Nan Robertson, who wrote *The Girls in the Balcony: Women, Men, and* The New York Times. Her book included the lawsuit brought by female employees against the newspaper in 1974. The title refers to the place in the nation's capitol to which women in the Washington Press Corps were relegated. Molly not only spoke to the group; she joined it.)

But back to Elvis: Molly and Maryln had heard of one another but never met. Maryln was writing for the *Dallas Morning News* and Molly was still with the *New York Times*. Molly had been standing behind Maryln in a line circling the yard where the King lay in repose. They eventually introduced themselves to one another.

"When we finally got through walking around Graceland and looking at Elvis all laid out, we realized we had to find a place to stay," Maryln said. "There was a Shriners convention in town and every hotel within eighty miles was taken. We paid a cabdriver an enormous amount of money to take us to the Memphis Chamber of Commerce, where we begged and whined and cajoled until they found a room for us at Memphis State University. Actually it was more like a suite. We shared a bathroom, but we each had our own room.

"By the time we got settled, the adrenaline had us both so wired we couldn't think about going to sleep. You have to understand I had never seen a corpse before. Jews don't have open caskets, and we had been going around and around, looking at Elvis in that incredible copper-lined coffin. By the time it got to be evening Molly says, 'I can't sleep without a beer,' And I said, 'I can't sleep without a book.' So then we walked around Memphis until we both found what we wanted."

Their friendship continued long after Molly returned to New York.

"We stayed in touch, and when she knew she was coming to Dallas [to work for the *Dallas Times Herald*], we wanted to remain friends." But they worked for rival newspapers, so they couldn't talk about what they were working on. They talked about food instead. As it transpired, Molly, being from Texas, was familiar with Cajun food. Maryln, being from Mobile, was all about Creole cooking, the secrets of which she shared with Molly.

Cooking cemented friendship for them—although at one point, Maryln was ready to plant Molly in cement shoes. She recounted the circumstances with feigned indignity: "Anyone from the South will tell you when you are trusted enough to get a recipe, you keep it to yourself. You don't go running all over town telling everybody about it—unless you give credit to the original source. Not Molly. She took my recipes and ran with them. The next thing I knew everyone thought they were HER recipes. I taught her how to make West Indies salad, shrimp boil, and scalloped oysters. And you know what she did? I'll tell you what she did: She had a dinner for Alexis Herman and served MY shrimp boil. Every time I turned around there was Alexis Herman talking about this *fabulous* shrimp boil she'd had at Molly Ivins's house. Harrumph!"

To demonstrate the absence of residual hard feelings, Maryln shared her recipes for West Indies salad and scalloped oysters—with *all* the ingredients, along with permission to share them here.

MARYLN SCHWARTZ'S WEST INDIES SALAD

"You make this and it's a killer every time," Maryln said. "I don't know what it is about layering the ingredients this way, but I promise you if you do it this way, it's the best thing you ever tasted."

INGREDIENTS

1 medium onion, chopped fine, divided use

2 pounds white lump crabmeat, rinsed and picked for cartilage

⅓ cup *cold* water

⅓ cup vegetable oil

¼ cup white vinegar

A sprinkling of kosher salt

DIRECTIONS

In a large bowl, spread half of the chopped onions evenly across the bottom. Spread the crabmeat on top of the onions. Evenly distribute the remaining onions in a third layer. Pour cold water and vinegar evenly over the crabmeat and finish with the oil. Add salt. *Do not stir or mix the ingredients.* Cover and refrigerate overnight. Remove from refrigerator, stir once to combine ingredients, and serve on lettuce. Serves 2 to 4.

★ ★ ★

MARYLN SCHWARTZ'S SCALLOPED OYSTERS

INGREDIENTS

48 oysters

2 cups Progresso Italian bread crumbs

1 cup grated Parmesan cheese

3 tablespoons chopped parsley

Juice of 2 lemons

¾ cup olive oil

1 garlic clove, crushed

½ to 1 tablespoon crushed red pepper flakes

Kosher salt to taste

DIRECTIONS

Preheat oven to 350°F. Place oysters in a shallow baking dish. Combine bread crumbs, cheese, parsley, lemon juice, olive oil, garlic, red pepper, and salt. Top oysters with the mixture. Bake until oysters curl, about 15 minutes. Remove and place under broiler until lightly browned. Serves 4.

★ ★ ★

15

Dinner—A Family Affair

PEOPLE UNFAMILIAR WITH THE SWEETS/IVINS commitment to the five-second rule might never have returned to a meal at Molly's table had they known about our "oops" moments. Both the "get the shrimp off the floor" and the "rinse the blood from the onions" incidents were reminiscent of the Sweets Family Thanksgiving Dinner Secret. It moved Molly to feel culturally deprived, since the Ivins family apparently lacked a history of such moments.

Melba Sweets, my mother, belonged to an organization called the St. Louis Committee on Africa. In the late '60s and early '70s students from sub-Saharan Africa were often left on their own on holidays, so committee members invited students without plans to share the holiday.

One year Mother invited a woman from Egypt, a man from Ghana, and another from Ethiopia. The best china was hauled out, the linen tablecloth was ironed, and matching napkins were appropriately placed for a seating of ten.

We had a turkey roughly the size of Vermont, and because my father didn't like turkey, we also had a standing rib roast. Both were the focal points for a full-court press of Brussels sprouts, mashed potatoes, oyster dressing, plain stuffing, braised carrots, collard greens, and a sweet potato casserole laced with orange zest and pecans.

Did I mention the family dog, Chips, a boxer of considerable size?

Remember Chips.

My grandfather, my mother's father, always arrived for these celebratory dinners in an already slightly schnockered condition. Inebriation notwithstanding, he was the designated table-blesser. Our guests, accustomed to according their elders more deference than we did, punctuated Grandpa's long-winded prayer with an occasional "amen," which only egged him on to pray longer. Just then, a sound not unlike like that of gumbo falling from a refrigerator shelf emanated from the kitchen. One of my brothers immediately interjected a resounding "Amen!" at a pause that permitted Grandpa to hiccup and my mother to hastily retreat kitchenward.

There she found Chips with the entire rib roast in his mouth, his escape stymied by a locked screen door that prevented him from absconding altogether into the backyard. In a preternaturally soft voice, Mother summoned me. "Ellen," she said sweetly, "could you help me, please?" Inherent in her tone was a requirement to respond instantly. As I cautiously opened the swinging door leading from the dining room, Chips was reluctantly relinquishing his loot. Mother retrieved her miraculously unbroken Noritake platter, rearranged the kale leaves, and shot me a look that said, "Not a word of this." With a few more flourishes, she returned to the dining room, all smiles, bearing a perfectly browned turkey surrounded by wine-poached pears on the big platter. I, trailing close behind, carried the roast on the smaller platter, tooth marks camouflaged beneath butter-laced whole mushrooms and decorative sprinkles of freshly chopped parsley.

I never uttered a peep about the Sweets Christmas near-disaster either—until I wrote about it for the *Denver Post* a few years ago. That Thanksgiving dinner, like the gumbo dinner Molly and I laughed about for years, was a resounding success. At both meals there was much laughter and conversation. Everyone went home sated and none the worse for partaking of food off the floor.

Food memories formed most of the glue that held our friendship together, Molly's and mine. The more we talked about remembered meals, the more we realized what an important role food had played in our respective lives, albeit entrenched in very different social strata. She was to the manor born. Her father, whom friends all called Big Jim, was an attorney for Tenneco, one of the world's biggest oil companies at the time. By Molly's account he was a paid-in-full member of the Houston power elite—rich, powerful, racist, and mean.

Her brother, Andy, the youngest of the three Ivins siblings, has more positive memories of cookouts in their River Oaks home. Andy recalls backyard barbecues in particular. "Around 1964 we got a barbecue pit with a rotisserie and Big Jim would cook chicken on it," he said. "It was outside by the pool and we had a park-type bench where we would eat in the evenings.

"Big Jim" Ivins, Molly, and brother, Andy, share a laugh and a meal in an Austin restaurant in 1987. The locale is lost to memory. Ivins family collection.

"We'd have hamburger steaks with onions and a side dish of mushrooms. We always had a salad that came between the main course and dessert and only had oil and vinegar as the dressing and never anything else. We'd have baked potatoes with butter and salt and pepper and paprika, but never sour cream. Even at restaurants we would have to go through hell getting the chef to give him paprika.

"Big Jim also made serious Sunday breakfasts—fruit, cereal, eggs, coffee cake, bacon, and sausage. We'd all eat at the round table outside by the pool. Mag [Margot, materfamilias and Big Jim's wife] started cooking more when we moved to Maryland." Like Molly, Andy remembers not only his mother's turnip fluff, but her "goody-goody grits," both dishes that she added to her *Joy of Cooking*–based repertoire. Molly's menus *français* came later.

The Sweets and Ivins families had at least one thing in common: Andy remembers the family's 1950s-era meat grinder. My brothers and I fought over who would get to press solid chunks of raw beef through the top of ours and watch it squish through little holes as ground beef. Apparently Andy had the same experience in reverse—except as the lone male with two sisters, he got left out.

"We had a crank machine that you put some cut of meat in and it came out hamburger. I think that was Sara and Molly's job, but I remember watching and thinking what a great deal it would be when I got my turn to crank. The other thing I remember is that Molly and Sara were in charge of doing dinner dishes. Sara would always remember when she had either washed or dried last.

"Molly always got screwed on whose turn it was to do what 'cause she didn't bother to remember. My job was to empty the garbage."

While Molly's father was part of an elite power structure, my dad was the struggling publisher of a black weekly newspaper that frequently pissed off the power structure.

My family was also part of that demographic that never gave two hoots for heart-healthy calorie consciousness. Today only a pariah would suggest the kind of breakfast meal my aunt Jen used to prepare on Sunday mornings. She lived in Chicago, midway between our home in St. Louis and a black-owned farm in the middle of Michigan—our standard summer vacation destination throughout the 1950s. It was someplace we could go without the hassle of wondering where we could eat or sleep. We knew we would be welcome, for example, in Benton Harbor, dominated by an amusement park owned by the House of David colony, a religious sect that did not engage in racial discrimination. Sometimes we went to the Wisconsin Dells, another safe vacation place.

Aunt Jen's rolls were known throughout the Windy City. Her breakfasts of baked chicken, bacon, sausage, buttered rice, scrambled eggs, and those wonderful rolls are the stuff of favored reveries. In fact, almost everything warm and wonderful that I remember about growing up revolves around food. Aunt Jen and the Johnsons' farm put the soul in "soul food." So what the hell: Let's hear it for pariahs.

For the most part, Aunt Jen just cooked for herself and Uncle Howard. But on Saturdays, when she and friends had their penny poker nights, she might whip up a pot of chitlins, spaghetti, greens, and some cornbread. The smell of chitlins (you can call them "chitterlings" if you want, but folks will laugh behind your back) drove the kids to the barbecue joint around the corner, where ribs and chicken were generously served atop mounds of potato salad and coleslaw.

But Aunt Jen's rolls and baked chicken were an absolute Sunday-morning treat. She cut a couple of good-size fryers into pieces—chickens didn't come shrink-wrapped on a Styrofoam tray back then—dredged the pieces in salt, pepper, garlic powder, and paprika, placed them in a roasting pan, and topped each piece with a pat of butter. She then whisked together maybe a half cup of flour with about 2 quarts of water, poured it down the side of the roaster and covered the pan tightly.

She baked the chicken at 275 degrees for about two hours, or until the incredible aromas emanating from the oven proved too much for empty stomachs to bear. As the liquid evaporated in the roaster, the flour from the chicken and the flour in the water melded with the butter and chicken fat to form a light gravy. This was served with a choice of rice or grits, sliced tomatoes, and eggs, sunny-side up or scrambled.

The Johnsons' farm was another world. Food preparation there was geared toward the farmhands who did real work, not the vacationing pretend-workers we city slickers were. Sometimes the table was filled with homemade sage-and-pork sausage served alongside apple pancakes made with fruit from the Johnsons' trees. Thick slabs of sliced bacon came from hogs slaughtered and cured on the property. The Johnsons dug their own potatoes and hand-chopped them into little bits before adding onions—also grown on the farm—for hash browns. Chickens that had clucked noisily in the afternoon were crisp, golden-fried drumsticks, wings, breasts, and thighs by evening.

Those meals are cherished components of family reminiscences to this day—just as the entire family remembers the time I broke my arm when I fell off the back of a moving truck (don't ask; it involved a game of "chicken" where the winner was the idiot who could jump off and onto the bed of the pickup truck the most times and I was the only girl and had to prove I was as dumb as the guys) or the time a herd of turkeys forced Mom and me up a tree. It had never occurred to me that my mother could climb a tree. Chances are it had never occurred to her either, but there she was, eight feet off the ground, sitting on a limb and clinging to branches for dear life. That Sunday, roasted turkey and dressing were more delicious than ever.

Summer segued into fall, when we made our annual pilgrimage to Lincoln University in Jefferson City, Missouri, for homecoming. Standard fare there consisted of salad and Aunt Kay's chicken spaghetti. It's hard to pinpoint exactly what made the spaghetti so memorable. Maybe for us kids it was seeing that big pot atop the stove, aromatic steam rising from its simmering contents, knowing, as we did, that the humongous pot in which the spaghetti was made was the same one Aunt Kay used to bathe her daughter and me in when we were little bitty people.

Anyway, for the football enthusiasts, her chicken spaghetti provided welcome warmth after watching a chilly afternoon's football game. All she did was throw five or six chickens into the pot with bay leaves, a pound or two of onions, celery, salt, and pepper. When the chickens were done, they were relocated to a giant colander to cool. The remaining stock simmered as she added canned tomatoes, two whole bunches of chopped celery, several more pounds of onions, a huge jar of sliced green olives (pimientos and all), red pepper flakes, basil, thyme, a quarter cup of chili powder, a bunch or two of chopped parsley, salt, black pepper, and, of course, more garlic.

Once the chicken cooled, we kids got to help pull chunks of meat from the bones and throw it back into the pot. The bones were put in another pot to simmer some more to make additional stock for soup. Finally, Aunt Kay added Lord knows how many pounds of spaghetti. As it cooked, it absorbed the liquid until, finally, the pot was brimming with the finished product. Somehow she never cooked the spaghetti to mush, and it was never soupy or over-seasoned. Of all my food recollections, I don't remember precise measurements as being part of any of them: a bit of this and a bit of that generally did the trick.

Such are the memories of foods eaten in childhood—a childhood where much revolved around Sunday breakfast, weekday dinners, and Saturday meals that always consisted of either a pot of chili or a pot of beans—pig's feet and navy beans; ham hocks and lima beans; red beans and rice with smoked sausage. Saturday was the day Daddy took over the kitchen. The bean of the day was always accompanied by cornbread. Not any old kind of cornbread, but cornbread made with cornmeal, flour, eggs, and buttermilk, with a special addition: half a pound of bacon, cooked crisp and crumbled into the batter.

Daddy poured off most of the bacon grease and put the skillet in a pre-heated oven. When the remaining grease was smoking, he'd remove the skillet, pour the batter in, and return it to the oven. When the cornbread was brown on top, he'd take it out and turn it onto a rack, like a cake. The result was incredible. It had a crisp brown crust that rendered butter superfluous.

In fact, my father made two incredible dishes. The other was fried corn, which we ate on Sunday, usually with pole beans (cooked with the requisite ham hock and salt pork). He would go to the market in the morning and buy ten or fifteen ears of white corn. He and I would sit on the back porch and shuck it as he listened to a baseball game. Then he'd cut it off the cob and put it in a big bowl. After he heated up some bacon grease in the cast-iron skillet, he'd add the corn, a chopped green bell pepper, some cream, a pinch of sugar, a little salt, and a lot of black pepper (my mother kept a lidded clay pot with the words "bacon grease" atop the stove, flanked by two burners on our old Roper.

As the corn cooked, he'd stir and stir. By the time it was finally done, almost all of the liquid had cooked away. Only soft kernels of white corn remained, with flecks of green pepper. The centerpiece of the meal for everyone else was chicken, rubbed with garlic salt, black pepper, and paprika, dipped in buttermilk and flour and fried in lard. But the fried corn won my heart.

Mother was no slouch in the kitchen either. Especially memorable were her stuffed pork chops. Actually, they were thick fried pork chops topped with a thick slice of onion, a thick slice of tomato, and a thick slice of bell pepper into which she spooned parboiled rice. She then placed them in a tightly covered baking dish and baked them for 40 or 45 minutes. The result was a one-dish meal worthy of your best cardiovascular surgeon. Over the years, neither my brothers nor I have forgotten those dishes from childhood, and occasionally I'll make them as best as I can recall.

My father, Nathaniel, died in 1988, a year before I moved to Texas. One night at dinner after my arrival in Dallas, a friend took me to a restaurant for an introduction to Texas cooking of the relentlessly fried kind. When I saw fried corn on the menu, I thought I would burst into tears. Could it be?

I eagerly ordered a double portion. How was I to know I had ordered batter-fried chunks of corn on the cob? Somewhere, that night, I know my father was spinning in his grave. Eating healthy might be good for you, but I still can't see fat-free, low-cholesterol food-fad fanatics reminiscing over tofu casseroles or alfalfa-sprout sandwiches the way we remember Mother's pork chops, Daddy's fried corn, Aunt Jen's baked chicken, and Aunt Kay's chicken spaghetti.

MELBA'S BAKED PORK CHOPS

When my daughter, Hannah, was in charge of her first kitchen in Dallas, she put these on her menu and sold out every time. Although I don't particularly care for green bell peppers, they complete the flavor profile of this layered dish of pork chop, onion, tomato, and rice. Choose vegetables that, when sliced, will have roughly the same circumference as the pork chop because they will be layered one atop the other, finishing with a bell pepper ring that is filled with partially cooked rice. This dish is best served with a simple green salad with a blue cheese or feta dressing. Dessert should be something light, like a fruit cup or sherbet or a long walk. I first shared this recipe in a Mother's Day tribute in the *Denver Post*.

INGREDIENTS

¾ flour
1½ teaspoons kosher salt
2 teaspoons black pepper
1 teaspoon paprika
4 loin pork chops, cut 1½ inches thick
¼ cup cooking oil
2 large yellow onions, sliced ½ inch thick
4 ½-inch-thick slices of beefsteak tomato

4 ¾-inch-thick slices of large green bell pepper
Cooking oil spray
2 cups partially cooked long-grain rice
3 cups chicken stock
Extra paprika
¼ cup fresh parsley, chopped fine, for garnish

DIRECTIONS

Combine flour, salt, pepper, and paprika in a plastic or paper bag. Rinse and dry pork chops and dredge in the flour mixture. Shake off excess flour.

In a nonstick frying pan or a cast-iron skillet, brown pork chops in oil quickly over medium-high heat, searing them on both sides. Put the chops in a casserole or roasting pan large enough to accommodate them.

Preheat oven to 350°F.

On each chop, layer, in order, an onion slice, a tomato slice, and a bell pepper slice. Spray a ¾-cup measure with cooking oil and fill it with rice. Invert cup so that a mound of rice is placed inside each bell pepper ring. Sprinkle all with a light dusting of paprika. Pour chicken stock around chops and seal casserole with foil or a tight-fitting lid.

Bake 35 to 40 minutes covered, 10 minutes uncovered. Serve each chop with pan juices ladled over rice and a sprinkling of parsley. Serves 4.

★ ★ ★

MOLLY'S FRIENDS WERE A QUIRKY, ECLECTIC BUNCH who came to dinner in jeans and kicked off their shoes. Their language was frequently salty, and they often made Molly double over with laughter at delicious gossip or schoolgirl silliness.

Sure, she hobnobbed with the rich and famous, but she came home to the same merry band she had known over the years: Kaye Northcott, with whom she shared legislative reporting responsibilities at the *Texas Observer* and, later, the *Fort Worth Star-Telegram*; Courtney Anderson; her good friend Sara Speights; Austin attorney Shelia Cheaney; and later, television news producer Marilyn Schultz, whom Molly affectionately dubbed Schultzie. I came comparatively late to the party, but they allowed me in.

Each has a tale or two to tell, from Molly's early days as a reporter to her years as a three-time Pulitzer Prize finalist, through her induction into the American Academy of Arts and Sciences. One of Sara Speights's many memories of cooking with Molly revolves around the fact that no matter what the meal was, Molly was rarely ready, especially if a Julia dish was involved.

"Molly's food was always fabulous," Sara said. "But if I do a meal I always try to do as much as possible in advance. Not Molly. You'd arrive and she'd be working away in the kitchen, preparing some unbelievably complicated food, so we'd all be squeezing past one another to get the damn dinner done.

"Once Molly invited federal district judge William Wayne Justice, his wife, Sue, and the Episcopalian bishop over. For this meal she decided to take on *saumon en papillote*—salmon baked in parchment paper—that was just incredible. It was the sort of thing you'd pay a small fortune for in a restaurant, but here Molly was, making it at home."

In addition to being a friend, Schultzie was also a frequent cooking buddy and avowed newshound who did not fear a good fight. In the 1970s Marilyn, a veteran of network television news, sued NBC for wage, sex, and age discrimination. She paid dearly for this courageous move—both personally and professionally—although women who followed benefited. Although the suit was filed in 1971, right up to her death in 2010 she refused to talk about it publicly. Anyone who has had the temerity to face down corporate power—and won—can tell you the experience is not just emotionally draining. Depending on how dirty a former employer wants to play, it can also render you unemployable.

Her courage in leading a class-action suit against the NBC mother ship and its affiliates on behalf of women who wanted equal opportunity and pay forever changed the way media institutions set pay and promotion scales.

The lawsuit took a terrible toll on Marilyn, although she was in good company. Think Brooksley Born, one of maybe three people in the world who actually understood credit swaps and those incomprehensible, complex financial instruments called derivatives—pesky critters that caused a near-cataclysmic collapse on Wall Street a couple of years ago.

Several years before that financial meltdown, Born warned of the dangers associated with careless trading of derivatives. And what did her warnings get her? She was forced to resign as head of the Commodity Futures Trading Commission, an obscure, relatively unknown agency—until she called for regulation and the rooting out of fraud. What was she thinking?!

From left, Marilyn "Schultzie" Schultz, Shelia Cheaney, and Molly at one of Molly's many Sunday brunches. Ivins family collection.

Or consider FBI special agent Coleen Rowley, who exposed internal FBI problems and publicly criticized the agency for its clumsy handling of the 9/11 terrorist attacks. Does anybody even remember Cynthia Cooper, the World-Com vice president who exposed billions of dollars in accounting irregularities? Or Sherron Watkins, a former Enron vice president, who warned of the oil giant's potential collapse to no avail? They all lost their jobs as a result of doing the right thing.

There still isn't a lot of wiggle room for strong women who speak truth to power. Like most of Molly's female friends, all of these women easily qualified for steel magnolia status, including Schultzie, despite her Indiana roots.

When Schultzie died unexpectedly from multiple medical complications at the age of sixty-four, she was an associate professor of communications at Austin's St. Edward's University. She died on January 10, 2010, just a few weeks before the third anniversary of Molly's January 31 death in 2007. Marilyn's memorial service revealed dimensions of her dynamic personality none of us had known, such as the immense affection and respect she had for her students.

Just as few people had known about Molly and her love of cooking, friends who thought they knew Marilyn well were deeply moved by the video montage her students created in tribute to her.

SAUMON EN PAPILLOTE
(SALMON IN PARCHMENT)

Molly raved about this dish so much that I decided to try it my very own self. Building on a recipe from Whole Foods, and incorporating baby carrots, sliced shallots, and two baby zucchini with the basil and lemon, I did. Once. It was really expensive and I was terrified that it wouldn't work, but it did and I've never made it since. It is in fact a relatively easy recipe—albeit a pricey one, especially if you use Copper River salmon or one of the seasonal Alaskan varieties. If there are leftovers, layer the salmon with vegetable cream cheese and cucumber slices on a toasted bagel.

INGREDIENTS

6 (6-ounce) salmon fillets
¼ cup chopped basil leaves,
 divided into 6 equal portions
6 (16-square-inch) pieces of
 parchment paper
12 baby carrots
12 baby zucchini

Kosher salt and freshly ground
 pepper to taste
2 tablespoons extra-virgin olive oil
2 lemons, thinly sliced
Kitchen twine (it is untreated with
 chemicals)

DIRECTIONS

Place a large baking sheet on bottom rack of oven. Preheat oven to 400°F.

Cut two half-inch slices into the flesh of each piece of salmon; roll basil leaves and stuff into the slits in each salmon portion.

Place a salmon fillet in the center of each piece of parchment paper. Place one carrot and one zucchini on each side of the fish. Sprinkle fish and vegetables with salt and pepper. Drizzle each fillet with 1 teaspoon of the oil, then place lemon slices on top.

Gather the sides of the parchment up over salmon to form a pouch, sort of as if you're wrapping a gift, leaving no openings, and tie tightly with kitchen twine. Place packages directly on hot baking sheet in oven and cook for 20 minutes. Transfer to plates and carefully open packages to release steam before serving. Serve with rice pilaf and haricots verts, grilled asparagus, or your favorite spinach dish. Serves 6.

★ ★ ★

16

Managing Molly

JAN DEMETRI, MOLLY'S LONG-SUFFERING ACCOUNTANT, remained on the periphery of Molly's Austin inner circle, due, one suspects, to the need for her to keep her distance in order to maintain a professional relationship separate from their social one. It was just how things had to be. But she, too, knew about Molly's kitchen skills and is herself no piker when it comes to cooking.

Jan and Molly met through Sara Speights when Molly was still living in Dallas. Sara knew Molly needed help managing her finances, and Jan signed on. All information about income and bills came through her from 1980 until Molly died—as exasperating as it was at times.

"We'd either meet at my office or at someplace like Sweetish Hill [which still serves some of the state's most luscious muffins], and agree to put a certain amount of money in her checking account so she would always know how much she had, and then set some aside," Jan said. "I was never controlling, but Molly had a way of giving money away before she made it. If I told her she didn't have any money, she would say, 'Well, I'll just do three extra speeches.'" Pity the poor referee who had to mediate that particular accountant-client relationship.

What a lot of people didn't know, however, was that Molly had a serious philanthropic streak. There was only one caveat: no one was ever to know what she gave or to whom. It drove Jan nuts. "Molly's position on the matter was reminiscent of Rosie O'Donnell's declaration that she would fire her accountant if she ever appeared in *Forbes* because of her wealth and philanthropy," Jan said. "Only where O'Donnell built arts programs, Molly gave free speeches for any ACLU chapter, anywhere. All the organization had to do was pay her way, feed her, and provide a place for her to lay her head. Managing Molly wasn't always easy, and she wasn't always easy to work for or with. But as stubborn as she was capable of being, she had a good heart. A really good heart."

And a big one. She was determined that her blood-kin nieces and nephews have a college education, and she saw to it that that happened. But she gave more than money. Molly never married and couldn't have had room for kids given the pace she kept. Instead she "adopted" the children of friends. They became nieces and nephews too.

Among them were Michelle and Candace McNeely, daughters of Molly's longtime friend Dave McNeely. The girls first met Molly when their ages could be measured in single digits. Dave and Molly had been friends since their overlapping days at the *Houston Chronicle* in 1965, a forty-year friendship that ended with Molly's death. They had met when she was a journalism student working summers at the *Chronicle* and he was a political reporter at the paper. He went on to cover politics for the *Dallas Morning News*, the *Dallas Times Herald*, and the *Austin American-Statesman*.

Dave spent a lot of time in Austin in the early '70s, and was among the crew that gathered on the balcony of the building that housed Dave Richards's law firm and the *Texas Observer*. McNeely remembers those visits as though they were yesterday.

"One of my frequent stops was to see Molly and the *Observer* crowd," he recalled. "At that time, they were housed in an old two-story house at the corner of West Seventh and Nueces Streets. Sometimes in the afternoons when I was in town, I'd call over to the *Observer* to see what was going on. Molly would often say, 'Come on over,' adding, 'and you might bring along a six-pack of Bud.'

"So I would, and we'd hang out on that great second-story porch, look south toward Town Lake, exchange political and personal stories, and, of course, drink beer."

When McNeely's marriage faltered, Molly invited Candace to spend several days with her in Denver, where by then Molly had become the *New York Times*'s Rocky Mountain bureau chief. Candy, as she was called then, remembers conversations about divorce and the importance of not taking it personally. Molly remained Dave's friend through that divorce and became a friend to his next wife, Carole Kneeland—going the extra mile and helping to lead the singing and dancing at their backyard wedding.

Carole died of breast cancer in 1998.

Today Candace, who has legally changed her name to Mariposa, has two specific memories of meals with Molly. They shared a very grown-up conversation about how each felt to be an involuntary observer of an unpleasant divorce, with Molly being her usual attentive listening post. Although there was a twenty-year difference in their ages, they were essentially talking as peers because both were riding the same emotional roller coaster.

"The memorable thing is that she was seeking my help," Candace/Candy/Mariposa said. "I was the expert, the sixteen-year-old giving advice to the thirty-five-year-old. I had already watched my parents go through what her parents were going through at the time."

The other remembrance, several years later, was considerably less intense.

"I was visiting her in Denver when she was the *Times*'s Rocky Mountain bureau chief. I don't remember what Molly had cooked, but it was something wonderful, and we had watermelon for dessert. We had planned to sit outside and eat it and see how far we could spit the seeds, Texas style—only the weather was too cool. So Molly decided we'd spit seeds inside with a painting on her wall as the target, and we did that for the longest time. She was the one who made me realize grown-ups weren't so different from kids after all.

"One way I keep her memory alive is by incorporating her terms of endearment into conversation whenever possible with friends and strangers. I don't call people 'sugar plum' as much as she did, but I do use 'honey' and 'sweetie pie' a lot. I even called my sister 'darlin'' a lot, even though we fought like cats and dogs."

Mariposa's sister, Michelle McNeely Mueller, is now in her forties, but she still laughs when she recalls some of the inscriptions in books from Molly. Her favorite appeared in *Nothin' but Good Times Ahead* and is dated 12/23/93. It reads: "For Michelle—who at the age of 12 shamed me into shaving my armpits—and I have been doing it religiously ever since, I promise. With great affection, Molly Ivins."

Michelle says she can't remember a time when she didn't know Molly. "But, really, other than Molly getting really pissed off at Sam Kinch at one of the Armstrong campouts because he didn't clean the deer meat well for the group-effort stew and there was still hair on it (it was so gross, and Molly gave him hell for it), I don't remember seeing her angry. The other thing I remember was helping Molly roast a whole pig, and her trying to convince us that the eyeballs were indeed a delicacy—if you want to call that a food memory!"

Kate, a daughter of *Denver Post* reporter Jack Cox and now in her thirties, has vivid Molly memories too. Her best recollection dates to ninth grade when her parents packed her off to spend a week with Molly in Austin.

"She hosted a dinner party in honor of my visit," Kate said. "I mean, I was only fourteen and she invited several people, including a lovely gay couple. When I look back on it, I realize she was trying to widen my world. I didn't think anything of it then. It was such an experience for me. In the morning she would bring me a glass of fresh-squeezed orange juice. We'd go to the market and shop, then she would cook all day long. She treated me like an adult. She'd cook and we'd eat together. She loved being in the kitchen. I thought I had died and gone to heaven and I'll never, ever forget it; it was a defining experience, and because of her I now know a lot more about what it's like to have a personal lifestyle. She had a good life but she also had a gift for knowing what the good life was."

Molly's involvement continued over the years. When she visited New York she took Kate to dinner with the young man who became her husband.

"We went to L'Absinthe, her favorite restaurant, with some of her New York friends," Kate said. "By then I was maybe twenty-two, twenty-three, and she bought wine for the table. I thought I was totally out of my league but she made me feel comfortable. Another time she took me to the Plaza and the whole two hours we were there all we did was complain about [President George W.] Bush. But the whole idea that she took two or three hours out of her schedule to have this long leisurely meal with Aaron and me was really special."

Kate Cox's experience was shared by numerous others. All were recipients of a very special kind of Molly treatment, including becoming a namesake.

When I moved to Colorado, Molly gave me a list of names of people to contact. Jack, now retired from a reporting career with the *Denver Post*, became a colleague and a friend. When Molly came to visit me in Denver one summer, I had a barbecue for her. Jack brought his other daughter, Molly, who was named for Miz Ivins. For much of the evening Molly visited with the small band of people she had asked me to include, but Molly and I took care to include Molly II in conversation. When she said her good-byes, she made a point of giving her namesake a big hug and, one must presume, some last-minute "atta girl" words of farewell.

Ben and Molly Stoff are the son and daughter of Michael Stoff, associate professor of history at the University of Texas at Austin and director of UT's nationally recognized Plan II Honors program. They too were part of that extended family of nieces and nephews.

Although both Molly and Michael lived in Austin, they didn't meet until the 1980s at the annual Conference on World Affairs at the University of Colorado in Boulder. Founded in 1948 as a forum on international affairs, CWA has expanded over the years to encompass an eclectic list of participants, ranging from astronauts, political figures, musicians, and surgeons to authors, storytellers, historians, and philosophers.

Michael was part of this heady convocation of minds—but more about that later. The point here is that Michael and Molly became close friends. By then Molly was well known in Texas but not on the national scene; she was just starting on her first book, *Molly Ivins Can't Say That, Can She?* The title grew out of a letter of complaint sent to her employer at the time, the *Dallas Times Herald*.

There she was, toiling away, writing, agonizing over which columns to include, which to exclude—moving her at one point to grouse to Stoff, "What the hell was I thinking? Writing a book is *hard!*" He agreed, having navigated that struggle several times himself. He became part of the Final Friday circle.

"Molly and I became close when she met my kids. They were maybe six or eight at the time," he said. "She became their Texas godmother. She had the gift with kids. She was really tall, you know, so when she met them she got down on her knees to talk to them, putting herself at their eye level. Once, she took them on a camping trip. I endured it, but they loved it. I remember her leaning over a fire and grilling sausages of some kind. It was another way to connect with these little children, giving them the sense of really belonging. My son is thirty-two now and my daughter is thirty-three, but they still have this wonderful memory of their Texas godmother. Even then they loved how she could be a Smith girl one minute and pure Texas almost in the same instant."

The friendship between Molly and Michael Stoff was sufficiently comfortable that she invited him to dinner once when her father visited. It is not classified information that Molly lived in an uneasy truce with "Big Jim," a name conferred on the basis of his larger-than-life personality—a powerful corporate executive, an avid sailor aboard his own yacht, and a domestic tyrant who never harmed her physically but did more than a little emotional damage.

Michael Stoff saw her unease up close. "I knew Molly didn't have the greatest relationship with her father, so when she invited me to dinner I initially demurred," he said. "My best friend, Stuart Schoffman, was visiting from Israel and teaching at UT, so I asked if he could come too. 'Please,' she said; she was insistent. I realized the real issue was she didn't want to not invite her father for dinner, but she didn't want to be alone with him either. She needed a buffer.

"Here were food, friends, and family thrown into the same pot together. It was the quietest I'd ever seen her. So the food became a buffer as well: food was used to grease the social wheel."

It was also a strategic move on Molly's part. Schoffman, an author, a screenwriter, and an authority on Israeli history and politics who formerly wrote for *Fortune* magazine, fit right in. Molly knew Michael had written extensively about the Manhattan Project and the bombing of Nagasaki. Her father was a World War II veteran. Big Jim, Schoffman, and Stoff found common ground, and in a delicious touch of irony, war became neutral territory.

"As it turned out, when Molly's father learned Stuart and I were historians, we spent most of the evening eating and talking about the atomic bomb! And there she was, quiet as a church mouse. I laugh every time I think about that evening—dinner, a leg of lamb, and the atomic bomb. After her father left, she turned to us and quietly said, 'Thank you.'"

No one could have known then that in 1998 Big Jim would be diagnosed with cancer and would commit suicide after deciding he could no longer face life as a terminally ill cancer patient.

In 2010 a play based on Molly opened in Philadelphia with her character writing a column about her father. The play, *Red Hot Patriot: The Kick-Ass Wit of Molly Ivins*, starred Kathleen Turner, who channeled Molly to a T. It revolved in large measure around a true story.

Molly had started writing what was to be a personal reminiscence when she received word of his death. The column became his eulogy. On the one hand she acknowledged his frightening outbursts of temper, but on the other she attributed her inner strength to having learned to stand up to him.

Molly's generosity of spirit was as impressive as her quietly philanthropic bent. And, in the interest of full disclosure, I must here acknowledge being a recipient of Ivins largesse. Once, after I had been whining about how office politics at the *Dallas Morning News* had pretty much derailed a plan to have the paper send me to cover a tribute to black American jazz musicians in France, Molly, without saying a word, arose from the green leather settee in her spacious living room, cut through the kitchen to her office, and made a call—which was strange because it wasn't like her to up and, unannounced, leave me in mid-sentence to go call somebody. She didn't even like to talk on the telephone.

A part of me was annoyed that she was so bored with my complaint that she simply walked off. I figured maybe I had been whining a little too long and opted to pout in the privacy of the guest room. Before I could schlump off, she returned with a scrap of paper. On it were the name, address, and telephone number of former Smith classmate Susan Concordet. It seemed that Molly had called Susan at home in Paris (France, not the one in Texas) to see if she could recommend someplace affordable for me to stay. Of course, Susan replied. She and her husband owned a pied-à-terre in their Montmartre apartment building. I could stay there. No problem.

Molly even offered to share her frequent-flyer miles to get me there. As it turned out it wasn't necessary, but it was typical of what she did for others. At the last minute she sent me a check for $500 "just in case."

Molly was making money and she didn't mind spending it on the ACLU; on nonprofits that helped the poor, the homeless, and battered women; or on friends, especially when it came to dining out. At times it left Jan Demetri, Molly's accountant, apoplectic. Her soft spot for Molly is reflected in her zealous guardianship of a collection of folders she found after Molly's house had pretty much been emptied. Stacked atop a pile of papers to be tossed were folders with recipes and menu plans clipped and torn from magazines and newspapers. "At first I didn't think anything of it until I saw that each folder had been assigned different foods," she said. "When I opened them there were all these recipes with notes scribbled in Molly's unmistakable chicken scratch."

Sure enough, one legal-sized manila folder is brimming with recipes dating to 1966. They are classified course by course—soups, appetizers, entrées, salads, meats, stews, even a separate one for paella. Each is a little culinary treasure trove. The notation for an Italian recipe for spaghetti *alla pescatora* is deemed "not so good, at least with canned tomatoes." The one for linguini *al pesto* is adjusted to Molly's specifications, substituting a half cup of Parmesan for the one tablespoon called for. Mushrooms, truffle-style—*funghi trifolati*—is pronounced "yummy!" but carries an admonition: "Don't go too heavy on the anchovies."

After reading them I wanted to go home, whip out pots and pans, and cook for days, especially after rummaging through the folder marked "Molly's Very Good Recipes." That one included Jacques Pépin's poached red snapper; a 1999 recipe from *Fine Cooking* magazine for a savory carrot-and-ginger soufflé, and another of undetermined origin for something called "Grandma's Chicken."

Successive ripped pages from an old *New York Times* feature focused on a Thanksgiving menu for eight that included, in addition to the traditional bird, a celery root bisque with thyme; mashed potatoes with mascarpone and cara- melized leeks; maple-glazed sweet potatoes; scalloped squash; a red-pepper corn gratin with Cheddar crust; cornbread stuffing with ham, chestnuts, and sage; and green beans with wild mushrooms.

You just know that at some point she prepared the entire menu—maybe for one of those Orphans and Strays meals or at her brother's home. Grease spots and smudges suggest serious use. I also now have a copy and see a red- pepper corn gratin and mashed potatoes with mascarpone and caramelized leeks in some unsuspecting dinner guest's future.

17

Everything Is Relative(s)

WHETHER IT'S THE FIRST-TIME VISIT to the Big Apple, ordering from a menu in French, or visiting the nation's capital under the guise of a sightseeing excursion, all of Molly's honest-to-goodness nieces and nephews have experienced a memorable meal with Molly.

Darby, the only daughter of Molly's brother, Andy, and his wife, Carla, now lives and cooks in San Antonio, where she cheerfully acknowledges her indebtedness to Molly on several levels. Here you learn the origin of Molly's nickname, "Mole"—a moniker that evolved from her propensity for adjourning to her room to read for hours on end.

Like Molly's "adopted" nieces, Darby remembers Molly through her generosity and her love of cooking, especially Thanksgiving meals cooked at the family home in Boerne. These days Darby does her own cooking, with beer-in-the-butt chicken holding a special place in her store of Aunt Molly memories.

"I just thought that was the funniest thing," she said with a laugh. "See, you rub the chicken all over with whatever seasonings you have, then you cook it over a can of beer. Well, no, first you have to . . ." For whatever reason, she can't quite bring herself to provide a graphic description of the methodology—which involves balancing the butt-end body cavity of a whole chicken, legs down, atop a can of beer, then maintaining the balance and roasting it on a grill or in the oven. It makes for a delicious, moist bird, and it was another Molly favorite.

Darby more easily describes the 2004 trip to Washington, DC, with her doting aunt. The unsuspecting eighteen-year-old had no idea it was the launch of a sensitization process that never stopped. Darby thought she was going to see sights and tour the nation's capital—which they did, in a way. They were really in DC to participate in a major abortion rights rally. Women had come from all over, and police estimated "almost" one million marchers.

Molly went to great lengths to explain to Darby why they were there and how, when the power of one becomes strength in numbers, one person matters.

"Like I knew what the hell I was doing at the time," Darby said. "I'd lived such a privileged life; I'd never had a political opinion of my own about anything, but I got the gist of it. Although I didn't fully appreciate it then, I realized later she was politicizing me. Here were these thousands of people in the street marching to make a point.

"After the march we ate at this beautiful Italian restaurant with dishes on the menu I'd never heard of. I remember that one of the people at the table was Molly's friend Myra MacPherson [whose son, Michael, and daughter, Leah, were among Molly's stable of "nieces" and "nephews"]. I loved listening to them talk about issues. I know it made an impression."

And that, of course, was the point. Joining Darby and Myra were eight other diners, including Myra's husband, Florida state senator Jack Gordon; Betsy Moon, Molly's aide-de-camp; and friends from California and New York. All held forth at Teatro Goldoni, one of those swank K Street see-and-be-seen eateries and a perfect eye-opener for a sheltered kid from Texas. Myra, an accomplished author and former *Washington Post* political reporter, met Molly in 1972. Myra was working on her first book, *The Power Lovers*, a look at politics and marriage. She had met and interviewed Bob and Nadine Eckhardt when Bob was representing the Eighth Congressional District of Texas, which included part of Houston. They invited Myra to their home and invited friends for cocktails, where Myra held forth as only she could. She has a treasure trove of stories from her years at the *Washington Post*.

"I had earlier been in the Houston Astrodome taking in a curious scene: Maharaj Ji, the teenage religious nut craze of the moment, was holding court, and there was radical antiwar relic Rennie Davis kneeling and crawling forward to touch this guy's feet," she said. "In the middle of recounting my Maharajah experience, a man with a tall blonde woman turned to me and launched into this really weird spiel.

"'You know what's wrong with the Veet Cong? Just ain't very Christian,' he says. 'Here they are fightin' in their bare feet and black pajamas and our boys are up there in their B-52's napalming the hell outta them with their Bibles by their side, Christian like.'"

Molly (right) shares congratulatory greetings with author Myra MacPherson at a reception following Myra's 1987 marriage to Florida state senator Jack Gordon. Ivins family collection.

Myra, figuring she'd encountered one of Texas's notorious right-wing nuts, suddenly saw the tall blonde smile and realized she'd been punk'd by the one and only John Henry Faulk. The tall blonde with him was Molly.

"The two of us became Thelma and Louise for the rest of my trip, with John Henry in tow and without the bad ending. We went driving all over Texas and ended up being fast friends."

Darby was treated to this and other Molly-based stories that evening, moving her to observe, "I think Mole attracted people to her because she was so willing to go the extra mile. It made me want to cook for her. I knew she had as much passion for cooking as she did for writing, so one day I got courageous and cooked sautéed scallops in a tomato sauce for her. I put some spices in that I probably could have done without, since I didn't exactly know what I was doing, and I don't think she liked it, but she ate it because she didn't want to hurt my feelings. That's what it boils down to—no pun intended—cooking food for people you love."

The notion of food as a form of communication wasn't lost on Darby either.

"I can't imagine Molly cooking just for herself—only for others," she continued. "She almost always came to us for Thanksgiving and cooked with my mother, but she was up and gone the next morning because she had to write a column due that day. I don't think people ever really appreciated how that kind of pressure takes its toll after a while."

In her relentless quest to reach her inner thin person, Molly made repeated visits to Rancho La Puerta in Southern California, where—of course—she took cooking classes. On these sojourns she usually returned with a new recipe. Once she brought Darby a Rancho La Puerta cookbook, which Darby treasures. Darby, who once sported a near-Goth look with black nail polish, dyed-black hair, and an uncertain but not-quite-hostile persona, has blossomed into a gregarious, self-assured young woman.

Darby's brother, Drew, has his own remembrances. "Aunt Molly loved cooking meals that brought up good memories in her life. I remember eating many French meals for this very reason. I knew France was a shining star in her life's panorama simply from the way she would tell stories over each French dish she prepared. I loved hearing her joy in explaining where in the country it came from, its history, and any personal story attached to it."

It seems that all of the cousins have a particular trip to remember, and niece Margot Hutchison is no exception. Margot, daughter of Molly's sister, Sara, is a wife and mother living in San Diego. She easily remembers visits Molly made to New Mexico when Margot and her family lived there. In addition to Trivial Pursuit smackdowns, there was that subtle element of horizon expansion that Molly was so good at providing. For example, Molly got Darby interested in cooking when she gave her her first cookbook, *The Man Who Ate Everything*, by Jeffrey Steingarten (the longtime *Vogue* food critic who abandoned lawyering to write about food). Knowing Molly, the gift had a message. Steingarten's award-winning work is part travelogue, part cookbook, and part lesson in critical thinking. It was perfect on many levels for a smart young woman unfamiliar with the world's gastronomic wonders.

"Molly got me interested in cooking," Margot said. "And every Easter I still make the potatoes au gratin from that book."

One of her best memories sounds a lot like a variation on a theme of the experience Darby had. Only this time, instead of the nation's capital, the scene was the Big Apple. Both excursions were designed to open a door, to encourage a willingness to try the different, the new—without making the point by stating it outright. As an example, Margot cited a visit with Molly in Manhattan: "I went to New York to visit and Molly took me to this incredible seafood restaurant," Margot said. "There were fish on the menu I'd never even heard of. I was from landlocked New Mexico. I'd never had fresh seafood. I was about ten or twelve and I'll always remember her smile when she asked me what I thought of the restaurant and the meal. I gave her this wide-eyed look and announced, 'Gosh, Aunt Molly, this is almost as good as Long John Silver's!' I mean, here I was in this fancy schmancy restaurant, comparing it to Long John Silver's. Hey, you gotta remember—I was only ten."

Molly took Margot and her family to many a restaurant, including the exclusive A. R. Valentien at the Lodge at Torrey Pines, a consistent favorite. But there were also visits to Molly's home.

"I remember sitting in her kitchen and having her show me how to cut a mango while telling me about a chef she had dated and how he had showed her how to do mangoes.

"Another time, after we moved to San Diego, she took us to Torrey Pines, where we ate fabulous food. I'd never heard of carrot sorbet, and there I was eating it between courses. We'd sit and talk politics. She had just done her cooking school in southern France so she'd be prepared for this assignment she had for some magazine to write about the Australian wine country. She was in heaven."

But the Australian trip was as much to visit Margot's brother, the nephew who was most geographically removed from the family.

BEER-IN-THE-BUTT CHICKEN

I first heard of this particular method for cooking a whole chicken in the '70s, when my counterculture neighbors all had grills. It became a standard cooking technique across the board—whether you were a non-cook, a lazy cook, or an accomplished cook, this was a godsend. Use whatever seasonings suit you—barbecue, Old Bay, lemon pepper, whatever—and don't go all skittish about rubbing the chicken's interior. It won't feel a thing.

INGREDIENTS

¾ cup salted butter, softened
1 tablespoon paprika
1 teaspoon garlic powder
1 tablespoon kosher salt

3–4 tablespoons of dry spice rub
1 (4- or 5-pound) whole chicken
1 can beer

DIRECTIONS

Remove neck and giblets from chicken and set aside to freeze later for soup stock. Rinse chicken well and pat dry with paper towels. Combine butter, paprika, garlic powder, salt, and spice rub to form a paste and rub chicken inside and out. Set aside.

Open beer and drink about half of it. Really. Okay: pour half of it into a glass and drink it. (I was just trying to save dirtying a glass.) Place beer can on a kitchen counter or other clean, flat surface and lower the bird cavity over the beer can. Transfer bird-on-can to the grill and place in the center of the grate, balancing chicken on its legs, creating a tripod-like effect.

Cook the chicken over medium-high indirect heat by banking coals on one side of the grill and roasting chicken on the other, with the grill cover closed. Baste with beer intermittently for about an hour and a half or until juices run clear when thigh is pierced with a skewer or a sharp knife with a narrow blade. Using mitts, transfer bird and beer to a cookie sheet to rest for 10 or 15 minutes. Get medieval and tear into it—or remove it to a platter and cut it into parts. Serves 4 to 6.

★ ★ ★

PASTA PRIMAVERA

This recipe comes from Rancho La Puerta, a favorite retreat of Molly's. In part she went to get skinny, but eventually she settled for going just because the setting was lovely and she could really relax. Reprinted with permission from *Vegetarian Spa Cuisine from Rancho La Puerta and Deborah Szekely*.

INGREDIENTS

3 cups water

8 ounces whole wheat, spinach, or tomato medium pasta shells or fusilli

1 large zucchini, cut lengthwise in 2-inch strips

1 large yellow squash, cut lengthwise in 2-inch strips

¾ cup Pesto Sauce with Lemon (see recipe next page), divided use

1 large red or green bell pepper, cut in thin strips

2 medium tomatoes, coarsely chopped

2 green onions, coarsely chopped

2 tablespoons fresh parsley, chopped

¼ cup freshly grated Parmesan cheese

Black pepper, freshly ground (to taste)

DIRECTIONS

In a large pot bring water to boil. Add pasta; boil 6 minutes or until almost tender. Add squashes and boil 1 minute. Drain pasta and vegetables well. Transfer to a large bowl and toss with ½ cup pesto. Add bell pepper strips, tomatoes, green onions, parsley, and Parmesan. Toss until well combined. Season with pepper. Serve at room temperature. Can be refrigerated, covered, up to 3 days. Makes six 1¼-cup servings of 200 calories each.

★ ★ ★

PESTO SAUCE WITH LEMON

INGREDIENTS

4 garlic cloves

3 cups fresh basil leaves, packed
tightly

2 cups spinach leaves, trimmed
and packed

3 tablespoons Parmesan cheese,
freshly grated

2 tablespoons pine nuts

¼ teaspoon black pepper, freshly
ground

¼ cup extra-virgin olive oil

2 tablespoons fresh lemon juice

DIRECTIONS

In a food processor mince garlic. Add basil, spinach, cheese, nuts, and pepper, and puree. With machine running, slowly pour in oil and juice. Process until smooth. (Refrigerate covered for up to 2 weeks, or frozen up to 3 months—pour 1 teaspoon olive oil over pesto before freezing.) Makes about 1 cup or eight 2-tablespoon servings of 92 calories each. Reprinted with permission from *Vegetarian Spa Cuisine from Rancho La Puerta and Deborah Szekely* (Rancho La Puerta, 1994).

★ ★ ★

Molly and Hannah Sweets, who was a chef in Fredericksburg, Texas, at the time, congratulate themselves on salvaging what Molly thought was a ruined beurre blanc. Ellen Sweets collection.

18

Westward Ho, Ho, Ho

MOLLY AND I HAD LOTS OF PLANS, some sillier than others. One was to eventually relocate to Marathon, a little town in West Texas, and open a pseudo greasy spoon that would serve wonderful food. No white linen, no stemware, maybe not even matching plates and flatware. Just tables filled with pecan-crusted catfish, smothered chicken in onion gravy, perfectly roasted chickens, fresh-picked vegetables, and cloud-soft biscuits doused with butter churned from the milk of local cows.

We would come up with menu ideas. My daughter, Hannah the Chef, would execute them, and I would greet guests pleasantly or otherwise stay out of the way. One sure offering would be coq au vin.

Close by our dream café Molly and I would pool our resources—hers substantial, mine meager—and plant a double-wide (hers) and a yurt (mine) on a patch of West Texas real estate in Marathon, where she did in fact buy a double lot. When her health took its final turn south, she ended up selling it to political strategist Harold Cook, a friend who, like a handful of other Austin renegades, was doing his part to Democratize that arid neck of the woods, as in "Let's turn Brewster County blue." In the best Molly tradition, it was the kind of sale ranchers probably did a century ago with a smile and a handshake. Like a lot of other friendships, this one evolved from a meal a long time ago.

Cook was working at the time for Representative Debra Danburg, arguably the most liberal snuff-dipping Democrat in the Texas Legislature at the time. Molly, who was writing for the *Fort Worth Star-Telegram*, stopped by the office to chase down some story or another. She and Harold struck up a conversation.

One thing led to another and the two began to hang out, a coalition built on mutual political interests—solidifed, naturally enough, at a political event.

But let him tell it: "Debra had been scheduled to participate in roasting Glen Maxey [the first openly gay member of the Texas Legislature] at a fund-raising dinner for the Lesbian Gay Rights Lobby at Scholz Garten, but she had to cancel at the last minute, so I filled in. Molly was emcee for the event, and she introduced me as a legislative aide for Debra Danburg, which, she said, was "just like being Murphy Brown's secretary." (This popular and sometimes controversial 1990s sitcom was set in a newsroom where investigative reporter Murphy Brown was plagued by a string of hilariously inept secretaries, often portrayed by high-profile celebrities.)

"I started my speech by reading a mock letter from Danburg, which she'd supposedly written and which started out, 'Dear Glen, I hate it that I couldn't be with you and LGRL tonight. I would have been there if I could, but I got another offer that sounded like more fun, so fuck you.' Molly decided that anybody who would say the f-word in public was A-OK in her book, so we stayed late, got drunk, and after that I was a regular."

The friendship grew. Cook even made chili in Molly's kitchen, having learned to cook out of desperation and self-defense while a student at the University of Houston. Too broke to eat out and too proud to scrounge meals at his parents' house, he taught himself, delving into the kitchen bible of the '50s and '60s—the red plaid *Better Homes and Gardens Cook Book*. He particularly remembers an evening when he made chili for her.

"She kept standing over my shoulder and tasting stuff, suggesting more of this or more of that. I told her I don't like backseat drivers and to leave me the hell alone and let me cook my chili."

Over the years the two spent time together in Marathon. She enjoyed piddling around, clearing cactus and moving rocks from point A to point B to make parking space. He became a piddling-around pal, primarily helping with the heavy lifting. Molly told Cook about wanting to build a writer's shack on the property, but acknowledged that because of her illness, the six-hour drive from Austin was just too much and she wouldn't use the house as much as she would have liked.

She decided instead to pool resources with her brother, Andy, for a place in the Hill Country village of London, only three hours away. They planned to have a few chickens, maybe a cow or two, and a vineyard, the results of which would be an insouciant Chardonnay bottled under the label "Château Bubba."

Molly offered to sell her piece of Marathon property to Cook because she felt he understood the spirit of the place and would care for it as she would have wanted. It would have been just like Molly to give it to him had Jan Demetri, her accountant, not intervened. Instead she sold it for the same sum she had paid for it several years before. Who knows how much it's worth now. But, once again, that was Molly.

Cook ponied up the cash, but they didn't even do a formal sale for at least another year or so—it was essentially a handshake deal in the best Texas tradition. There's an excellent chance that neither of them bothered with details long enough to find a notary public. Instead Molly insisted on a formal ceremony transferring "moral and spiritual responsibility for her property." This not-so-solemn rite was performed up the road, at the home of Ty and Kate Fain. It was originally scheduled to take place at the actual property, but the peripatetic West Texas weather refused to cooperate. Instead, at a New Year's Eve gathering Harold placed his left hand on a *Texas State Directory* and pledged to take care of the place and continue the frivolity and ridiculousness Molly had initiated.

As it's turned out, he has indeed built the writer's shack that Molly envisioned. The porch is almost as big as the cabin—to accommodate a crowd of friends sitting around talking politics, laughing and telling lies, just as Molly would have wanted.

═ **19** ═

Le Petit Dejeuner

MOLLY LOVED BREAKFAST. It was serious business, even if eaten at noon. As long as some egg incarnation was involved, it was breakfast. Breakfast for me usually arrived around noon-thirty and consisted of maybe a fried egg on spaghetti or a fried egg on a bowl of chili or a fried egg on whatever was left over from the preceding night—beef stew, baked chicken, lamb chops, or oh, Lord—pork chops.

For most of us scrambled eggs are scrambled eggs are scrambled eggs: fry the bacon, take it out, plop the eggs in, stir to the desired doneness, and flop the mass onto a plate.

Not so with Ivins.

One Sunday morning I awoke to earsplitting kitchen clatter. Curiosity prompted a stumble into the kitchen to identify the source of the noise.

When I arrived in the doorway, Mol was removing butter and cream from the fridge, followed by a quick detour to the little patch of chives she grew by the fishpond in her atrium. After chopping chives, she grated a little pile of Asiago cheese.

She had already brought six large eggs to room temperature. She then cracked them one by one, first into a small Pyrex bowl (lest one bad egg spoil the batch), then into a larger stainless-steel bowl.

Initially I thought this activity might be a prelude to crepes, but I didn't see flour. Rather than interrupt, I stood, puzzled. Counter space was filled with spoons, whisks, measuring cups, and bowls. This production, I soon learned, was the prelude to *ouefs brouille*—the French version of scrambled eggs.

In the context of Molly's everlovin' francophilia, the bustling started to make sense. One of the many things in which we concurred completely was the importance of taking all meals seriously.

When my daughter was in high school, she loved inviting friends over because she and I prepared cooked-from-scratch meals. We were living in the little town of Summit, New Jersey, where the parents of most of her classmates spent more for dinner than I made in a month. Her buddies couldn't believe it. I cooked every day for just the two of us. It was insane, but it was also my therapy. I often wonder if—or at least how much—our cooking together influenced her decision to become a chef. She had already decided to become a ballerina after seeing the Dance Theatre of Harlem perform. Little did I suspect at the time that she would actually eventually train at the DTH school, perform with the junior company, and go on to dance professionally with the Alvin Ailey American Dance Theater. She also became a chef in Cape May, New Jersey; Dallas, Texas; and Aspen, Colorado—where, after twelve years in a hot kitchen, she quit to become a bartender.

I think about that progression often, remembering typical weekdays that began before seven: make breakfast, go to work, get off at five, pick her up for the forty-minute drive to ballet class, return home, cook dinner, pick her up from ballet, eat, check her homework, and collapse into bed. As long as things went well at work, I could cook a daily meal. When things went wrong, I prepared several meals at a time to ameliorate borderline homicidal rage.

Hannah always knew whether I'd had a good or bad day by how vehemently I sliced and diced, each knife cut assigned to the head or throat of the offending supervisor. Once, after completing her homework, Hannah emerged from her room to find a different entrée on each of three of the four burners: chili, Puttanesca sauce, and chicken smothered in a three-onion gravy, one of those knuckle-sucking Southern recipes I learned from my father. I had half of a white onion, part of a red onion, and several green onions in the refrigerator. I chopped the hell out of all three. Hannah stood a safe distance away and weighed the wisdom of speaking.

"That bad?" she asked.

"That bad."

"Okay."

"I'll call you when dinner's ready."

"Okay."

I grew up in a household where we sat down to dinner together six days a week. My mother shopped almost daily for fresh vegetables. My father, one of seventeen children raised on a farm, bought our meat from a butcher. He brought it home midday if he came home for lunch. Otherwise my mother shopped at the family-owned grocery store near us. The butcher had a few false starts when he thought he could palm crap off on her, but then he saw the error of his ways and began selling a much-improved quality of beef, pork, and lamb.

So in the 1960s, when I lived in England, the daily shopping routine wasn't alien to me. I shopped every day because my husband, Eric, and I didn't have a refrigerator. Stopping at the greengrocer after popping in at the butcher's for chicken or chops was part of the routine. Molly didn't like for food to languish in the refrigerator either. She too had shopped daily when she lived in France, soaking up the language and loving the culinary wonderfulness that surrounded her. It never let her go.

As for the morning of Much Kitchen Noise: Molly's clatter, chive snipping, and cheese grating were deliberative, contemplative processes, clearly weighted toward the meticulous end of the cooking spectrum, unlike the Sweets version of scrambled eggs at the opposite end.

In the Sweets family version, scrambled eggs were prepared using the greasy bacon grease technique. It featured a mess of chopped green onions dosed with several hearty shakes of black pepper. Unscrambled eggs were unceremoniously dumped onto the wilted onions afloat in bacon grease in a very hot cast-iron skillet. The whole shebang went from skillet to plate in five minutes max. In the summer, sliced garden tomatoes and whole wheat toast were accompaniments, occasionally preceded by a wedge of fresh watermelon, cantaloupe, or honeydew.

And then there was Molly's interpretation: *oeufs brouille*.

So now six eggs are in the bowl on a big, heavy chopping board. The chives are in a little pile on one side of the bowl, and the grated cheese is on the other. Out comes a stockpot.

A stockpot? For six scrambled eggs?

To neutralize my by-now-palpable curiosity, Mol hands off a fresh loaf of brioche. Sometimes in the kitchen Molly was a woman of very few words. "Four slices," she says.

I obey.

On this particular Sunday she is unusually short on conversation and just points to the knife stand. Knives have been recently sharpened—glory hallelujah—and I set to work. Meanwhile Molly's *oeufs* preparation is coming up on the thirty-minute mark as imported unsalted butter sizzles in the stainless-steel bowl that she placed over the stockpot, which now contains boiling water—a double boiler on steroids, only instead of a narrow-sided saucepan on top, the bowl allows the eggs to be easily whisked and fluffed into creamy, buttery goodness.

Such concentration, such focus. For six eggs.

Without my realizing I realized it, it occurred to me that Molly's semi-surly, quasi-crabby demeanor was a variation on a theme of my way of working through an issue. Aha! It was Sunday. She had a column due Monday. She had no idea what she was going to write. Slicing tomatoes, grating cheese, snipping and chopping chives, toasting brioche, and scrambling eggs helped clear the cobwebs and free the mind to receive an idea.

When Molly worked in the kitchen she occasionally talked to herself. Not as if she was having a complete conversation, though. More like she was rearranging thoughts in her head. Sometimes she'd just grunt. That's what she was doing now: Molly mumbles. I learned during her conversations with herself that it was best to be scarce. So, slicing done, I headed for the living room to read the paper and watch for the red fox family.

Honest.

For years Molly had a family of red foxes that lived in some hidden quadrant of her substantial corner lot. Foxes, she explained, mate for life and, unsurprisingly, have baby foxes. I saw them walk by her wall-sized picture window on two separate occasions. Once, Mr. and Mrs. Fox were out on their own for an evening constitutional. Another time, the Foxes strolled by with Muffy and Chip, their juvenile offspring. As Molly explained, the names she conferred were deemed appropriate for the creeping gentrification of her South Austin neighborhood.

When Molly overhauled her once-modest Travis Heights bungalow, the kitchen redo included a counter with suitable seating for two. The counter faced a picture window with a bird feeder centered smack-dab in the middle of the sight line, the better to see sparrows, cardinals, mockingbirds, blue jays, and other birds she frequently identified from a field guide kept close by, next to the cat's dish. She called all the finches by the same name: Atticus.

Little Kaye Northcat, Molly's cranky gray tabby, took her meals on the counter near the window because Athena, the naughty poodle of insatiable appetite, ate anything within reach. Athena could not, however, get to Little

Kaye's dish on the counter. A few feet to the left of the window hung a hummingbird feeder. Greenery to the far right was planted with lantana and milkweed to attract butterflies, especially Monarchs. I returned to the kitchen when I began to smell toast. Sitting in one of the two window seats and appreciating this urban pastoral scene abbreviated the wait for the world's longest egg scramble. Mimosas helped.

At last fluffy steaming scrambled eggs, lightly toasted brioche, orange marmalade, and café au lait graced the counter. Breakfast was lovely. Mid-meal, out of nowhere, Molly said, "It's truly amazing, if there's one thing those goddamned Republicans know how to do, it's take care of their own."

I did what I do best with someone who clearly knows more about what she's thinking than I possibly could: I nodded, said something erudite like "Uhnh," and waited for her to continue. She was, as usual, royally pissed with a Bush. This time it was Bush the First. It had something to do with the increasing concentration of wealth in the hands of fewer and fewer people. Molly believed in the redistribution of wealth, just not the way Bush did. She believed it should go from the rich to the not-in-the-least-bit rich.

A forkful of eggs, a crunch of toast, a sip of café. Finally she spoke.

"We got a Congress that's useless as tits on a boar hog and a president who vetoed the first increase in the minimum wage in more than a decade," she mumbled. "Duddent make a lick a goddamn sense." After knocking off part of the second mimosa, or maybe the third, she stalked to her office. Presently the staccato sound of keyboard clicks began. The idea had gelled. I cleared the counter as quietly as possible, but apparently not quietly enough. "Just leave it," a disembodied voice said from two rooms away. I returned to the couch to read the paper and, with any luck, to glimpse a red fox.

OUEFS BROUILLE

This dish really is worth the time it takes to make it. Topped with chives and a skosh of your favorite grated cheese, it makes a very civilized morning meal. Or you can skip the cheese and drizzle the eggs with a bit of white truffle oil; Molly was quite possibly the only person I knew at the time who kept white truffle oil in the fridge. No, she was the *only* person I knew who kept it at all. This breakfast merits a mimosa. Cut the recipe in half for 2; otherwise it serves 6 French diners or 4 Texans.

INGREDIENTS

12 large eggs

½ cup cream (*not* milk, *not* half-and-half, *not* 2 percent, *not* skim!)

6 tablespoons cold, unsalted butter, cut into little cubes and divided

Sea salt and freshly ground pepper

2 teaspoons white truffle oil

2 tablespoons finely chopped chives

12 slices from a loaf of brioche, toasted

DIRECTIONS

In a bowl, whisk eggs and cream.

Melt 2 tablespoons of the butter in a large stainless-steel bowl over a stockpot with about 2 quarts of boiling water.

Add eggs and cook over low heat, gently stirring with a silicon spatula and scraping the bottom of the bowl until eggs begin to set, about 5 minutes.

Add the remaining butter, a little chunk at a time, all the while stirring and scraping the bottom and sides of the bowl, until the eggs are thick and cooked through but still soft, about 5 more minutes.

Season with salt and pepper; transfer to plates. Drizzle with truffle oil, sprinkle with the chives, and serve at once with the brioche.

★ ★ ★

In this 1985 snapshot Molly and her mother, Margot Ivins, prepare Thanksgiving dinner in the New Mexico home of Molly's sister, Sara Ivins Maley. Ivins family collection.

= 20 =

Home Cookin'

MOLLY AND I SPENT A LOT OF TIME REMINISCING about family and food, hers served in the upscale River Oaks section of Houston, mine in the then-segregated river city of St. Louis. As we got to know one another better, we discovered that to varying degrees, we had some things in common. She grew up Episcopalian; I was confirmed in the only all-black high Episcopal church west of the Mississippi. (Segregated housing forced everyone to live together, whether you were a teacher, doctor, lawyer, postal carrier, or welfare recipient.) Her father, by her description, was an unreconstructed bigot; my father was a publisher and a confirmed Republican, back when Republicans were, relatively speaking, the good guys who had freed the slaves ninety years earlier. Molly and I both grew up knowing a lot of people but having few close friends. We further had in common the fact that we were rebellious—she against a tyrannical father, me against a perfectionist mother. She loved to read. I learned to love to read because my mother's version of punishment was to send me to my room—where there were two well-stocked bookcases.

I got punished a lot. I was a congenital contrarian. I had a smart mouth. I got kicked out of the Girl Scouts for smoking and cursing. I disobeyed my parents when they forbade me to (a) play stickball with the boys and (b) to play in the Catholic schoolyard a couple of blocks away. I then lied when I hit a ball through one of the school's windows, where I went to play anyway. I hated shoes and walked around barefoot, which made my mother apoplectic. I questioned church teachings, I challenged my teachers and rolled my eyes and muttered under my breath when I disagreed with my parents. I spent a lot of time in my room.

My mother never told me I had to read from those books, but I didn't have a radio and no one had a personal television in the 1950s, and few had a smart-mouthed daughter.

Molly retreated into books too. And Margot, her mother, knew her way around a kitchen as well. Both of our families had someone who cooked evening meals, but left to their own devices they lived by the *Joy of Cooking* and *The Good Housekeeping Cookbook*, both reasonably informative culinary guides, but no competition for the wide range of ethnic, regional, and international options we have today. Well, there was one difference: Melba Sweets didn't have a Junior League cookbook in her modest collection.

Like Molly's family, we had a dinner schedule, even, surprisingly, some of the same dishes. In our house, Mondays were either meatballs and spaghetti or spaghetti with meat sauce; Tuesdays were calf's liver, sliced thick, with bacon and tons of onions. The liver had to be sautéed medium rare, never cooked all the way through. Wednesday's fare consisted of fried or baked pork chops and was anticipated with great enthusiasm in either incarnation.

Thursday at the Sweetses' was almost always a stuffed pepper day, unless eggplant was in season. Then it was eggplant stuffed and baked with either ground lamb or beef, unless we had it on Friday, when shrimp or crabmeat supplanted red meat. Otherwise Friday was a fried fish day. Saturday was pot o' beans day—chili, black, navy, baby limas, black-eyed, Great Northern. Sunday was chicken day: fried, baked, roasted, or stewed with dumplings.

My father said he belonged to the African Methodist Episcopal Church, which came as news to successive ministers who saw him only when he dragged my brothers and me to the annual Father's Day pancake breakfast.

Andy, Molly's beloved younger brother, remembers a weekly meal rotation in his house too. It included hamburger, steak, and, yes, liver and onions. Like Molly, he chuckles over his mother's turnip fluff, which, he says, was not as awful as it sounds. Mostly, though, he remembers Molly's love of the out-of-doors—and her stubbornness.

One of those memories revolves around a rained-out family camping adventure. Andy, his wife, Carla, and their three preteen children packed up tents, butane grill, and all the appropriate gear for a weekend on a small river in West Texas.

"It was either late fall or early spring, I'm not sure which anymore," Andy said. "We'd planned one of those campouts where Molly'd be the cook. Well, that night it started to rain, then it poured. Carla gave up, got in the car, and went home. I tried to tough it out, but it was raining so hard the tents were starting to leak. I finally gave in, packed up the kids, and tried to get Molly to come with us. Her tent was leaking too, but she refused to leave."

Reluctantly, Andy left in the car they had used to haul camping gear. "When we came back the next day she was lying in a giant puddle of water," Andy said. "I thought, 'Oh God, she's dead.'

"I kept thinking, 'Omigod, I never should have left her,' but she was so doggoned determined to tough it out," Andy said. "I was used to her being stubborn, so I just said 'Okay.' Still, I was scared of what I'd find, but there she was. Her eyes fluttered open and she said something really goofy like, 'Good morning.' When I asked her why the hell she didn't get up, she said, 'My body warmed the water just right when the rain stopped. If I move I'll be freezing.' That was Molly."

On other outings there would be food and plenty of it.

"Of course we could never have just plain steak or hamburgers; there was always some fancy cheese or some special ingredients. Once she even did shrimp on the fire. But her favorite was beer-in-the-butt chicken that she did with roasted potatoes. We'd share cooking duties, then sit around the fire with Molly telling stories while the kids sat mesmerized. Sometimes they'd be up until sunrise, asking her questions and listening to her stories.

"I know she broadened their world with those stories," Andy continued. "She taught them to be more open, to be informed, to think for themselves, to travel and listen to other points of view—and that was a wonderful thing."

Andy recalled those days as we sat in the barn on the ranch he owns in London, Texas. He and Molly bought it together. This was the property they had planned to put a few cows on, plant those grapevines, and eventually bottle their insouciant Chardonnay with the provenance of Château Bubba.

As we sifted through boxes of photographs, he periodically choked up as he uncovered snapshots of Molly with her mom, with him, with nieces and nephews, with her father. He lingered over the 2006 Thanksgiving photograph of him, Carla, and Molly, taken at the Four Seasons in Austin. It had turned out to be their last Thanksgiving together.

The family is scattered now. Darby is closest, in San Antonio, working for a public relations firm there. In Chile, Drew works for a nonprofit educational venture between the US State Department and the Chilean government. Like an uncle and his father before him, Andy's other son, Dax, committed suicide in 2005. It was a devastating period in Molly's life. Dax's death was almost too

Molly's last Thanksgiving, in November 2006, shared with her brother, Andy, and his wife, Carla, at Trio, the fine-dining restaurant at the Four Seasons Hotel in Austin. Ivins family collection.

much to bear. Molly had not only set money aside to finance college for each niece and nephew, she had also invested much of herself in nurturing them all—first as children, then as young adults. It was the only time I ever saw her truly inconsolable.

What had been a spacious dream home in the quiet town of Boerne became a house of sadness. Andy and Carla sold it and moved to the London property where Molly and Andy had once dreamed of raising a small herd and planting their vineyard.

We continued to rummage through photographs. The mention of Dax's death cast a pall over our sweaty undertaking in the barn, so I redirected it to food as Andy smiled over a photograph of his mother and his sister Sara in Sara's New Mexico kitchen. He smiled, and shaking his head, quietly said, "Turnip fluff."

21

Food Stamps and Fun on the Dole

WE USED TO LAUGH WHEN WE'D HEAR PEOPLE discuss the importance of eating naturally, organically, locally, as though those practices were a quasi-revolutionary concept; as if people hadn't done that for generations, until factory farms assumed center stage in the food theater. My parents organized seasonal family outings where we drove to the Eckert farm across the river in Illinois to pick peaches. Mother chose them one by one. We'd bring basketsful home, peel, pit, and slice them, then make hand-cranked peach ice cream to go with homemade peach cobbler. We all took turns at the old-fashioned ice cream maker.

I remembered those years as I struggled to raise my daughter. Although I was a single mother, I was determined that she and I would pick fruit together, but I rarely had the time. In the spring of 1980 I became an unemployed single mother. The mayor who had appointed me to a job failed to get reelected that April. His replacement replaced me. He had to. I refused to tender my resignation, forcing the new mayor to fire me. As a fired former executive, I was entitled to unemployment benefits. My tax dollars at work for me for a change.

If there is such a thing as a good time to be unemployed, it's spring. I reported immediately to the unemployment office and signed on for food stamps. Didn't even think about looking for a job until early August. My four months on unemployment were the best 120 days ever. Eight-year-old Hannah and I found all sorts of free things to do. Instead of buying bread, we bought flour and oil and milk and baked our own—onion, cheese, whole wheat, and, yes, white bread. We couldn't afford meat. We went to the Soulard Farmers Market late on Saturdays, when they practically gave away produce. We had already received gift memberships to the botanical garden, art museum, and zoo, so we went to each in rotation throughout the summer. We made egg salad and tuna salad sandwiches on our homemade bread and, to save gasoline, rode bicycles to Forest Park—St. Louis's answer to Central Park—for picnics. Sometimes we went downtown to the levee and watched tugboats guide barges up and down the Mississippi.

One night in 1977, when my mother and father were out of town and I was under the influence of a controlled substance (so maybe it was 1976), I decided to create a garden in a portion of my parents' backyard. For years the yard had belonged to Mr. Chips, a boxer of some size, so the soil was well fertilized, black and rich with big fat worms. Once the rows were prepared (and sanity more or less returned), Hannah accompanied me to a nursery and we chose what we would plant. Throughout the spring and summer we pulled weeds and watered rows. When eggplants, bell peppers, yellow squash, zucchini, tomatoes, and onions were ready, she picked them and we made ratatouille. She couldn't wait to eat the spinach she picked. When there was enough okra, we pickled it or cooked it with tomatoes and onions or made shrimp Creole. Before the sun killed off the spinach and lettuce, we picked cucumbers and made simple salads with canned tuna and baby green beans. When tomato plants threatened to consume the block, we canned the fruit and used it to make our own spaghetti sauce the following winter. It is now and ever shall be my belief that kids who plant, nurture, and tend food can't wait to eat it.

Early-morning visits to Shaw's Garden (now Missouri Botanical Garden) earned us fresh-picked bananas for breakfast when the banana trees bore fruit. We also went to Eckert's, where we picked strawberries in the spring, peaches in the summer, and apples in autumn, just like I had done at her age. We ate as much as we picked. We made strawberry jam and gave it away for birthday, get-well, and Christmas gifts. As autumn set in, we picked apples and made chutney. In winter we made chowchow from cabbage, onions, peppers, garlic, salt, and vinegar. When food stamps didn't stretch far enough, I posted a note in the lobby of our apartment building and offered to cook for neighbors, cash on the barrelhead.

A couple from Louisiana who lived in our building hired me to make gumbo for a dinner party. Hannah set the table, arranged flowers, and peeled shrimp. When we were done, we couldn't wait to get back to our apartment. We opened the envelope with our pay in it.

We had apparently not charged enough, because instead of the $100 we had agreed on, the envelope contained $150. Now we could sock some away, then go to the movies and eat popcorn and buy ice cream cones. Now we could buy groceries we wouldn't otherwise have splurged on—capers, Gouda, fresh mushrooms, a mixture of veal and pork and fresh ground round for meat loaf instead of cheap ground beef of ambiguous origin. The closest grocery store was Straub's, a boutique market not generally frequented by people on food stamps. It was also my mother's preferred destination for buying meat and seafood.

On one particular Saturday afternoon she was in one line while I was preparing to check out in another. She was so worried that I would whip out those little multicolored coupons that she actually began shaking her head, as if to say, "Please don't do that while I'm here." She was so unhinged that she summoned my daughter over, gave her cash, and sent her back to the line we were in. Saved an easy $50 in 1970s-era food stamps.

That story cracked Molly up.

April, May, June, and July came and went. The botanical garden's banana season ended. Signs appeared announcing that the zoo train would soon run on an abbreviated schedule. Children's classes at the art museum scaled back to weekends in August. Time to find a job. One evening, while we were riding our bicycles from Baskin-Robbins, I bumped into Art Hoffman, a friend and neighbor who told me about a job possibility. A new vice president for public relations at Bell Laboratories wanted ex-reporters to translate tech talk into English.

Emboldened by Art's information and fortified by hops and barley, I wrote, detailing my intimate familiarity with telecommunications technology (i.e., I'd used a telephone all my life) and my enthusiastic willingness to apply wit, intelligence, charm, and the aforementioned technological expertise on behalf of that august institution.

They actually hired me.

Marilyn Laurie, who was elevated to vice president in spite of having the bad judgment to add me to the Bell Labs payroll, was cruel enough to read part of the letter at my farewell party about a decade later, confessing that she had summoned me for an interview just to find out who this person was who had written such well-crafted bullshit.

So I went back to work. But at least Hannah, then nine, had learned that food came from the earth, not from plastic bags or shrink-wrapped Styrofoam.

HANNAH ROUNDED OUT THE TEXAS PHASE of her culinary career as executive chef at a restaurant called August E's in the historic town of Fredericksburg, about eighty-five miles west of Austin.

Molly and her family promptly came for Thanksgiving dinner. The restaurant, situated at the time in a turn-of-the-century log cabin just outside town, featured what the owners called "nouveau Texas cuisine." Hannah even had the temerity to introduce once-a-week sushi to locals. My favorite recollection of Thursday-night sushi revolves around a family arrival just before sunset. As they were being shown to a table, the son, about ten, said "Dad, what's sushi?" The father, attired in neatly pressed Levi's and wearing a smart ten-gallon hat, didn't miss a beat. "It's raw fish, son, and yure gonna lak it."

As much as anything else, I suspect the Ivinses' Thanksgiving dinner in Fredericksburg was Molly's way of showing support for Hannah in her first crack at executive chefdom. I also suspect that Molly wanted to see for herself if Hannah was telling the truth when she said she had hired a one-armed waitress. She had, and the young lady waited on us. The Fredericksburg employment pool was not very deep, Hannah explained, and she liked this woman's spirit. And I liked any meal where I didn't have to spend two days preparing something that was demolished in less than two hours.

Thanksgiving at August E's featured turkey, prime rib, stuffing, gravy, spinach, mashed potatoes, and a superb mac 'n' cheese made with Asiago, Cheddar, Parmesan, Gruyere, and truffle oil. Hannah used orzo instead of traditional elbow macaroni. Molly loved it and insisted that Hannah come to Austin to give a personal tutorial.

Meanwhile, it took all the self-control Molly possessed to repress convulsive laughter as our personable young waitress served us, two by two, and as efficiently as a two-armed waitress would have.

That's the thing about Texas tales; even when they're not lies they sound like they ought to be.

A few months later, Hannah, fully intending to teach Molly how to make her mac 'n' cheese, instead ended up demonstrating how to repair a broken beurre blanc, a delicate, buttery white sauce. Hannah still recalls the meal.

"We were sipping Chardonnay and talking away—or rather I was talking and poor Molly was listening to me moan and groan about life in a professional kitchen. I can't remember if she left the sauce on simmer too long or the heat was too hot or what. Anyway, the emulsification broke, becoming a greasy buttery mess that more resembled ghee than a sauce.

"She was going to pitch it, but I said we could fix it. All I needed was a sauce-pan, a little white wine, and some heavy cream. I found a copper saucepan and we went to work. I let Molly pour in some white wine, which we reduced until it was almost all gone. Then we added cream and reduced it until it was thick. It was like doing a science experiment, and Molly was so intense about it, especially after we started slowly, slowly whisking the new sauce into the broken sauce. As soon as it emulsified, we served it over steamed asparagus. Of course it was delicious."

August E's (named for a landowner who once lived in Fredericksburg) has since moved into the center of town—motivated, quite possibly, by cows. Let me explain: August E's owners built a lovely deck perfect for dining alfresco, Texas weather permitting. Weather aside, there was an occasional problem with wind shifting direction and wafting across the adjacent cow field toward the deck. The collision of food fragrance and the indelicate aroma of cow poop was not conducive to fine dining.

Having had enough of Texas heat, Hannah moved to Aspen, Colorado, where she traded froufrou food for mixology. Although she can cook concentric circles around me, we still consult with each other. Her culinary expertise extends eons beyond chili, gumbo, and Brunswick stew, but she still calls for advice when she wants to make the dishes we made together; and when she visits she expects me to serve oxtail stew and red beans and rice before she leaves. Food, which bound my family in so many ways, still binds my daughter to me; Molly to her mom's turnip fluff; me to Melba's pork chops; and Molly and me for almost two decades.

HANNAH'S ORZO MAC 'N' CHEESE

This is the macaroni and cheese Hannah made for the Thanksgiving dinner Molly's family shared in 2004. If you're on a diet, skip this recipe.

INGREDIENTS

2 pints heavy cream
1 cup mascarpone
3 cups Fondi di Toscana (or 1½ cups Havarti and 1½ cup Asiago)
1 cup grated Parmesan
¼ teaspoon kosher salt
½ teaspoon freshly ground black pepper

¼ teaspoon nutmeg
¼ cup fresh chopped parsley (1 tablespoon truffle oil if using Havarti and Asiago)
1 pound orzo
¼ cup unsalted butter, cut into quarter-inch pats
½ cup Panko breadcrumbs

DIRECTIONS

Preheat oven to 425.

In a large saucepan, reduce cream by half over low heat.

Add mascarpone and whisk until smooth. Using a wooden spoon, fold in Fondi di Toscana (or Havarti and Asiago) over medium heat until blended. Stir in Parmesan. Add salt, pepper, nutmeg, parsley, and truffle oil. (If using Fondi di Toscana, truffle oil is not necessary.) Cover saucepan and set aside.

Cook pasta to just under al dente (or half the time suggested in the instructions on the box) and drain thoroughly.

While the pasta is still hot, transfer it to a stockpot and, using a wooden spoon, gently stir in the cream and cheese mixture. Transfer to a buttered 3-quart casserole. Sprinkle breadcrumbs on top and bake for 15–20 minutes or until golden brown. Serves 6 to 8.

★ ★ ★

MARGOT IVINS'S TURNIP FLUFF

This is an adaptation of Molly's mom's original recipe. None of Molly's friends had heard of it before sampling it at Molly's Christmas dinners.

INGREDIENTS

2 pounds turnips, peeled and cut into cubes

1 tablespoon plus ½ teaspoon salt

2 tablespoons unsalted butter, melted, or bacon grease

2 tablespoons butter

1 egg, separated

1½ teaspoons lemon peel, grated

¼ teaspoon freshly ground black pepper

¼ teaspoon dried basil leaves, crushed

½ teaspoon Tabasco

1 egg white

1 tablespoon brown sugar (optional)

DIRECTIONS

In a medium saucepan add water to cover turnips and 1 tablespoon salt. Bring to a boil and reduce heat to a simmer for 15 minutes or until turnips are tender. Drain and mash.

Preheat oven to 350°F.

Using bacon grease or butter, heavily grease a 1-quart baking dish. To the turnips add butter, egg yolk, lemon peel, black pepper, basil, Tabasco, egg white, and the remaining ½ teaspoon salt. Mix well.

In a small mixing bowl, combine the separated egg white with the additional egg white; beat until stiff. Fold into turnips. Spoon into baking dish. Sprinkle top with brown sugar, if desired. Bake for 20 to 25 minutes or until golden brown. Serves 6.

★ ★ ★

22

Laissez les Bon Temps Rouler, Y'all

ON MANY OCCASIONS GUMBO, a perennial Molly favorite, was the Saturday meal in Austin—gumbo, rice, cornbread, and a green salad, maybe pralines, or, if Molly was in the mood, she'd bake a pie. In peach season we had cobbler. Some guests opted for wine, but any Cajun worth his roux would tell you beer is the beverage of choice with this particular dish.

One Labor Day weekend we had a full frontal weekend food blowout. Friday night: grilled chicken, dueling potato salads, coleslaw, grilled asparagus. Gumbo on Saturday. Sunday we were invited out. Ditto Monday. I had taken a vacation day and driven down on Thursday so we could shop the day before we were to cook. We knew that to serve gumbo on Saturday and throw a barbecue on Friday we had to be in the kitchen first thing Friday morning. And we were.

From 9 a.m. to noon we made the gumbo.

By 2 p.m. we were done with the potato salads.

Knives? Check. Chopping boards? Check—one for Molly, one for me.

Beer? Red Stripe. Chardonnay? In the immortal words of that former governor of Alaska, you betcha.

Now it was time to start the *Friday* evening meal, the one we'd consume in about six hours. Theoretically it was a piece of cake. About two dozen chicken thighs had to be rubbed with olive oil, Dijon mustard, pureed garlic, lemon juice, and black pepper and allowed to marinate for a couple of hours before being grilled and basted with beer. We planned two potato salads—this time Molly made a mayo-free Italian one from my friend Susan Simon's recently published cookbook. I made the other one the old-fashioned Southern way, with celery, onion, mayonnaise, dill pickle relish, black pepper, and overcooked potatoes. Asparagus was shaved and tossed with olive oil, ready for the grill. Deviled eggs and sliced tomatoes completed our farewell-to-summer cookout menu.

Garlic-laden coleslaw was based on a recipe I had pried from Betty Ablon, a Dallas chef who once owned a successful catering business. She still has a sign in her kitchen that warns, "We serve food with our garlic." Molly and I shared responsibility for piping in the deviled egg filling.

Yeah, that's right—piping.

I stopped spooning the yolk mixture into the whites as soon as I learned you could snip off the corner of a Ziploc bag and squeeze the contents into the egg half. Most folks would just spoon in the egg yolk goo, but once again, Molly had been watching way too much Martha. Which also explained why an artful arrangement of deviled eggs was alternately topped with caviar, capers, anchovy slivers, or a dusting of paprika. They were served, of course, on her mother's deviled egg plate. Within three hours my potato salad, the deviled eggs, and Molly's mayo-free potato salad were carefully covered with plastic wrap and refrigerated, and the mayonnaise-vinegar dressing on the slaw was doing its slow dance of flavor melding.

The only thing left was to crank up the gas grill.

Yes, well . . .

When you open a grill and discover the bottom shelf has fallen out and rust dust fills half of the gas jets, it is a sign that the grill should probably be replaced. If there is any doubt, the presence of a vacated bird's nest pretty much clinches it, especially when bird poo has cemented the nest to the remaining jets.

Fortunately, we started early enough in the day that there was time to roll the old grill out of sight and head for the nearest barbecue supply store. This was before the Internet let our fingers do a different kind of walking. A quick Yellow Pages consult and a few calls later we located a couple of places in the vicinity that were still open.

Bye-bye, nap.

Now, I'm all about low-rent shopping, as in Sears or Lowe's or Home Depot. Hell, Big Lots. Better yet, I would have been happy with one of those big things made from cut-up oil drums. But that would take us back to the wood-and-charcoal scene that Molly was determined to avoid.

Anyway, Miz Molly is already guiding Truck Bob in the general direction of some high-end store where, if barbecue grills were cars, the one with the lowest price tag would have been a Saab convertible.

Girlfriend is determined to cook with gas. She already has a propane tank. She's used to gas. It's her dime. Gas it is.

We enter and I head straight for the corner with a big red "Sale" banner over it. "Sale": almost one of my favorite four-letter words. The unit I spy has three shelves inside and three knobs that will register "high," "medium," and "low." There's even a shelf on one side for warming sauce, and another on the other side for utensils and other grill-related stuff, like beer. It's perfect.

She's looking at a monster with knobs and windows reminiscent of a 747 control panel. It requires not one but two propane tanks and comes in just under four figures. I veto it. The woman who allows birds to nest in her grill doesn't need two propane tanks and an $800 grill. The salesman says the store's staff will put it together for $25 and load it into the truck; says it'll take maybe twenty to thirty minutes. No worries. Guests are coming at 7. It's almost 5. What's thirty minutes? Except Molly starts that "we can put it together" so-called feminist nonsense. In my mind's ear I hear Tonto saying, "What's this 'we' shit, Kemosabe?" Molly thinks maybe we should look elsewhere. This idea also makes me nervous.

Go somewhere else? Did she really say "go somewhere else"? Eight, ten, maybe fifteen people—who knows anymore?—coming in less than two hours and we're going to go somewhere else? On the Saturday before Labor Day? Haggle over $25 for assembling a three-tiered barbecue grill that would take us until Thanksgiving to put together?

She relents, thank God.

It's now 5:30.

Bye-bye, shower.

We arrive back in Travis Heights, park Truck Bob, unload the *assembled* grill, hook up the propane tank, fire it up, and glory hallelujah, there's fire.

For about thirty seconds.

Then nothing.

The propane tank is empty. Molly shakes her head and mutters, "I'll just be goddamned." As I pop the top on a new bottle of Red Stripe, and she refreshes a glass of Chard, she turns to me and says, "Whose fool idea was it to grill this fuckin' chicken anyway?"

"Yours."

"Liar," she replies, launching one of her singular from-the-belly-up laughs.

Molly starts making calls to places in the neighborhood where she knows propane tanks are sold. Of course the first two or three calls she makes confirm what we already anticipated: propane tanks are in high demand on Labor Day weekend. Each place is either closed or out of tanks. Finally she finds a service station relatively close by. There is one left. We head out to effect an exchange at the border. As it turns out, the guy is holding it for someone who is late picking it up. The prospective buyer hasn't appeared and he hasn't called. It's just after 6. The shop closes at 6:30. Molly offers the guy cash plus $20.

Full tank secured.

By the time we get back to the house, fire up the grill—*really* fire it up—it's almost 7.

Change clothes? Oh, probably not. Let's just do with another glass of wine and another Red Stripe, which is, if you recall, also good for basting.

The first arrivals appear a little after 7:15, bearing cheese, crackers, olives, and nuts. Iowa-born and farm-raised, Doug Zabel arrives with a casserole of baked beans based on a recipe straight from his mom's kitchen. Successive diners bring appetizers, booze, and dessert—the omnipresent guacamole, blue corn tortilla chips, more cheese, fresh fruit, brownies and lemon squares. More white wine, more six-packs. Before long a dozen or so of us are nattering away. I'm on the patio tending chicken thighs slowly progressing from amber to golden to an almost mahogany brown.

By 8:30 the chicken is done. A little before 9 we settle down to eat, talk, laugh. We catch up on the latest from the Lege, who voted for/against what in Congress, who's shtupping whom, whatever. This continues for another hour or two. Then it's time for dessert. Elliott Naishtat and Doug Zabel offer a toast to the cooks.

Someone suggests we must have been in the kitchen all day. Nah, Molly and I say almost simultaneously. Nah, just something we threw together. No big deal.

ELLEN'S REALLY GOOD GRILLED CHICKEN

This recipe is gonna scare the beejebers out of the hypochondriacs among us, because nobody believes you should leave chicken out for more than six seconds lest you contract some dread disease. I'll just tell you what we did, and you do what you're comfortable with. Of course it's legitimate to ask why anyone should trust cooks who scoop food off the floor and feed it to their dinner guests, bleed on onions, or serve roasts tooth-marks down at a holiday dinner. Just remember: meat taken straight from the refrigerator to the grill cooks unevenly because it cooks from the outside in, which means the part nearest the bone is the coldest. By the time the outside is all golden brown and beautiful, the inside is still pink. Chicken that is the same temperature throughout cooks more evenly. (By the way, boneless is not only comparatively tasteless, it is harder to eat with one's hands and hardly worth the additional expense.) Potato salad, slaw, and beans make great accompaniments in the summer; in winter, pair with ratatouille and rice.

INGREDIENTS

1 cup Dijon mustard
6 garlic cloves, pureed
1 tablespoon paprika
1 tablespoon black pepper
Juice from 6 lemons
1¼ cup soy sauce, divided use
¼ cup rice wine (or white) vinegar, divided use
3 tablespoons olive oil
2 tablespoons water

16 to 18 chicken thighs, excess skin and fat trimmed (use kitchen shears, but remember to wash them afterward with hot soapy water and rinse them well—the scissors, not the chicken)
2 12-ounce bottles or cans of beer
1 tablespoon garlic powder

DIRECTIONS

In a small bowl, combine mustard, garlic, paprika, and black pepper. Whisk in lemon juice, ¼ cup soy sauce, 1 tablespoon vinegar, olive oil, and water. In a shallow casserole large enough to hold the thighs in layers, pour the mixture over the chicken thighs, distributing it equally. Using both hands, rub the mixture into each thigh and refrigerate covered for at least 4 hours (preferably overnight), skin side up. Remove from refrigerator 45 minutes before grilling.

In a bowl (or a large plastic spray bottle) combine the remaining soy sauce, vinegar, beer, and garlic powder to make the basting sauce. Refrigerate overnight so the beer will go flat. Remove 1 hour before you put the chicken on the grill.

Heat grill to medium low. Place thighs skin side up and grill for 20 to 25 minutes, checking periodically. When chicken starts to brown, turn and baste (or spray) the pieces with beer marinade. Have a sip yourself from a standby bottle. Take care that the fat from the skin doesn't flare up. If it does, drizzle on more beer. Have a sip. Keep doing this every 15 minutes until the chicken is a rich golden brown, using additional beer if necessary. Let chicken rest for 20 minutes before serving. Serves 8.

★ ★ ★

BETTY ABLON'S GARLIC COLESLAW

You can either buy a small head of purple cabbage and a small head of green cabbage and shred them along with a carrot for this salad or make life easy and buy vegetables already shredded. Remember, you're cooking for friends, not campaigning for a Michelin star. Molly might not agree, but when we've been pressed for time, even she has acquiesced. Finally, if you don't love garlic (or if garlic doesn't love you), don't even think about using the amount of garlic called for here. This is not for people who are ambivalent about this first cousin to the mighty onion.

INGREDIENTS

¼ cup granulated sugar
⅓ cup white vinegar
½ cup mayonnaise
6 garlic cloves, peeled and forced through a press

1 teaspoon kosher salt
Freshly ground black pepper to taste
2 1-pound packages of shredded slaw

DIRECTIONS

Combine sugar and vinegar and whisk until mixed. Add mayonnaise. Stir in garlic, salt, and pepper. Combine thoroughly with slaw mix. Refrigerate for at least 2 hours. Stir well and correct seasonings before serving. Don't breathe on anybody who doesn't eat it. Serves 4 to 6.

★ ★ ★

SUSAN SIMON'S INSALATA DI PATATE CON APPERI E ACCIUGHE (POTATO SALAD WITH CAPERS AND ANCHOVIES)

My friend Susan Simon divides her time between Italy and New York. She has written several deliciously utilitarian cookbooks based on her Italian experience, one of which, *Insalate: Authentic Italian Salads for All Seasons*, includes this perfect summertime recipe. Molly and I made it several times. It's especially good with grilled fish and chicken.

INGREDIENTS

2½ pounds small white potatoes
½ cup extra-virgin olive oil
2 teaspoons red wine vinegar
¼ cup coarsely chopped fresh flat-leaf parsley

2 tablespoons capers
2 anchovy fillets, minced
Salt and freshly ground black pepper to taste

DIRECTIONS

Cook potatoes in a large pot of boiling water for about 20 minutes, or until a paring knife easily passes through them. Drain, reserving some of the cooking water. Carefully peel the potatoes while they're hot. Cut them into ¼-inch-thick slices and put them in a large bowl.

Combine the olive oil and vinegar and add to the still-warm potatoes. Toss to combine thoroughly. If the mixture seems a bit dry, add a few tablespoons of the hot potato water. Let sit for 10 minutes.

Add parsley, capers, and anchovies to the bowl. Toss to combine. Taste for salt and add with pepper as needed. Serves 6.

★ ★ ★

23

The Minnesota Dead Guy

MOLLY RECEIVED MYRIAD HONORS, as reflected in stacks of engraved plaques. True to her entrenched facility for self-deprecation, she frequently used them as trivets on her dining table. Every now and again when "the girls" gathered, someone invariably asked whom they were dining on that evening— at which point Molly would retrieve a plaque and announce the donor with a flourish as she gathered the requisite number of "trivets." It might be from an ACLU chapter, the Sierra Club, the Colorado Bar Association, or the Texas Democracy Foundation. Such utilitarian use of awards was not done out of any disrespect to the presenters; it was more a practical matter. The way she looked at it, these awards were of more value protecting her handcrafted dinner table than they were hanging on her walls.

We traded war stories, like the time I scooped the police beat reporter by covering a triple homicide—earning me my first above-the-fold A1 news story. It was a keeper in the best old-school style: three dead and one infant who was subsequently determined to be alive when a cop gingerly reached out to cover the blood-spattered baby and it let out a squall that startled the tough guy so completely that he shrieked, prompting others to shriek and prompting the infant to cry even louder. Come to think of it, I'm pretty sure I told that story over dinner, but not meat loaf—and for sure not meatballs and spaghetti.

Although her dearest newspaper love was the pugnacious *Texas Observer*, Molly also did early time at the *Houston Chronicle*, serious time at the *Minneapolis Star-Tribune*, and hard time at the *New York Times*. In Minneapolis her tenure was distinguished by one assignment in particular. It is one of those stories Molly told on herself, so here goes:

At some point in her three-year tenure as the *Star-Tribune*'s first-ever female police reporter, Molly was dispatched to cover a homicide on a very cold starting-to-snow-again Minnesota day. When she arrived, totally inappropriately dressed for the occasion—after all, this was her first full-time, post-Columbia gig and she wanted to make a good impression—she promptly discerned that to interview the cops on the scene she would have to get to the bottom of a shallow but nonetheless treacherous ravine, where the recently departed lay.

Wearing a smart pair of heels, a sturdy down-to-the-knees winter coat, a black cashmere sweater, a straight black wool skirt, gloves, and pearls, Molly was perfectly attired to cover a homicide in New York's Central Park, but not one in the Land of 10,000 Lakes. In the winter.

As she gingerly descended, step by cautious step, her heel snagged on a rock or a root and gravity took over, landing her in a belly flop on the body—and further contaminating a crime scene already compromised by inclement weather. The stunned silence created by her abrupt arrival was punctuated by a police lieutenant who reportedly snarled, "Who the fuck is that?"

In the ensuing years she otherwise comported herself professionally, covering city and county stories. But Minnesota was not a much better fit than New York City would come to be. For one thing, it was very, very, very cold. She liked to say that other than the dead guy in the ravine, her only big Minneapolis crime story featured a Norwegian consul accused of shoplifting a package of wild rice. When she left Minnesota for warmer climes she was appropriately honored: the Minneapolis Police Department named its pig mascot "Molly." Ever one to view life through the prism of humor generously laced with irony, she was flattered.

When Molly returned to Texas, she and Kaye Northcott became coeditors of the *Observer*, still one of the nation's gutsiest independent publications. It was the perfect place for those who didn't care about money, because the *Observer* didn't have any. The gamin-like Northcott has a soft-spoken demeanor that conceals a rapier wit and a wicked sense of humor. Kaye and Molly shared many meals together, primarily because Molly loved to cook and Kaye didn't quite so much. It was an epicurean yin/yang configuration that worked well for both. As coeditors they covered the state legislature—Molly the House, Kaye the Senate.

For all her journalistic feistiness, when you Google "bleeding heart," Molly's photograph should pop up.

Case in point and a true story:

Kaye had a dog classified (by her) as a "Texas Blackhound," a Weimaraner–black Lab mix unlikely to be listed in anybody's AKC registry. She had managed to give away all of the puppies from a litter sired by her dog, J. Edgar.

Magnolia Blossom went to Kaye's sister. Sport found a home with Dave Richards and his then-wife, Ann. (Sport once ate a marijuana cigarette and proceeded to dig a big hole and circle it many, many, many times before plopping into it and falling into a sound, weed-induced doggy sleep.) One puppy remained.

So, the night before Kaye was to leave on a much-needed vacation, Molly dropped by to say bon voyage. In the course of friendly farewell chatter, Molly asked about the remaining puppy, the one that had somehow acquired a blob of poop on its forehead shortly after its birth.

Knowing exactly how her vulnerable guest would react, Kaye casually shared a bit of information with "entrapment" written all over it: since she, Kaye, was about to go out of town for the weekend, she would just take this darling little puppy to the pound. If they found a home for him, wonderful, but if not, well, with any luck *maybe* he'd be there when she returned.

Molly, convinced that the pup would probably *not* be there, offered to play foster mom for the weekend. Thirteen years later she still had the dog, which she'd named Shit. Kaye says the moniker was not appreciated.

"I think that poor dog knew its name was just wrong. I mean, nobody says 'shit' in a nice way. Molly realized that word of the dog's name was bound to reach her editors, and the New York Times would have a hard time understanding how they'd managed to hire someone who named her pet after fecal matter. The dog's neuroses probably escalated when she moved to New York and, for some reason, changed its name to 'Sitter.'"

Although Kaye can't remember a single instance in which she cooked for Molly, she does remember food-related events. One in particular occurred during the "Ides of March" weekend on Bob Armstrong's ranch some forty-five miles northwest of Austin.

Armstrong, a member of the Texas Legislature from 1963 to 1970, went on to become land commissioner, a member of the Texas Parks and Wildlife Commission and, ultimately, assistant secretary of the interior under President Bill Clinton. He and his then-wife, Shannon, started the campouts more than forty years ago, as a means of sharing their spread with those who might never spend time on a working ranch, let alone own one.

Four hundred acres of the 628-acre spread have been placed in conserva-tion, which means they can never be developed. "You can run cattle, and you can have a campout, but you can't build anything on them," Armstrong said with a chuckle. "It's also nice because it's really hard to find."

Armstrong met Molly when he was still in the Lege, and remembers her being a regular at Dave McNeely's camp, probably because Dave attended the first-ever Armstrong campout, in 1971, and has missed only one or two in the forty years since the event's inception. Dave and Armstrong had known each other since Armstrong's 1970 run for land commissioner. Dave was his press secretary, travel aide, and all-round Guy Friday.

"Bob celebrated his victory the following February, as I recall, for his sup-porters from around the state and members of the Texas capitol press not averse to sleeping on the ground and using the great outdoors for their toilet needs," McNeely said.

"During the time Bob and his next wife, Linda Aaker, were in Washing-ton in the mid-1990s, and when he was deputy secretary of the interior under President Bill Clinton, Bob, a couple of other friends, and I were responsible for getting out the word and manning the ranch until the Armstrongs could fly in for the campout.

The Armstrong Weekend Campout, as the event came to be called, com-prised about ten camps scattered across the ranch site. One was the reporters' camp, somewhere else the political progressives staked their space, and so on—environmentalists, trial lawyers, fiddlers and other musicians—unabashed liberals of every stripe. Northcott's ticket to this celebratory outing was Sara Speights, who had once worked for Armstrong and later became a close friend.

It was, by all accounts, a great family weekend. Almost everyone brought tweezers because somebody's kid was always falling into cactus, necessitating removal of needles from a butt, back, thigh, or foot. Atop a cedar flagpole the camp flew a giant Texas flag because the March camp date almost always coin-cided with Texas Independence Day.

"We'd get all patriotic, sometimes much to the distress of Yankees who weren't accustomed to people shooting off guns in the middle of the desert," Kaye deadpanned. "They damn near jumped out of their skin. Don Kennard—he was a state senator then—always roasted a pig, and watching folks who were waiting for the pig to be done was like viewing a scene from *Lord of the Flies*, with people circling, skulking, wanting to be the first to have at that pig.

Ours, where Molly was, was a kind of gourmet camp. We'd have steaks and fancy stews, and somehow an unofficial competition evolved where people would try to out-cook one another.

"Sometimes it would be so damn cold you really didn't want to be outside, but there we were, slogging around from one camp to another, trying to see who had the best food or the most beer or both. Molly's specialty during this particular period was beer. But she had spent a year studying in France, y'know, and had taken some cooking classes, so she made this beef thing with red wine—it had a name, beef burgundy, or something like that. We called it beef stew, but she let us know it was really *boeuf bourguignon*. She did another thing she called *pot-au-feu*. We called it chicken stew. But hey, both had wine, so how bad could they be?"

Molly was also on hand for the annual Patterson Lake frog gigging outing, organized by Randy Parten, another soldier in the lefty brigade—son of J. R. Parten and arguably the only liberal oilman Texas ever had. "We'd go out with pointy sticks and gig frogs," Northcott explained with editorial detachment— like an artisan describing a recently mastered quilting stitch. "The idea was to nail 'em with this pointy stick, whap 'em on the side of the boat to kill 'em, then bring 'em back to the camp where somebody would clean 'em, dress 'em, and fry 'em up."

Kaye actively participated only once. After that she just ate what others gigged.

24

You Gonna Eat That?

TEXAS STATE REPRESENTATIVE ELLIOTT NAISHTAT was one of those who knew Molly more as Savvy Ally Molly, friend and cook. His journey to the Texas legislature is one of those curious tales that helps clarify the confluence of Elliott, Molly, and food.

Known as a relentless champion of progressive causes, he has served more than twenty years in the Texas Legislature. Not bad for a Democrat who defeated Bob Richardson, the only Republican who had the nerve to oppose him; he's run against Libertarians since then and won handily. Not bad for a guy who never intended to be in Texas for a year—let alone four decades. And certainly not bad for a native New Yorker who wears Save the Children ties and has extraordinary radar for free meals.

The sixty-seven-year-old bachelor represents the 49th District, an elongated sliver of legislative real estate that runs through central Austin. It includes low-income, multiethnic, and inner-city neighborhoods, a few pockets of affluence, and the University of Texas.

And if you're wondering how a self-described pacifist Jew from Brooklyn ended up in the state legislature, it's okay; there are still times when he wonders the same thing. For one thing, it was the '60s when his tale began—1966, to be exact.

When Naishtat reported to his draft board in that year, he learned that an alternative to Vietnam was Volunteers in Service to America—VISTA. So instead of fighting the war in Vietnam, he opted to fight LBJ's War on Poverty. He was told he'd be doing battle in San Francisco. Life, he reckoned, was sweet. He had never been west of Pennsylvania and looked forward to the two-week orientation in San Antonio. The sweetness came to a screeching halt when he learned that he wasn't California-bound after all; he was being assigned to Eagle Pass, a dusty border town on the Rio Grande—roughly equivalent, from Elliott's point of view, to half past the end of the world.

"I figured there had been some terrible mistake," he said. "It looked like Mars. I mean, where were the buildings, the traffic, the noise? I looked around and thought, 'This is my punishment for not wanting to fight the war.'"

He didn't view it as punishment for long. Brought up in a family with a strong sense of social justice, he saw legal work that needed to be done on behalf of the local community and began to do it—all the while taking relentless ribbing from Texans who found him as curious as he found them.

Gonzalo Barrientos, a former migrant worker who later served as a state senator for twenty-two years after a decade-long stretch as a state representative, became a friend and mentor. Together they organized the first Head Start program in Maverick County.

(Yes, Texas gave us the word "maverick." The Maverick family refused to brand their cows, so anytime a stray wandered onto their property, the family claimed it.)

Working together, Barrientos and Naishtat brought water lines and sewers to the barrios, they introduced immunization and tutoring programs, and they generally pissed off the existing power structure. They were interlopers, outside agitators. The people might have appreciated them, but a lot of local power brokers didn't.

Texas politics worked its way into Elliott's blood. Not satisfied with the limitations of working at the grassroots level, he set his sights on where the real power lay: making the laws that create social change on behalf of those without the money or the power to alter their circumstances. Texas and its bizarro politics had invaded his psyche.

Texas and politics. Ever a curious combo.

By 1986, *attorney* Naishtat, now a graduate of the University of Texas with a law degree and a master's degree in social work, was working for *Senator* Barrientos, drafting legislation on the same issues they had worked on for VISTA—battered women, improved access to health services, protection for migrant workers, and services for the elderly. But for Elliott the battlefield had changed from barrios to the House floor, which brought him into Molly's sights as her kind of agitator: deceptively understated, truly determined, conscientious, and effective.

There he was, this Jewish kid from New York, who never meant to stay in Texas a minute beyond his three-year tour of duty as a VISTA volunteer. He would soon meet his best friend, Malcolm Greenstein, a VISTA volunteer who worked in San Antonio and Colorado in the '60s.

Malcolm, a native of Rhode Island, also had some adjustments to make. Nowhere could he find a decent bagel. To demonstrate his grasp of Texas realities, Malcolm made a major move after VISTA: he opened Austin's first bagel shop, Murray's Bagel Nosh—named for his dog.

It was not exactly a resounding success, but not because he didn't produce a worthy product; he did. His bagels were sold at Whole Foods in its early days. He just didn't have much of a grasp of the profit concept—he failed to understand the importance of pricing the product to make more money than he spent.

He and Elliott both ended up living in the Clarksville neighborhood. Guess who was neighborhood association president?

Elliott Naishtat.

The two met and commiserated on their respective Texas experiences. They found they had more than the Atlantic Coast in common. They had traveled extensively in other countries; both were heavily endowed with a sense of social justice; and each subscribed to the notion that if you weren't part of the solution, you were part of the problem.

Malcolm had already established his bona fides as part of the solution with his efforts on behalf of migrant workers in southern Colorado. He was among those who encouraged Elliott to run for the legislature. Word on the street was that the incumbent representative was vulnerable. Egged on by friends and that Don Quixote quest to do good for good's sake, Elliott crisscrossed the Forty-Ninth District, walking door to door, telling people what he believed in and why—going so far as to honestly say he believed in a state income tax, something Texans have rejected for as long as anyone can remember.

"Gonzalo had told me that I had a shot at beating [three-term incumbent] Bob [Richardson] as long as I never talked about an income tax and never told anybody I was from New York," Elliott says. "I knew I would have to bite the bullet and at least mention the possibility of a state income tax. I had to be honest."

"Honest" and "Texas Legislature": words not often employed in the same sentence when describing the state's governing body.

He was especially endearing to Molly for several reasons—he espoused causes she believed in; he chose his battles carefully; and like her, he could get along with adversaries, even when they opposed efforts important to him or teased him about wearing ties that came from the Save the Children project. More to the point, she could always count on the handsome bachelor to round out boy-girl-boy-girl seating at her dining table. Finally, because she didn't like leftovers, she could also count on him to take them home. Elliott, who weighs maybe 150, is a food-consuming phenomenon. I have always suspected him of having the metabolic rate of a ferret.

Once, despite protests from Molly about my penchant for fatty foods, she caved at the mention of my father's smothered chicken in onion gravy. As usual, we needed diners, but not the ones who sit around the table and bemoan the cholesterol content and caloric value of everything on the menu. Every time I hear one of these tiresome monologues I'm reminded of *Babette's Feast*, a wonderfully convoluted tale of food, austere religion and the people who practiced it, and the struggle to absolutely not register enjoyment of anything, let alone food.

Bright green freshly steamed broccoli was Molly's counterweight to my calorie-laden contribution (I wanted to call it my "arteriosclerotic comfort food contribution," but *Austin American-Statesman* reporter Mike Sutter had already used that description). Although I am partial to thighs, a few breasts were also browned as a concession to those who insisted on white meat.

On our shopping expedition we could find only unusually large chicken breasts. I make this point because Molly wanted her guests to understand why they were cut in half, and that anyone who wanted to double up should feel free to do so. Just the mention of "big smothered breasts" laid the foundation for one tacky crack after another.

After several rounds of bad breast jokes and the usual verbal jousting, the evening wound down. Molly, being true to her diet of the moment, left half of her very large (chicken) breast on her plate, prompting Elliott to gesture toward it, his azure eyes raised in mock supplication. We knew what was coming. In a gesture not unlike a third-grader seeking permission to be excused to the restroom, he at last posed the question we'd all been waiting for.

"Uh, Molly," he said softly, "you gonna eat that?"

SMOTHERED CHICKEN IN ONION GRAVY

Late in my teens I learned that chicken was called "the gospel bird" because it was often served on Sundays. My grandfather said poor blacks on plantations—and later during the Depression—were happy to have one day a week when they could eat "real" food instead of miscellaneous animal parts—neck bones, ham hocks, and chicken wings before Buffalo drove the price sky high. In our house smothered chicken was a winter variation on our standard fried or grilled Sunday chicken dinner. We ate it with rice, gravy, and greens or spinach.

INGREDIENTS

10 to 12 chicken thighs, skin on, excess fat trimmed

Salt

Black pepper

Paprika

Garlic powder

4 cups all-purpose flour, divided use

1 cup canola oil, divided use

2 yellow onions, sliced thin

4 cups chicken stock

2 teaspoons salt

1 teaspoon black pepper

DIRECTIONS

Rinse chicken thighs and dry them with a paper towel. Sprinkle with salt, pepper, paprika, and garlic powder. Dredge each thigh in flour and shake off the excess. Save ¾ cup of flour for gravy.

In a large cast-iron or nonstick sauté pan, preferably one with a lid, brown chicken in ½ cup oil over medium-high heat, then remove it to a platter and set aside.

Scrape loose any bits that have stuck to the pan. Except for ½ cup, stir the flour that has been set aside into the remaining oil and stir until it turns a rich, dark brown, creating a roux. Take care not to let any of the chicken bits stick. When the roux is a dark brown, add onion slices. Stir until they begin to wilt. Slowly stir in chicken stock. Stir intermittently until the mixture starts to thicken, about 5 minutes.

Return chicken thighs to the pan and cover. Reduce heat to simmer for 15 to 20 minutes. Check once or twice to make sure the chicken isn't sticking. Season with salt and pepper. Uncover, simmer for another 10 minutes, and serve. Serves 6.

★ ★ ★

25

Thank God It's Friday

FOR MORE THAN THREE DECADES AUSTINITES of a certain political stripe have gathered for Final Friday, a monthly assemblage of politically progressive types. These gatherings, which started out as First Friday, bounced around for several years until there was some concern about the event's survival prospects—at which point Molly stepped in and offered her house until a permanent destination could be established. Her house remained the "temporary" location for more than five years.

I met Molly when Final Fridays were still at La Zona Rosa, a local watering hole that served decent food and music and was once owned by artist/entrepreneur Gordon Fowler. (Gordo, as he is still known to friends, is married to Texas-born, Louisiana-raised blues babe Marcia Ball. Both were close to Molly. Marcia rounded out Molly's memorial service with a rousing performance of "Great Balls of Fire.")

From La Zona Rosa, Final Fridays moved to Ty and Kate Fain's. When they moved away in 1998 it migrated to Molly's house. You never knew who might turn up. It might be feminist author Gloria Steinem, economist Paul Krugman (before he became a Nobel laureate in 2008), Peter Yarrow (of Peter, Paul, and Mary), populist judge William Wayne Justice, or Lady Bird Johnson's former press secretary, Liz Carpenter. They moved among the revelers freely and without fanfare.

It was indeed a merry band of political progressives who convened monthly for sing-alongs, slam poetry, storytelling, music making, or just plain old-fashioned conversation. Subject matter might cover state legislature gossip, small talk about weather, or rants about right-wing crazies or the Bush administration, which were not always mutually exclusive.

Final Fridays live on, with seasonal changes in destination. They now occur under the imprimatur of the *Texas Observer* as a tent welcoming all like-minded souls. There are a few ground rules: they no longer continue into the wee hours of the morning as they once did. The standing time frame is 7 p.m. to midnight. At one time everything said on those evenings was off the record, and to the best of my knowledge, few violated that constraint. With fewer reporters and more "civilians" participating these days, those rules have shifted.

Author, columnist, and populist Jim Hightower, who had known Molly since the late '70s, was a frequent face in the crowd. Molly and Jim were also veterans of several cruises organized by the *Nation* magazine. The publication hit on the idea to invite readers to go on a six-day sail with writers and political activists ranging from Barbara Ehrenreich and Tom Hayden to Arianna Huffington and Ralph Nader. The cruises included symposia and panel discussions held in the ship's amphitheater, where Las Vegas–style shows would otherwise have held sway. The *New York Times* dubbed the *Nation* cruises "The Love Boat for Policy Wonks."

"Of course, at Final Friday food took a backseat to whatever else was going on," Hightower said. "You weren't so much coming to dinner as you were participating in an evening of food and good conversation. I usually brought appetizers like baba ganoush and prosciutto-wrapped dates stuffed with Manchego cheese, stuff like that."

Other contributions were more prosaic. I brought fried chicken, red beans and rice, and biscuits from Popeye's—calories and cholesterol be damned. When I didn't have money to splurge at Popeye's, I made a totally kick-ass tuna salad. In the summer someone always got ambitious and brought a huge platter of deviled eggs. In the winter one had to take care not to trip over cords leading from wall sockets to Crock-Pots full of chili, beef stew, or spaghetti.

Final Fridays at Molly's were eventually discontinued due to an overpopulation of curiosity seekers who behaved badly. Hangers-on who didn't know George Walker Bush from Luke Skywalker surfaced. As news spread of Molly's terminal cancer, attendees began to include the prurient curious.

Once, as Del Garcia and I stood talking near the front door, a couple broke away from their companions, another couple with whom they'd been talking. Neither Del nor I recognized any member of the quartet. As the woman moved toward Molly's bedroom door—Molly had quietly excused herself and gone to bed as she increasingly did when her energy level flagged—I saw the woman turn back to the other couple and mouth the words, "Is she in there?" At this point I moved toward her and asked if she was looking for the bathroom and pointed her toward it. No, she replied, she wanted to know if Molly Ivins was behind that closed door. As calmly as possible I asked why she felt she needed to know that. At this point her husband nudged her and suggested they leave. There was no mistaking the extent to which I agreed with him.

It was 2005 and the beginning of the end in more ways than one. In its heyday Final Friday had been something to behold. Melancholy Ramblers. Hootenannies. Slam poets: Molly was on to this renegade art form ahead of a lot of others. Spike Gillespie was in the forefront.

Spike and Molly met not too long after Spike (her real name) moved to Austin in 1991. Spike took a job waiting tables at Magnolia Cafe South—"South" to distinguish its sister restaurant of the same name on the *good* side of town.

Located on South Congress near Molly's Travis Heights neighborhood, Magnolia South attracted, shall we say, an eclectic clientele—neighborhood regulars, cops, musicians, the hookers and homeless after a successful night of panhandling.

Spike, now a published "Arthur" (Molly's words), public speaker, quilter, wedding officiant, and president of the Office of Good Deeds, treasures those days.

"Molly would come in and we were always excited to see her," she said. "But we wouldn't say anything because we were used to seeing visiting celebrities, and we wanted to respect her privacy. She thought she was traveling incognito, or as inconspicuously as a six-foot-tall strawberry blonde can, so we let her have it that way. One night she came in for dinner with her mother. Somehow in the course of the meal she knocked over a glass of iced tea. Everybody rushed to clean it up. I might have even made some lame joke along the lines of 'Molly Ivins can't spill that, can she?'

"Anyway, we had this waiter named Lindsay from Australia, a UT journalism major, and he was beside himself to see her. Although I was covering her table, he couldn't wait to be the one to clear her plates. So when I checked on the table and saw they were gone, I said, 'Hey, Molly, your plates are gone; did you put them in your purse or something?' It was really pretty funny because Molly had just been telling her mother that she liked to eat at the Magnolia because nobody knew who she was—and I had to tell her that *everybody* knew who she was. When she came in people were jockeying to wait on her. We were just too cool to let on."

Molly liked Spike's spirit. As it transpired, Genevieve Van Cleve, a fellow poet, invited Spike to join her one Final Friday evening.

"I didn't want to come across as some big starfucker, so I said no," Spike continued. "But then I found out what the evenings were really about and went the following month. In fact, before she got sick, I was one of the earliest people to take a kid. My son, Henry, was about eight or nine then and he loved to go. We'd bring his friends and they'd play in Molly's bedroom. He thought that was the coolest thing."

'Round about that same time Spike was looking for someone to write a blurb for a new book of her poems. She mentioned this to Mike Smith, Molly's research assistant, and he urged her to ask Molly, which of course Spike couldn't bring herself to do. Instead she passed the manuscript on to Mike, figuring Molly would probably never bother.

A month or two later, Molly asked Spike to read a poem. She declined, arguing that she didn't have any new material—at which point Molly said, "Yes, you do." With that she fetched the manuscript. Spike read and was a hit. Molly subsequently wrote the dust-jacket blurb.

Spike became part of a regiment of volunteers who chauffeured Molly to and from medical and hospital appointments. One of her early assignments occurred just after Molly's first round of surgery.

"After we left the hospital she invited me out to one of those ladies-who-lunch places," Spike said. "We had a lovely visit and a really good meal. When the check came I thoroughly intended to pay my share—but Molly insisted that I was her guest, and it was a good thing too, because I never had any money.

"As it turned out, though, Molly only had twenty dollars. Because she had just left the hospital, she didn't have any credit cards either. Between us we came up with enough loose change to pay the bill and put it all in that little black folder they leave on the table. So we're in this fancy joint and I'm with this millionaire 'famous Arthur,' and there's change spilling out all over the place. Then this snooty waitress, her voice dripping with frigid sarcasm, sneering, 'Do you need change?'"

Molly and Spike had become friends.

"I'll always be grateful for all the lunches she took me to," Spike said. "Wherever we'd go, whether it was Eastside Cafe or Fonda San Miguel, the restaurant owners and staff all knew her. She was as gracious with the staff as she was with the owners. She was never too good for the so-called little people. I think of her whenever I cook because I have potholders she gave me. [Liz Faulk, Molly's assistant at the time, started making them to pass the time when Molly was sick during chemo treatments.]

"Molly gave me some advice once, and I've always remembered it. She said, 'If you're a hungry writer, save pennies so you can buy cat food, but drink water before going to bed; you can trick your stomach into believing it's full, but you can't sleep if the cat is yowling.'"

KICK-ASS TUNA SALAD

Whenever I'm asked to participate in a potluck gathering I check the refrigerator and pantry first to see what's already workable, which is why it's always good to have certain staples—canned tuna, Dijon mustard, garlic, capers, anchovies and/or anchovy paste, pasta, rice, mayonnaise, canned tomatoes, thyme, and bay leaves. This recipe also works for leftover grilled or baked tuna and is best made and refrigerated at least several hours before serving.

INGREDIENTS

1 tablespoon Dijon mustard
1 teaspoon anchovy paste
¼ cup fresh lemon juice
1 or 2 garlic cloves, peeled and
   squeezed through a press
3 tablespoons white wine vinegar
1 tablespoon water
¼ cup olive oil
2 tablespoons mayonnaise
1 teaspoon freshly ground black
   pepper
1 12-ounce can albacore white
   tuna, drained
1½ cups celery, chopped

¼ cup red onion, chopped fine
2 tablespoons fresh parsley,
   minced
¼ cup nonpareil capers
2 tablespoons chopped black
   olives
½ teaspoon dried dill weed
½ teaspoon dried savory
1 teaspoon Old Bay, Zatarain's,
   or Tony Chachere's Creole
   seasoning
2 hard-boiled eggs, chopped
Kosher salt and freshly ground
   black pepper to taste

DIRECTIONS

In a small mixing bowl, or a wide-mouth jar with a lid, combine mustard, anchovy paste, lemon juice, garlic, vinegar, water, olive oil, mayonnaise, and black pepper. Whisk (or shake) well and set aside.

In a larger mixing bowl, using a fork, toss together, tuna, celery, onion, parsley, capers, olives, dill weed, savory, seasoning, and eggs. Add salad dressing and mix thoroughly. Add salt and pepper to taste. Refrigerate for at least 3 hours. Stir to mix ingredients again before serving. Serves 2.

★ ★ ★

26

The Great Leonard
Pitts–less Dinner

SO THERE WE WERE, MOLLY AND I, driving along in Truck Bob, conjuring up a reason to have a celebratory dinner for someone. Anyone. Any reason.

Although she did indeed plan and organize real dinner parties with structure and properly paired wines, she and I would often stop halfway through preparing a meal and realize she had no idea who might eat it. Although it was not unusual to completely lose track of how many people might turn up as a result of our haphazard way of inviting guests, we had yet to plan a meal and not invite *anyone*.

Once we outsmarted ourselves by planning a birthday surprise dinner for Malcolm Greenstein. Not that there was anything particularly smart about what became a series of misbegotten episodes.

In any case, we couldn't top the birthday celebration and roast that friends threw for his sixtieth, where Molly was the moderator. By the time the program began, we were all pretty well oiled, including Molly. But she extolled his virtues, his generosity, his striking resemblance to a fit and trim Santa Claus, his commitment to social justice, and his rejection of worldly goods.

Case in point: When my daughter was in her mid-twenties, I think she and Malcolm's television were the same age. Perhaps in response to merciless chiding from friends, he has since bought a flat-screen color TV and subscribed to cable. He also owns a cell phone, thanks to his partner, Stan, and, after a two-year deliberation, he replaced his old convertible with a new one. Used, of course.

He might own two suits, but I can only recall seeing him in one. You always know when he has to appear in court. The suit and tie or a jacket, tie, and slacks come out. The volume on his home stereo system hasn't worked for years, so he listens to NPR on two small radios—one in the bathroom and one in the kitchen.

Instead of spending on, oh, say, a third suit, for the longest time he took a six-week vacation every year—usually to unusual destinations.

On one of his trips to what was once the Soviet Union, he sought out his mother's village, now part of Ukraine. Fluent in Spanish, he's traveled to Mexico a dozen times, once encountering a gringo scam artist from Muleshoe, Texas. He lived with a family whose political activist daughter got crosswise with Mexican authorities and was jailed for her activism. Greenstein intervened by notifying Amnesty International of her plight. She was subsequently released.

When the South African Truth and Reconciliation Commission hearings were held, on one occasion he was the only white person in the room. He who is in no way handy with tools nonetheless volunteered to help build homes for Global Village in Uganda (each volunteer was asked to bring a tool that could be left behind for future construction; he brought a level—as it turned out, that was the only one). Had all hell not broken out in Iran, he had planned to go there in 2010.

In 2005, Malcolm and Travis County Court judge Eric Sheppard were recognized as the driving forces behind renaming the Travis County Courthouse for Heman Sweatt. In a historic case decided by the US Supreme Court in 1950, the *Sweatt v. Painter* lawsuit changed the way Texas (and the country) dealt with race and education and set the stage for desegregating the University of Texas School of Law.

(Heman Sweatt was a graduate of Wiley College in Marshall, Texas, one of the oldest historically black colleges west of the Mississippi. His initial 1946 application to law school at UT was rejected. This refusal was at the core of a "separate but equal" challenge that the NAACP successfully brought before the US Supreme Court in its historic *Brown v. Board of Education* [which struck down segregation in public schools].)

Once ensconced in Austin, Malcolm was among those who made their way to Final Friday gatherings at La Zona Rosa. It was called the "out-of-power happy hour" because the crowd pretty much consisted of Democrats adrift in what was then a sea of Republicans. Malcolm met Molly through that crowd and they became friends. Which brings us back to Molly and me contemplating the anniversary of Malcolm's birth. What a good idea, she opined, to have a surprise birthday party.

We knew Malcolm was a big Leonard Pitts fan, and Molly had read somewhere that the syndicated columnist was to speak in Austin. Intrepid reporters that we were, we agreed that I would track Pitts down at the *Miami Herald*, where he worked, find out when he would arrive and how long he'd stay, and we'd invite him for dinner with Elliott, Del Garcia, Doug Zabel, Malcolm Greenstein, Molly, and me.

As it turned out, the same weekend Leonard Pitts was due was also the weekend political consultant Ed Wendler and his partner, artist Mercedes Peña, were having a pig roast at their rambling house in Lockhart, about twenty-five miles south of Austin. So much the better, we decided. We'll fetch Brother Pitts, swoop down to Lockhart with him, and boy, won't Malcolm be surprised.

Only someone got the weekend dates wrong.

No Leonard Pitts.

Mercifully we hadn't told Malcolm, so we just wished him happy birthday and that was that. If he suspected anything he never let on.

Fast-forward a year or so. Pitts was coming to Austin again, this time to speak at UT. Once more, and with great resolve, we made plans.

Grand, glorious, meticulously orchestrated plans.

I hopped in my trusty burnt orange Nissan and hightailed it south on I-35. Molly and I developed a menu. Hearts of palm salad with champagne-shallot dressing; *boeuf bourguignon* with buttered noodles sprinkled with freshly chopped parsley. Molly made one of her favorite desserts, a fresh pear tart. Red wine, Pellegrino, and Belgian beer would be poured.

Molly and I shopped the day before, this time with The List intact. No fooling around. This was serious business.

Leonard Pitts was coming.

We had it nailed this time.

Molly was up at 8 a.m., chopping shallots, browning meat, slicing mushrooms. Throughout the afternoon the kitchen windows remained steamed from one aspect of the meal or another: parboiled pearl onions, scraped carrots, baby potatoes. There were pears to be peeled and dough to be rolled.

This would be a meal to remember. We even had a seven-member guest list: Elliott, Malcolm, Del Garcia, Mercedes Peña, Ed Wendler, Molly, me. Leonard Pitts would be *número ocho*.

This time I was the sous-chef, cleaning behind chef Molly, following her instructions until, at last, the salad greens were rinsed, wrapped in paper towels, and refrigerated; the beef burgundy rested comfortably; the pear tart sat beautifully browned. The table was set with the good china and shiny sterling flatware.

No effort was spared for this much-admired syndicated *Miami Herald* columnist.

A nicely pressed white linen cloth with matching napkins covered the table. Courtney Anderson's hand-painted wineglasses sparkled, positioned at the tip of each dinner knife. With considerable anticipation we all assembled in the living room, sipping wine and waiting.

7.

7:30.

8.

No Leonard Pitts.

I knew he had the address; I'd given it to him, along with specific directions for the cab in case the driver was unfamiliar with the crazy way streets can zigzag in and out of pattern.

We glanced alternately at the front door and then at one another. Small talk got smaller and smaller and finally descended into uneasy silence.

About an hour past his anticipated arrival time, I retreated to Molly's office to call the hotel. He hadn't checked in.

I had his home number.

I called.

He answered.

Damn.

Alas, Malcolm remembers the evening too well.

"I had plans for that Friday, and Molly kept saying, 'No, no, you have to cancel, you have to cancel. So I did. I had no idea what the big deal was, I just knew that when we finally were about to sit down, I noticed there were seven of us but eight place settings. It wasn't until much later I found out Leonard Pitts was supposed to have been there."

Apparently the person who was supposed to organize the arrival had botched the weekend dates.

He was scheduled to come the following weekend.

Botched? Again?

Ouch.

How could this be? Were we really that incompetent? (And here I hear that Tonto voice intoning, "What's with this 'we' shit, Kemosabe?" There was no "we." I got the date wrong.)

Mea culpa.

As in the best American psychodrama, which this had become, the dinner plan ended as well as could be expected. The meal was delicious, albeit slightly subdued. Molly's glare didn't help. I haven't organized a celebratory dinner for anyone since then.

The following weekend, the one when Pitts really *was* in town, Molly had to give an out-of-town ACLU speech. I had yet another crisis with my ninety-year-old mother and had to go to St. Louis. Mercedes and Ed had other plans. No one was falling for this Leonard-Pitts-is-coming-to-dinner nonsense again.

At least Malcolm and Pitts finally met. In his usual measured way, Malcolm had done due diligence and learned that Pitts, who easily stands six foot one, was a Lakers fan. An NBA game was to be broadcast that Sunday, and Malcolm invited the soon-to-be-Pulitzer-prize-winning columnist to his house to watch the game. On Malcolm's twenty-four-inch television, the one with an intermittent semblance of color and no working remote control.

Molly decided that from that year forward we would have an annual commemorative dinner. We would set the table for eight, but have only seven diners, sort of like setting an extra place for Elijah at Passover.

Her inscription in my copy of *Who Let the Dogs In?* reads, in part, "For many years of laughter, hospitality and Leonard Pitts—less dinners."

=== 27 ===

Plans? We Don't Need
No Stinkin' Plans

MOLLY HAD WAY TOO MUCH FUN PLANNING meals for others, especially people she really, really liked. They were a diverse group whose common thread was concern for making life better for those least able to do so for themselves, people like political strategist Harold Cook; environmental advocate Doug Zabel; civil rights attorney Dave Richards and his wife, Sandy; *Texas Observer* publisher Carlton Carl; attorney Shelia Cheaney, executive director of Jane's Due Process—Texas's only nonprofit dedicated to providing legal advice and assistance to pregnant teens; and multimillionaire philanthropist Bernard Rapoport, who with his wife, Audre, were ardent Molly fans and have been most generous.

Sometimes there was a plan, a purpose, a theme for meals at Molly's house. Once, in casual conversation about ethnic foods, I mentioned the fact that the Greek salads we eat in the United States bear only passing similarity to the salad that Greeks eat—there's no lettuce in their version—and she promptly decided we should do a Greek dinner—some elements store-bought, some homemade. No point, for example, in trying to improve on the stuffed grape leaves from Central Market.

We fearlessly tackled braised lamb shanks and white beans on one evening, then roasted chicken thighs with fresh rosemary and artichoke hearts the next. For once we agreed that potatoes roasted with lemon and garlic would work better than rice—well, rice pilaf, a blend of long-grain rice and orzo. Our meals were often spontaneous and unrehearsed. Dinners just tended to evolve. Every now and then, however, synchronicity occurred wherein plan and purpose collided in a good way. As it did with African Chicken.

Just as I enjoyed making Molly's favorite French meals with her, Molly was almost always game for sampling my ethnic culinary explorations. One was a hit I created from melding two recipes for chicken and peanut stew: a Bahian one called Ximxim de Galinha from Heidi Haughy Cusick's *Soul and Spice* cookbook, and the other, Senegalese *mafe* from Jessica B. Harris's *The Africa Cookbook*. Both books have been used so often they fall open to the pages where preferred recipes reside.

I call my amalgamated concoction African Chicken. We decided to make it and invite people we knew to be receptive to new tastes and flavors. The evening's purpose ended up being twofold. We had heard through the grapevine that our friend Malcolm was smitten with a new flame.

All we knew about this special person was that her name was Stan. We figured we were sure to like a woman named Stan. That she had captured Malcolm's undivided attention was impressive. We held our collective breath, hoping he would bring her along. Sure enough, he asked if he could invite a "friend."

As nonchalantly as possible, Molly assured him it would be fine. Okay, he added, but there might be a hitch. One of Stan's dearest friends was gravely ill. If he died, she for sure wouldn't come. If not, well, she probably would because the December day we had chosen for our experiment in African dining was her birthday.

Now that Malcolm was *maybe* bringing her to us, we had to make her feel welcome. Wait a minute. Did someone say birthday? All of a sudden our plan had an even bigger purpose: minimize sadness. Oh, yeah, and hope she didn't have a peanut allergy. We now not only had a new dish to sample, we had a big fat reason for sampling a new dish with a new friend.

We now had a birthday dinner to prepare.

The day before the dinner we headed to Central Market for chicken thighs and jumbo fresh shrimp with the heads on, the better for making shrimp stock. Then it was off to Fiesta (our local ethnic supermarket) for ground dried shrimp, a crucial ingredient.

On to Half Price Books for cards and cookbooks, often the gift of choice for friends.

Off to Sweetish Hill to buy a birthday cake.

Then to buy candles. The ones that won't go out. You blow and blow and blow, thinking they're done but they keep coming back.

Wait.

What to drink?

Champagne.

It's a birthday party.

We were becoming giddy with anticipation and hoping it wouldn't turn into a Stan-less dinner like the Leonard Pitts fiasco.

Stan did join us. She had no idea that the gathering had morphed into a birthday party in her honor. There were husband-and-wife attorneys Bob Ozer and Janet Dewey, Doug Zabel, Elliott Naishtat, Molly, Malcolm, Stan, and me, seated around that wonderful round table.

Molly made a simple green salad with various baby lettuces tossed in a garlicky lemon-based vinaigrette—she rarely used store-bought salad dressings.

Our centerpiece was a honking great pot of chicken simmered with onion, tomato, mint, ginger, and the secret ingredients—coconut milk, dried ground shrimp, and chunky peanut butter.

The fun of the meal was getting people to identify the ingredients. Tomatoes, onion, sweet potatoes, and chicken were no-brainers, and Zabel, who knows his way around a kitchen, discerned peanuts, not, mercifully, by going into anaphylactic shock. Some truly observant person volunteered bay leaves, another no-brainer, especially since one had ended up in his bowl. Nobody got mint, dried shrimp, or coconut milk.

As our "guess what's in the stew?" game wound down, Molly brought out the cake and we burst into song, with Molly's distinctly atonal voice soaring over a robust, champagne-enhanced chorus of "Happy Birthday."

Stan was stunned.

"It was so unexpected," she said. "I was just excited that I was actually going to meet Molly Ivins, actually going to her house as a dinner guest, and here she greeted me like she had known me all along and was pleased that I was there. Then to find out the dinner had become a party for me—I was pretty darned overwhelmed."

It was one of the happiest dinner parties Molly and I had, and we had quite a few of those spontaneous theme-in-search-of-a-movie meals.

AFRICAN CHICKEN

Ingredients we had to scrounge for a decade ago can be easily found today. I think beer is the best accompaniment for this dish, being a Red Stripe beer gal myself. Ask the store's wine guy for a wine recommendation. I serve this over yellow rice in a shallow bowl. Try to make it a day or two before you plan to serve it; it's another one of those dishes that improve with resting. A simple green leaf salad tossed with hearts of palm in a light vinaigrette rounds it out nicely.

INGREDIENTS

10 to 12 chicken thighs, skin on, but excess fat trimmed

2 large bay leaves

2 large yellow onions, one pureed, one chopped

2 garlic cloves, peeled and minced

6 cups water

1 15-ounce can diced tomatoes

1 teaspoon dried mint

1 teaspoon thyme

1 teaspoon ground ginger

¼ cup dried ground shrimp

1 cup chunky peanut butter

1 sweet potato, peeled and cubed

1 pound large shrimp, peeled and deveined, tails removed

½ cup *unsweetened* coconut milk

Kosher salt and freshly ground pepper to taste

Long-grain rice for 6, cooked according to instructions, with ½ teaspoon turmeric added for color

DIRECTIONS

In a large stockpot (preferably a cast-iron enameled one that can go from stovetop to table), place chicken, bay leaves, pureed onion, and garlic. Add water. Bring pot to a boil, then immediately reduce heat and simmer, covered, for 20 minutes.

Remove chicken to a platter to cool.

To the same pot add tomatoes, mint, thyme, ginger, ground shrimp, and chopped onion. Simmer, covered, for 25 minutes, stirring occasionally to make sure nothing sticks. Add a cup of water if necessary.

Place peanut butter in a small bowl. Ladle about 1½ cups of liquid from the stockpot and gradually stir into peanut butter, diluting it until it thins. Whisk into pot. Add sweet potato. Simmer for 10 minutes, covered.

When chicken is cooled, discard skin, pull meat from bones in large chunks, and add it to the pot. (If preparing the dish in advance, at this point remove the pot from heat, cool, and refrigerate.)

To serve, slowly heat stew and simmer on low heat for 15 to 20 minutes or until sweet potato is cooked through. Add shrimp and cook until they curl and turn pink. Reduce heat and stir in coconut milk. Add salt and pepper to taste. Serve immediately over yellow rice. Serves 6 to 8.

★ ★ ★

ROSEMARY-ARTICHOKE CHICKEN

I first had this dish in Nafplion, a seaside village in Greece. When I saw chicken and artichokes on the menu, I promptly ordered it. "No, madame, so sorry," the waiter said. "The artichokes are finished." I thought he meant the restaurant had run out of them. Instead he was telling me the artichoke season was over. There were no more. They were gone until artichoke season came 'round again. You can add canned ones to this dish if you don't want to cut and peel a zillion baby artichokes to get what you need. Substitute orzo for rice, and a Greek salad for green beans or broccoli. The variations are limited only by your imagination.

INGREDIENTS

6 to 8 fresh rosemary sprigs
8 chicken thighs
15 whole garlic cloves, peeled
2 tablespoons flour
1 cup dry white wine
2 cups chicken stock
1 cup water
8 lemon slices
1 cup Italian seasoned bread crumbs
1 15-ounce can baby artichoke hearts, drained

DIRECTIONS

Preheat oven to 375°F.

In a shallow casserole that will hold the chicken pieces comfortably (they will shrink), layer the bottom with rosemary sprigs.

Rinse the chicken thighs and pat them dry. Place them in the casserole, scatter garlic cloves over and around them, and set aside, covered with a clean dish towel.

In a mixing bowl slowly whisk together flour, wine, chicken stock, and water. Pour mixture over the chicken thighs and top each with a lemon slice. Sprinkle bread crumbs on top. Bake, covered tightly, for 20 minutes. Uncover, add artichoke hearts, and continue baking until chicken is golden brown. Serves 4.

★ ★ ★

28

. . . and a Partridge in
a Bean Stew

SOMETIMES MOLLY WOULD GET A WILD HAIR and decide to tackle some ridiculously complicated dish for no reason other than because it was there.

Such was the case with cassoulet, a classic, centuries-old French dish said to have originated in the southwestern Languedoc region. There are two dishes that I think must be related to one another in some absurdist way: Paul Prudhomme's turducken and Julia Child's cassoulet. Anytime a recipe fills six pages in a cookbook I immediately start shopping for shortcuts. Both turducken and cassoulet take an inordinate amount of time to prepare, and both require patience.

Lots and lots of time; lots and lots of patience.

For years cassoulet, a hearty white bean stew, was considered a peasant dish. There are three major versions: Cassoulet de Castelnaudary, which features pork; Cassoulet de Toulouse, whose main meat is lamb and sausage; and the decidedly high-end Cassoulet de Carcassonne, made with partridge. The dish can contain duck, chicken, sausage, pork, ham hocks, veal, lamb, or a combination of two or three of those meats.

Beans must be soaked, simmered, and layered with meats and vegetables, then cooked slowly in a covered dish. Having an enameled cast-iron pot like those made by Le Creuset or Martha Stewart—omigod, here she is again—isn't mandatory, but it is ideal. A well-seasoned cast-iron Dutch oven will work well, too.

I first experienced cassoulet in England, where friends prepared it in a wood-burning oven that came with their home—a big stone affair surrounded by a wall that dated to the 1066 Norman Conquest. Honest. Henry and Paddy Goddard lived in a house that, when the last of their line dies out, reverts to the National Trust because of the Norman Wall.

When I related the tale of how my former husband and I met the Goddards, Molly promptly decided we should make cassoulet in tribute to them.

About meeting Paddy and Henry Goddard: my husband at the time, Eric, and I were out for a Sunday-afternoon walk and, as it transpired, trespassing on Goddard property. Their land was adjacent to a small national park, and we thought this rambling stone edifice was park property, especially when we saw the front door standing open. There was also a spread of outdoorsy magazines on a table in the entryway that seemed consistent with public property.

So in we went, snatching up reading material along the way. To our left was a great room with overstuffed sofas and more magazines. We promptly settled in to rest a bit. That was when we noticed the full bar against the wall opposite the sofa into which we had so comfortably sunk. Sets of cocktail and highball glasses were arranged next to an ice bucket. With tongs. Either this was an unusually hospitable park ranger or we were in a private home. The real clue came when we noticed that the magazines had labels addressed to "Patricia Goddard," "Mr. and Mrs. Henry Goddard," and "The Goddard Family."

We were attempting a stealth exit when a voice trilled, "Hullo? Is someone there?" We stopped in our tracks. As the woman we would come to know as Paddy descended the stairs, showing no surprise at all, she said, "I say, were you looking for my husband?"

I suspect she thought we might be a husband-and-wife team looking for yardwork. When we apologized and explained, probably way too much, she laughed and offered to show us around.

It was the beginning of a friendship launched with a cassoulet dinner baked in their three-hundred-year-old wood-burning oven. Their son eventually visited my mother in St. Louis.

Upon hearing the end of my cassoulet story, I recall, Molly said something along the lines of "Oh, goody!," but it might really have been more like "Hot damn!" and clapped her hands at the thought of spending two and a half days making this wonderful wintertime casserole.

I didn't have the heart to tell her I took shortcuts—I used canned cannellini beans, rinsed, of course—and canned tomatoes. At least they were San Marzanos. Even with shortcuts, preparation takes a nice chunk of time.

But no, Molly had to buy flageolets, the French white bean that dates to the nineteenth century. She then soaked and gently simmered them with salt pork and a ham hock. My contribution consisted of cutting the ham hocks into pieces once the meat was falling off the bone, then sautéing kielbasa in rendered duck fat. Naturally we also had to have duck confit. Once again, as I saw what was to have been Saturday supper fading into Sunday dinner, I realized an early Monday-morning departure for the drive back to Dallas was definitely in my future. Eating a bean stew laced with white wine, pork, and duck and then driving two hundred miles afterward was quite out of the question.

The meats had to be browned separately—as did the onions, garlic, and celery. Molly's response to my search for dried thyme leaves prompted a detour to her atrium herb patch to snip fresh sprigs.

Oh—did I mention we were making *Julia's* cassoulet?

Dear God, what was I thinking?

Assembling the layers of beans, meat, and vegetables required that they be topped with bread crumbs.

You know what's coming, don't you? Dry bread in the oven, melt butter, chop fresh parsley (I'm sure it's not necessary to say my version has dried parsley and seasoned Progresso bread crumbs), and generously sprinkle the homemade bread crumbs atop the casserole just before committing it to a preheated oven.

It took less time to film *Gone with the Wind*.

Sometimes we just chopped; sometimes we just sautéed. Whether creating cassoulet or making meat loaf, we talked about food as therapy, sustenance, community, social glue.

We wondered why so many mani-pedi shops were run by Vietnamese.

We laughed about the incongruity of the phrase "jumbo shrimp" or how you can search the "four corners" of a round earth.

We bemoaned the decline of the language, trying to figure out how something could be "one of the only" anything. We wondered where on the color spectrum Karl Rove's conscience would fall. She said mauve. My vote went to dog-turd brown.

We lamented the extent to which political correctness had corrupted the honest exchange of information.

At one point halfway through day two we were pretty much done with deconstructing obtuse topics, as evidenced by Molly turning to me and saying, with a mischievous eyelash flutter and badly concealed humor, "Whose stupid idea was this, anyway? We ought to be having de Gaulle to dinner and not some gang of reprobates."

Of course we still had no idea which reprobates would consume our masterpiece, so we started off determined to invite people we hadn't included before, but decided in the end we really wanted the same crew we always turned to.

They were blown away that we'd made this incredible one-pot meal just for them, this marvelous amalgam of flavors and textures that commands a hefty price in French restaurants—where, I promise you, only the highest of high-end eateries go to the trouble we went to. And that, in my humble opinion, makes cassoulet a bargain at twice the price.

Remember this if you're fortunate enough to find it on a menu.

A bargain at twice the price.

CASSOULET, SORTA

Go ahead and wade through Julia Child's recipe if you're channeling her or Molly. You want duck? You got bucks? Fine. Buy duck breast or confit already prepared. Buy *Julia's Menus for Special Occasions* or tuck into all five pages of the original recipe from *Mastering the Art of French Cooking*, now in its zillionth printing. But I promise you, my way is easier, equally satisfying, and can be assembled in an afternoon. Nonetheless, cassoulet, like any other stew, is better if it sits overnight. My version is for people who love to cook but don't have the kind of time women in 1950s Paris— or America—had. All this dish needs is a hearty red wine, a green salad, a baguette, and fresh fruit for dessert. Trot out your specially designed baguette pan and make your own if you're so inclined. Me, I want to do my part to keep pastry chefs employed.

INGREDIENTS

8 slices good smoked bacon
3 celery stalks, chopped
4 large garlic cloves, minced or
    put through a press

3 small carrots, sliced diagonally
2 yellow onions, chopped, divided
    use
1 15-ounce can diced tomatoes

3 cups chicken stock
1 cup dry white wine
2 bay leaves
1 tablespoon dried thyme
½ cup dried parsley, divided use
4 14-ounce cans cannellini beans, thoroughly rinsed

8 *bone-in* chicken thighs
Kosher salt and black pepper
¼ cup rendered duck fat (available from fine grocery stores)
1 pound smoked sausage
1½ cups seasoned bread crumbs
½ cup unsalted butter, melted

DIRECTIONS

In a nonstick skillet, fry bacon slowly, allowing it to render its fat. When bacon is crisp, remove it to paper towels and set aside to cool.

Pour rendered fat into a large stockpot. Sauté celery, garlic, carrots, and *half* of the onions until vegetables are soft. Add tomatoes, stock, wine, bay leaves, thyme, and half of the parsley. Simmer uncovered for 15 minutes. Add beans and reserved bacon strips, crumbled. Remove from heat and set aside.

Allow chicken thighs to come to room temperature and rub them with salt and pepper.

In a large skillet heat the duck fat. Brown chicken thighs on both sides and set them aside on a platter.

Slice sausage and sauté with the remaining onions until onions are translucent. Remove chicken from bones in chunks. Discard skin.

Preheat oven to 300°F.

Stir contents and correct seasonings.

In a large casserole, ladle in some of the tomato-bean mixture. Arrange chicken and sausage on top and continue alternating beans and meat until you finish with a layer of beans, leaving about ½ inch at the top. Finish with bread crumbs. Drizzle butter over the top. Bake, uncovered, for 1 hour. Remove from oven and allow casserole to cool. Refrigerate overnight. The next day place casserole in a cold oven. Bring oven to 325°F and remove the casserole once it is bubbling. Break down the crust, forcing bread crumbs into the casserole. Add stock if mixture looks too dry. Sprinkle remaining parsley on top. Return to oven and bake until a second crust forms. Remove casserole and let it rest for 10 minutes before serving. Serves 6 to 8.

★ ★ ★

NOT QUITE JULIA CHILD'S
BOEUF BOURGUIGNON

This is the simplified version of the show-off beef stew that is a Julia Child hallmark. Hers is also, in my humble opinion, entirely too complicated. Molly and I at least agreed that the same effect could be achieved by going this simplified route. We debated whether it should be served with buttered, parsleyed boiled potatoes as the French probably would serve it, or with noodles. Molly was mortified that I even suggested rice, but I still say it is rice-worthy—after all, when all is said and done, it's only a very nice beef stew with wine. You will need a five-quart casserole.

This version has been modified a teensy tiny bit, But Molly, being the ardent Francophile that she was, would tolerate only so much fiddling with Julia's recipes. On the other hand, one can now buy frozen pearl onions, and there are exquisite frozen baby carrots that can be added at the last minute. Once again, I say, not everyone has the kind of time Julia and Molly were willing to invest in meal preparation. You decide what works for you. Finally, if you think this is time-consuming, try making Julia's original version from scratch! This recipe pairs well with Beaujolais, Côtes du Rhône, or, of course, Burgundy.

INGREDIENTS

6-ounce chunk of salt pork
1 tablespoon grapeseed (or canola) oil
3 pounds lean stewing beef, cut into 2-inch cubes
1 teaspoon salt
1 teaspoon black pepper
3 tablespoons flour
3 cups of a full-bodied, young red wine (not cooking wine; a Burgundy suitable for drinking)
2 to 3 cups organic beef stock

3 garlic cloves put through a press
1 teaspoon dried thyme (or three 3-inch fresh sprigs)
1 large bay leaf
1 pound fresh mushrooms, quartered
3 cups frozen baby carrots
10-ounce package of frozen pearl onions
¼ cup chopped fresh parsley
Parsley sprigs

Preheat oven to 400°F.

Cut salt pork into 1-inch slivers about ½-inch thick. Simmer, covered, for 10 minutes in 2 cups water. Drain and pat dry. Set liquid aside.

Sauté salt pork in oil over moderate heat long enough to brown lightly. Remove to a side dish with a slotted spoon.

Reheat fat until it is almost smoking before you sauté beef. Pat beef dry using paper towels; it will not brown if damp. Sauté, a few pieces at a time, in the hot fat until browned on all sides.

Return beef and salt pork to the casserole and toss with the salt and pepper. Sprinkle the flour on and toss again to coat the beef lightly. Toss beef 4 or 5 minutes more. (This browns the flour and covers the meat with a light crust.)

Stir in wine and enough stock to barely cover the beef. Add garlic and herbs. Bring to simmer on top of the stove. Cover the casserole and set in lower third of preheated oven.

Immediately reduce heat to 300°F and cook for 2 to 2½ hours or until meat is tender. Check to make sure there is enough liquid. Remove casserole and distribute mushrooms, carrots, and pearl onions over the meat. Simmer for a minute or two, skimming fat as it rises. You should have about 2½ cups of sauce thick enough to coat a spoon lightly. If too thin, boil it down rapidly. If it's too thick, mix in a few tablespoons of stock. Correct seasonings.

Cover casserole and simmer for 5 minutes, basting meat and vegetables with the sauce several times. Serve with potatoes, noodles, or rice. Garnish with parsley sprigs. Serves 6.

★ ★ ★

Molly and Kaye Northcott at a 1991 wedding reception. Photo courtesy of Kaye Northcott.

29

Bienvenidos a Tejas, Comrades

MOLLY LOVED TO TRAVEL, and she believed in reciprocating whenever possible. So shortly after she visited Russia on one of those trips where reporters were invited to "see" the Soviet Union, she helped organize a trip that attracted a gaggle of Russian reporters to Texas. To give them an authentic experience, the *Texas Observer* rented a bus and a margarita machine (or a Bloody Mary machine, depending on who's doing the telling) and set out to show the Russkies the *real* Lone Star State. To keep it even more authentic, the company included *Observer* reporter Kaye Northcott; contractor Joe Pinelli, a staunch Democrat and union man; Molly; and John Henry Faulk.

Faulk was a disciple of J. Frank Dobie, an outspoken opponent of intolerance and one of those Texas anomalies—a populist voice at a time when it was way less popular to be one than it is now. He kept that voice from the 1920s until his death in 1990.

Now, imagine having John Henry Faulk along in the 1970s with an unsuspecting busload of Russians, liberal Texans, and a margarita machine. Kaye Northcott remembers it probably better than most. She's a teetotaler.

"The whole time we were driving through these racist little towns, we, the hosts, were pissing and moaning about how corrupt politicians were in this town, and how rotten the cops were in that town. John Henry would lapse into preacher mode and tout America's greatness one minute and rail against its social shortsightedness the next, denouncing the poll tax and castigating Jim Crow laws."

Pinelli is a barrel-chested force of nature whose conversational style moves at something close to warp speed. He has one of those Texas accents that would probably require subtitles if he were in a movie. He's plainspoken, liberal, strident, and very, very funny. He does not have a "pause" button. The whole scene must have driven the overseas visitors nuts.

"Those poor Russians were convinced we'd all be swept into prison any minute for sedition," Kaye recalled. "We were equally sure we were being spied on all along the way—if not by the KGB, then the FBI, but probably both. What did we eat? Lord only knows. And between the distance in time and the alcohol consumed, I doubt anyone else remembers. We were just grateful we didn't end up in the hoosegow somewhere."

On yet another international occasion, Northcott wound up with Sylvan Bouillard, a French photographer. Kaye spoke no French, and he spoke the tiniest bit of English, but he was a wonderful cook. Molly acted as interpreter.

"She really saved my bacon once when we had a complete miscommunication resulting in the three of us having to eat *moules à la marinière* prepared for six. I thought Sylvan was preparing for Saturday dinner, but *he* thought he was preparing for Saturday lunch. It seems the French make a midday meal of mussels, salad, and a good loaf of French bread. So all of a sudden I had to call everyone and say 'lunch, not dinner.' But since it was Saturday and people had already made plans for lunch, I called Molly and she came right over to help us eat up those damn bivalves. I mean, they were good, but all I can remember was much wine and garlic and wads of parsley and Molly telling Sylvan how *delicieux* the fucking mussels were."

Before Sylvan left, Kaye took him to a Final Friday that left him totally confused. It was loud and crowded and several slam poets presented works that were in all probability incomprehensible except by intonation and dramatization. At the end of the evening he turned to me and expressed great appreciation, asking, "Is this a soiree? A salon? A buffet? How do you call thees? This is complete anarchy, but I like it."

MOULES À LA MARINIÈRE

This is a classic recipe that Molly and I put together one day when we got crazy at the Central Market fish counter. There were all these netted bags of mussels, sitting there, begging to be steamed. We couldn't resist. As a lunch meal, the French make *moules et frites*, but if you have neither the time nor the inclination to make French fries the French way, pick up a baguette on your way out of the store and sop to your heart's content. It's probably déclassé, but I polish off the stock with a soup spoon. Don't panic if some of the mussels don't open; that means you don't want to eat them anyway.

INGREDIENTS

6 tablespoons unsalted butter
½ cup chopped shallots
2 tablespoons chopped garlic
2 tablespoons chopped parsley
2 tablespoons fresh thyme

6 pounds mussels
½ cup dry white wine
2 cups organic chicken stock
½ teaspoon kosher salt

DIRECTIONS

Melt butter in a stockpot that has a lid and sauté shallots, garlic, and herbs over medium heat until shallots soften. Turn heat to high, add mussels, wine, chicken stock, and salt. Cover the pot. Steam 5 to 6 minutes or until shells are open and meats are not translucent. Serve immediately in large bowls and pour broth over each serving. *Pitch those that don't open.* Place a large bowl in the center of the table for discarded shells. Accompany with French bread, green salad, and white wine. Serves 4 to 6.

* * *

=== 30 ===

Oeufs à la Neige

AS PART OF MOLLY'S INNER CIRCLE Courtney Anderson participated in many of Molly's beloved dinners with a theme. The group usually included Shelia Cheaney, UT journalism professor Maryln Schwartz, and Kaye Northcott, who was editor of *Texas Co-op Power* until her retirement in 2010. The monthly magazine, published by Texas Electric Cooperatives, boasts a circulation of 1 million, the largest in Texas, and goes out to all homes that get power from the various rural companies. (In the 1930s a young Lyndon Baines Johnson shepherded electric cooperatives into being as a means to provide affordable electricity to rural Texas.)

All except Shelia, Athena (Molly's badly behaved, aristocratic French poodle), and Coco (Shelia's sleek, playful Weimaraner) cooked. Shelia, therefore, usually brought bread and wine. Courtney's forte was baking—specifically, apple pies—based on a skill learned from her daughter, Barrett.

Molly was also known for her potluck brunches. Guests were expected to come up with something *wonderful*. On one occasion Courtney knew immediately what her offering would be.

"I kept trying to think of a dish that would wow Molly, then I remembered her love for frenchified food. I dug up an old recipe my mother used to make. We called it 'floating island.' In French it was called *ouefs à la neige*. As I recall, it means 'eggs in the snow' or something like that—but in Sherman, Texas, it was 'floating island.' I'm pretty sure *oeufs à la neige* was not part of my vocabulary. I do remember that it was labor-intensive, but it came from a day when women who were so inclined would take time to make a nice meal."

Whether you call it "snow eggs" or *oeufs à la neige,* "floating island" or *ile flottante,* it is a light dessert consisting of a liqueur-drizzled sponge cake spread with jam, sprinkled with nuts, topped by whipped cream, and surrounded by a pool of thin custard.

"Molly was genuinely impressed, and I remember thinking, 'Well! How d'ya like that!'"

Courtney, a divorcée, grew up in Sherman, a town about seventy miles north of Dallas, near the Oklahoma state line. She moved to Dallas twice, once in 1968, then again in 1970. There she met Molly through her brother, Steve Anderson, and his wife, Linda. The two of them knew every liberal in Dallas. Both Molly and Steve, now Linda's former husband, knew their way around a kitchen. The food fad in the '70s was paella. Dinner parties fueled by beer, sangria, and a general joie de vivre frequently featured dueling paellas. Even then, joyous dining events had Molly at their epicenter. As her popularity soared and book sales skyrocketed, so did the Ivins largesse.

Courtney chuckles to herself as she recalls a dinner with Molly and friends at Mezzaluna, a long-gone Italian restaurant in the heart of Austin's then-burgeoning warehouse district. It was one of Molly's favorites.

"We loved ordering all those fancy-schmancy dishes we could barely pronounce. You gotta remember this was the tail end of the '80s, and Austin was not exactly known for its gourmet restaurants. So we got a big giggle out of dishes with names like Quaglie Ripene con Salsicca, Pesce Spada Siciliano, and Cotoletta di Vitello Balsamico.

"After completely fracturing pronunciations, we'd usually surrender and order in English—sausage-stuffed quail, grilled swordfish, and breaded veal cutlet. Back then they were even doing that chicken under a brick that became so 'in.' At the time we thought that was pretty hysterical but ordered it anyway, just to feel *Eye-tal-ian.* We'd go out for these dinners and the check would come and we'd reach for our wallets, but Molly would sweep up the tab with this grand gesture and, quoting Karl Marx, announce to the table, 'From each according to his ability, to each according to his needs.' It was always so funny how one minute she could do this deep East Texas accent, then lapse into her upper-crust *voulez-vous* accent at the drop of a hat."

On another occasion Molly organized a birthday dinner for Shelia Cheaney at Courtney's house. The plan was to have dinner, then walk down to Jeffrey's to see an exhibit of Courtney's work. Once there, they would toast the exhibit with a glass of champagne and return to the house for dessert.

A 1990s photo captured well-fed friends Courtney Anderson, seated; Marilyn Schultz, to Molly's left; me (behind Marilyn); and an unusually subdued Athena. Photo courtesy of Linda Lewis.

A friend made tamales, and Courtney, herself an accomplished cook, prepared sautéed spinach balanced on artichoke heart bottoms topped with pine nuts and toasted sesame bread crumbs that she finished with a drizzle of white cream sauce.

Molly made an incredibly elaborate chocolate cake. Everyone was keen to have at it. Courtney still salivates at the thought.

"It was called the Four Seasons Chocolate Fancy Cake. It's hellishly hard to make. There are a zillion steps and you use all this expensive chocolate and lots of butter and I don't know what all. I remember Molly saying it took her three days to make it.

"So off we went to Jeffrey's, but when we got there we learned that somehow things got screwed up and my paintings weren't being shown. The exhibit had been moved to New Year's Eve. On the one hand it was the millennium, so I got way better exposure than I would have on the original date. I was still kinda disappointed until I saw that cake. What a work of art!"

Austin attorney Janet Dewey, a friend and fellow traveler, was among the cake's admirers. Janet got to know Molly when they were doing a little upscale camping on a houseboat on Lake Amistad.

"Molly and I were preparing breakfast together. I'm not sure she'd ever given me much heed other than occasionally calling me 'Darlin',' and I suspect that was because she couldn't remember my name. But as I was peeling and slicing apples, I felt Molly's gaze fix on my apple action and say, 'Well, it looks like you've made a pie or two.'

"Suddenly, I existed. Molly always appreciated people with great stories, tall tales, courage, or, as luck would have it, cooking skills. She seemed to be able to divine personality and character through your movements with a knife, or concept of a dish. I think food talked for Molly. It was another form of communication. And preparing food and sharing meals was just another way to be with people and tell stories. Food, stories, stories, food.

"Anyway, the cake was a thing to behold. Molly served it as if delivering the Eucharist to sinful tongues. It was light and billowing, layer upon layer, nothing cloying or cakey, just soft angelic mousse, whispery layers of perfect soufflé-like cake, and rich, dark chocolate icing. Crackled caramelized sugar drizzled over the top delivered a delightful crunch in contrast to the cloud within. While not a shy group, not a one of us asked for more. Clearly for Molly, that cake was more than food. It was an offering. And it was *so good!*"

After some sleuthing—mostly in the wrong direction—I thought the recipe came from a Four Seasons *hotel* restaurant until I learned otherwise. As I grumbled about my difficulty in finding the recipe to Gayla Hoffman, a St. Louis friend and fellow foodie, she said she thought she had seen it somewhere. Lo and behold, it was in her copy of *The Four Seasons: A History of America's Premier Restaurant*, written by John Mariani and Alex von Bidder, the restaurant's owner.

The ingredients and instructions would have intimidated the living daylights out of a lesser mortal, but not our Molly. So for those of you who think you are a match for her resolve in the kitchen, have at it. Be sure to savor it with champagne and drink a toast to her as you take fork to pastry.

THE FOUR SEASONS CHOCOLATE FANCY CAKE

This is an exercise in patience and diligence and is done in stages. Please read the recipe through twice before cracking the first egg. You do not want to discover an error halfway through making it! Reprinted with permission from New York's Four Seasons restaurant.

INGREDIENTS

For the Bavarian cream:
3¾ cups milk, divided use
3 scant tablespoons (3 envelopes)
    unflavored gelatin
6 large eggs, separated
¼ teaspoon salt
1¼ cups sugar
¼ cup dark rum
1 cup heavy cream, whipped stiff
¾ cup crushed almond
    macaroons or vanilla wafers
    (about 10 to 12 small cookies)
⅓ cup finely chopped walnuts or
    pecans

For the orange chiffon cake:
1 cup plus 2 tablespoons sifted
    cake flour
¾ cup sugar

1½ teaspoons baking powder
½ teaspoon salt
¼ cup vegetable oil
2 egg yolks
6 tablespoons fresh orange juice
1½ tablespoons finely chopped
    orange peel
½ cup egg whites (from 3
    or 4 large eggs), at room
    temperature
¼ teaspoon cream of tartar
½ cup heavy cream, whipped stiff

For the chocolate almond cream
    coating:
2 pounds almond paste
1 cup cocoa
Confectioners' sugar for sprinkling

DIRECTIONS

To prepare the Bavarian cream, place 1 cup of milk in a medium bowl and sprinkle gelatin over the milk. Let stand for 5 minutes to soften. In a medium saucepan over medium-high heat, warm the remaining milk until tiny bubbles appear around the edge.

Meanwhile, beat the egg yolks with the salt and ½ cup of the sugar until blended. Stir in the milk and gelatin mixture. Gradually stir in the warm milk. Place the mixture in the top part of a double boiler. Cook over hot (but not boiling) water, stirring often, until the mixture coats the back of a spoon, about 15 minutes. Remove from heat, cool slightly, and stir in rum. Refrigerate, covered, until the mixture mounds slightly when lifted with a spoon, about 3 hours. (Alternatively, place the pan over ice water to hasten chilling. Stir occasionally until the mixture mounds slightly when lifted with a spoon, about 30 minutes.)

Line a 2½-quart bowl no wider than 9 inches in diameter with plastic wrap or foil. Set aside.

In the bowl of a large electric mixer, beat egg whites on high speed until soft peaks form. Gradually add the remaining ¾ cup of sugar and beat until stiff but not dry. Add the whipped cream and the gelatin mixture. Beat at low speed until just combined, about 1 minute. Turn into the prepared bowl.

In a small bowl, combine the crushed macaroons or wafers with the nuts. Mix well. Sprinkle over the top of the mixture in the bowl and gently press down. Cover and refrigerate for at least 8 hours or overnight.

To prepare the orange chiffon cake, preheat the oven to 350°F. Sift flour with sugar, baking powder, and salt into a large bowl. Make a well in the center. Add the oil, egg yolks, orange juice, and orange peel. Beat with a spoon until smooth.

Beat the egg whites with cream of tartar on high speed until stiff but not dry. With an under-and-over motion, use a wire whisk or rubber spatula to gradually fold the orange batter into the egg whites. Mix just until blended. Do not stir. Pour into an ungreased 9-by-1½-inch round cake pan. Bake for 30 to 35 minutes, or until a cake tester inserted in the center comes out clean. Place the cake upside down on a dry, clean kitchen towel. Cool completely, about 1 hour. With a spatula, carefully loosen cake from pan. Hit the pan sharply on a table. Remove cake and place it on a serving platter.

Spread the whipped cream over the top of the orange chiffon cake. Invert the bowl of Bavarian cream over the whipped-cream-topped cake. Remove the bowl and peel off the plastic wrap. The Bavarian cream will form a dome over the cake. Refrigerate until ready to coat.

To prepare the chocolate almond cream coating, in a large bowl knead the almond paste with the cocoa until thoroughly mixed and softened. Divide into 5 portions, 4 of equal size and 1 smaller portion for the topknot. On a large board sprinkled with confectioners' sugar, roll out the 4 uniform pieces, one at a time, into 8-by-7-inch sheets that measure about ⅛ inch thick. As each sheet is rolled out, place it on the covered Bavarian-orange cake, working from the bottom up and pinching the top to make gathers in it. Break off any excess that sticks out at the top. The whole cake should be covered by the 4 rolled-out sheets.

Roll out the remaining portion of chocolate almond cream coating into an oblong that measures about ¼ inch thick. Gather into a topknot and place on top of the cake. Refrigerate until ready to serve. Let the cake stand at room temperature for 20 minutes before slicing. Serves 16.

★ ★ ★

OEUFS À LA NEIGE

Courtney Anderson lost her recipe for this classic French recipe, so we found a close substitute in the one Gale Gand developed for the Food Network. Reproduced with permission.

INGREDIENTS

3 cups milk

½ vanilla bean

9 egg yolks

1¾ cups sugar, divided use

2 quarts water

6 egg whites

Crystallized rose petals
for garnish

DIRECTIONS

In a saucepan, bring milk to a boil with the vanilla bean in it. Let sit 15 minutes to infuse. Whisk yolks with 1 cup of sugar, then slowly add hot milk. Return to heat and cook gently to thicken. Strain into a stainless-steel bowl and place the bowl in a shallow pan filled with ice water. Stir sauce to cool and thicken. Chill, covered.

Simmer 2 quarts of water in a large frying pan but do not boil. Meanwhile, beat the egg whites until stiff but not dry. Gradually add the remaining ¾ cup of sugar and continue beating until glossy, about 30 seconds more. Place a large sheet pan next to the water and line it with waxed paper dampened slightly. Using a large star tip or 2 dessert spoons or an ice cream scoop, squeeze out rosettes onto the paper.

Using a spatula, lift the rosettes off the paper one at time and slide them into the simmering water. Poach for 7 minutes on the bottom, then turn over for 3 minutes, not allowing them to touch while poaching. Drain on a dish towel. Remove to a sheet pan and chill.

In a shallow glass bowl, saucer, or long-stemmed champagne glass, float meringue on a puddle of custard and garnish with rose petals. Serves 4 to 6.

★ ★ ★

CRYSTALLIZED ROSE PETALS

½ teaspoon water
1 egg white
16 rose petals from organic or confetti roses
2 tablespoons sugar

Whisk water and egg white in a medium-sized mixing bowl. Dip rose petals into mixture and stick them to inside rim of bowl to drain. Dip both sides of drained petals in sugar and place on a sheet pan with parchment paper. Let dry for 4 hours in a warm place.

=== 31 ===

Table That Emotion

CARLTON CARL RETURNED TO AUSTIN after twenty-five years in Washington, DC, to become publisher of Molly's favorite former employer, the *Texas Observer.*

He probably knew Molly longer and better than anyone other than Molly's brother, Andy, and their sister, Sara. Molly and Carlton met in high school when both were teenage social misfits of the same stripe: both living in Houston, both in love with reading and writing, both firmly ensconced in their respective school newspapers, both almost painfully shy. They gravitated toward one another. He looks today a lot like he looked thirty years ago, only grayer. He could easily be cast as Tevye in *Fiddler on the Roof.*

Carlton and Molly were from Houston's decidedly upscale River Oaks neighborhood and attended rival schools. He graduated from Kinkaid, a pedigreed, century-old, nonsectarian prep school that boasts of its position as Houston's oldest independent coeducational school. Molly finished at St. John's, also a private, nonsectarian school despite its religious name. She was on the newspaper a year ahead of Carlton, and he was assistant editor of his. They met, as he recalls, at a high school newspaper event. As has been known to happen in such circumstances, the two outsiders focused on what they knew they could do well. Both ended up at Columbia University, she for grad school, he for both undergrad and graduate studies.

Despite their privileged backgrounds, they were drawn to community service outside their elevated place on the socioeconomic spectrum. Continuing their parallel lives, they found summer jobs at the *Houston Chronicle.*

Carlton remembers those days well. "We got to the *Chronicle* and Molly headed straight for the morgue—which was what we called the newspaper reference library back then—to look up the paper's history. She found this book recalling the good old days of dirty newsrooms, where editors drank whiskey from a coffee cup, and lamenting how those days were gone, probably forever.

"At that point she looked up and saw Zarko Franks, the night city editor, pouring what was probably bourbon into his coffee cup. Her eyes lit up; she smiled and announced that she was going to like it at the *Chronicle* just fine."

The Carl/Ivins friendship sustained itself over the years, primarily through letters and internships where they hung out with reporters who went on to make names for themselves—including political columnist Dave McNeely, who became a close friend. They frequented the kind of ratty bar that at one time could be found in close proximity to any major daily. The one diagonally across from the *St. Louis Post-Dispatch* was called the Press Box. Its Houston counterpart was the Golden Stein. Dave McNeely remembers going there the year he worked at the *Chronicle*—the same year he met Carlton and Molly.

As the summer job season closed on their fledgling newsroom experiences, they returned to New York. Carlton's most specific food memory from those Columbia days involves hot dogs and beer at Columbia football games. "Athletic events at Columbia were always a kind of bad joke," he said. "Sports weren't a priority and the teams rarely won anything. But the hot dogs and beer were good."

In a display that was to become a hallmark of Molly's egalitarian approach to life, she took part-time jobs to earn extra money—always a puzzlement to Carlton, who often wondered why somebody from River Oaks was cleaning toilets in a bank building to earn mad money. But that, he said, was Molly. She never thought she was too good to do menial work. Carlton's final days at Columbia should have ended on a bright note, but in 1967, as his parents and brother drove to New York from Houston, his father had a fatal heart attack. Molly wrote a warm and comforting note that meant a lot at the time and made him appreciate her even more.

Molly pursued the reportorial fame she had predicted for herself back in her days as Mole. Carlton, after a successful career in Washington, DC, retired from his post as vice president of policy and strategy for the American Association for Justice (formerly known as the Association of Trial Lawyers of America). Carlton's turn to comfort her came some years later when her father killed himself; when her mother died of cancer; and when Dax, one of her much-loved nephews, committed suicide. When her father killed himself, she said she could almost understand it because he had always been healthy and in control of his life, and felt he couldn't adjust to being cared for by others. Dax, on the other hand, she said, had his life before him. His death hit her hard. Carlton was among those who offered consolation.

A friendship spanning almost half a century ended where it began—in Texas, but in Austin instead of Houston, and with Carlton as publisher of the paper Molly held so dear. By then she had become something akin to a state, if not a national, treasure. Her columns had grown to syndication in more than three hundred newspapers. She'd been shortlisted for a Pulitzer Prize three times, had been a National Book Award finalist, and had received too many honors and awards to detail. In 2001 she was named to the American Academy of Arts and Sciences, entering a pantheon of men and women honored for the wide range of expertise they bring to multidisciplinary analyses of contemporary issues. Elected by a committee of their peers, members range from astrophysicists to zoologists.

Carlton's link to Molly and food exists in its own unique way: the round table and matching chairs she commissioned now reside in the living room of Carlton's Victorian home in Martindale, a quiet community first settled in the 1850s. Not much has physically changed over time. If you've seen Clint Eastwood and Kevin Costner in *A Perfect World*, or Matthew McConaughey and Ethan Hawke in *The Newton Boys*, or the 2003 remake of *The Texas Chainsaw Massacre*, you've actually seen Martindale. All three movies were filmed there.

This is a town where residents numbering maybe nine hundred still parade down Main Street and adjourn to a Fourth of July potluck picnic in the park. Carlton hasn't yet decided what to do with it, but he owns a bunch of Martindale property. Molly and I made the forty-mile drive from Austin to see for ourselves: three vacant general stores, an abandoned bank, a cottonseed weigh station, several warehouses, a movie-set courtroom, a seed elevator, sixteen seed silos, and three hundred feet of land that fronts the San Marcos River.

I don't know about anyone else, but as I pointed out to Molly at the time, I want dibs on one of the storefronts. Martindale deserves a restaurant. These people only think they've seen smothered pork chops and chicken-fried steak. I can see it now. The Martindale Diner and Dive Bar, serving late lunch and late dinner. If my daughter could bring sushi to Fredericksburg, Molly and I could have brought baked pork chops, African chicken, *truite amandine*, and *clafouti* to Martindale.

Carlton threw his first official dinner party in 2009 in tribute to Molly and the table. Carlton, Mercedes Peña, and I each made our favorite meat loaf. His was an applesauce version, adapted from the recipe of the mother of a college friend. He'd made it at one time or another for Molly. Mine was a turkey interpretation of Paul Prudhomme's Cajun meat loaf, which I had also made for one of our many crazed Cajun/zydeco meals. Mercedes prepared a Cuban number with spicy chorizo sausage embedded in the center; she too had served it at one of Molly's multiculti culinary convocations.

Doug Zabel, a respectable cook himself, joined us, as did Dave Richards, who, with his wife, Sandy, and a few other friends, had accompanied Molly on her big float trip through the Grand Canyon. Seated around that beautiful table, we did what Molly intended folks to do: we drank beer and wine and regaled one another with Molly tales. "Remember the time she did that video about dildos?" (Raucous laughter.) "Remember the time she let those lovebirds out and forgot to turn off the ceiling fan?" (Guilty hysterical laughter.) "God, I loved the time she said that calling George [W.] Bush 'shallow' was like calling a dwarf 'short.'" (Giggles.) "Yeah, but remember what she said about [President Ronald] Reagan—the bee thing?" ("He's so dumb, if you put his brain in a bee the bee would fly backwards.") This went on until recollections were exhausted and it was time to return to Austin.

Until Martindale installs me to cook for the diner and dive bar—well, until Martindale gets a liquor license—it's enough to sit, listen to the mockingbirds, and remember the many Molly meals that preceded the dinner of dueling meat loaves.

Dancing with Dugger. Courtesy of the *Texas Observer*.

=== 32 ===

The *Observer*'s Observant Observer

MOLLY, BERNARD RAPOPORT, AND BERNARD'S WIFE, Audre, were a perfectly triangulated mutual admiration society. They shared the same sociopolitical views—he, even into his nineties, remains a smidge to Molly's political left.

"B," as friends call him, is probably one of the least known and most influential Democrats in the country. He stands a few inches over six feet. His booming, raspy baritone voice invariably precedes him by several giant steps, in contrast to Audre's carefully modulated tones.

Were it not for Rapoport support, there is a strong possibility that the *Texas Observer* might be a thing of the past. There is nothing immediately obvious that signals his existence as one of the nation's wealthiest men, and only the photographs on his office wall hint at the extent of his connections. He is generally known as a staunch supporter of, and generous contributor to, the Democratic Party, and presidents have sought his counsel. Israel's former prime minister Golda Meir was once a guest in his home.

Rows of framed eight-by-ten black-and-white photographs are a visual history of those he holds dear: civil rights activist Bayard Rustin; former senator Thomas Eagleton; presidents Carter and Clinton; astronaut John Glenn; West Virginia senator Jay Rockefeller. Many are signed "To my good friend Bernie." Bernard Rapoport has testified before Congress on several occasions, most notably in the late '80s, when he spoke on behalf of his friend, former House Speaker Jim Wright. Wright, who resigned his seat rather than face a protracted investigation, was accused of House ethics rules violations related to the sale of his book *Reflections of a Public Man*.

(As part of a long-standing practice, B had purchased a thousand copies of the book to distribute to friends and business associates. He argued that his purchase had nothing to do with raising funds for the Democratic Party or for Mr. Wright. An avid reader, he often bought books he liked in bulk and sent them to friends.)

He was also called before the infamous Whitewater grand jury in Little Rock, Arkansas, in 1996. While he was not the least bit intimidated by the experience, he was also not amused.

"Those guys really went nuts," he said, referring to the special prosecutor's office. "I knew they didn't have anything on me; they knew they didn't have anything on me. They were just big on muscle flexing. Ridiculous."

And to prove his point, B flexed a little muscle of his own by testifying without a lawyer. "They asked me why I didn't bring an attorney," he said, still bristling at the memory. "I said 'cause I didn't need one; I hadn't done anything wrong."

Although he isn't particularly comfortable talking about himself or his role as a power broker, he periodically relents, as he did once for the *Dallas Morning News*. He had been tapped for a singular honor—one even more important than the one conferred in 1998 when *Fortune* named him one of America's forty most generous philanthropists. That article grew out of a $15-million gift to his alma mater, the University of Texas, and $5 million to the Jerusalem Foundation.

Another beneficiary of his largesse is the *Texas Observer*. In a *Dallas Morning News* article, Ronnie Dugger, the *Observer*'s founding editor, acknowledged that Rapoport's support had been a determinant in whether the paper survived. Dugger, not ordinarily effusive, spoke with great warmth in discussing the *Observer*'s benefactor.

"Most of the people who make the kind of money he's made spend their lives protecting it, but not B. He has a commitment to the future, which manifests itself in his foundation. Just look at the list, and you'll know what I mean."

The Rapoports and Molly were a natural fit, and they made no bones about it. When I cornered B at the *Observer*'s annual high-dollar fund-raiser to tell him I was writing a book about meals with Molly, he let loose a hearty laugh and said, "Well, we've had plenty of those."

And indeed they had, usually at one of two preferred destinations, but frequently at an Outback Steakhouse—which is where I first met the Rapoports in Dallas. Once when he informed Molly that lunch would be at a local country club, Molly, reverting to droll-humor mode, replied, "Why? Did the Outback close?"

33

Salmon on the Fly

ALMOST ANYONE WHO KNEW MOLLY well has a food story, and Ellen Fleysher, otherwise known as "Flash," is no exception. They met many moons ago, when Molly moved east to work for what she insisted on calling the *New York City Times* and was dispatched to Albany to cover the legislature. The *New York City Times* hired her and sent her to Albany ostensibly because they liked her style in covering the Texas Legislature.

The operative word here is "ostensibly."

Flash, who speaks at ninety miles an hour, recalled the experience with dark humor.

"Molly, being Molly, wrote the same as she did in Texas, but the *Times*, which had hired her for her writing, proceeded to change her copy. Once she showed me a story she wrote about a [New York state] rep named Judah Gribetz.

"He was, shall we say, a rather large gentleman.

"Molly wrote that when he laughed his stomach shook like a bowl of Jell-O. [The *Times*] changed it to read that he had 'a rotund protuberance.' She thought that was hysterical. I said I couldn't even laugh, because the whole flavor of the narrative was wrong. I couldn't believe it, and this happened all the time.

"It was the beginning of her souring on the *Times*. Molly said she should have taken her cue from Shit. She swore that when she drove to New York he started howling and never stopped."

The good news is that for her abbreviated tenure as a New Yorker, Molly and Flash, who was with NBC at the time, had some mighty fine food times.

"I was always extolling chicken wings as the greatest thing ever to come out of Buffalo other than Millard Fillmore," Flash said. "I had always heard that the perforated postage stamp was invented during Fillmore's administration. As it turned out, it came from England and wasn't introduced until years later. Some guy with the [US] postal service went berserk over it.

"Anyway, there I was, telling Molly about old Millard and this post office guy who was having a conniption over the perforated postage stamp. Somehow the issue kinda segued into an idea for a salute to Buffalo."

Read "party."

"My job was to get the original chicken wing recipe from the Anchor Bar, where Buffalo wings are said to have originated," Flash continued. "That led me to Frank and Teressa Bellisimo, and eventually to their son, Dominic. So I get the recipe—including the one for the secret Roquefort dressing—and we said, Molly and I, 'Okay, we got the recipe; let's make wings and Texas mud pies.'

"I mean, this was a hearty meal, right? We got a ton of chicken wings, and we had the celery and the Roquefort and I got as big a supply of Molson and Labatt as we could afford."

As would befit such a regal repast, the Albany-based twosome shifted into high gear.

Guest list: Everybody.

Music: Nonstop polka, of course.

Decor?

"We decided we needed to have snow tires and tire chains all around the living room," Flash went on, clearly warming to the recollection. "Instead of candelabra we'd use antifreeze cans to replace Chianti bottles, which were all the rage then. It was fabulous, but the bottom line is we made thirty pounds of chicken wings. Thirty pounds. In the end we were both muttering, 'We're never gonna do this again.'

"There was not one chicken wing left, nor were there any mud pies. At the end of the evening I asked Molly if she had eaten any of either. She hadn't. Neither had I, but the party was a major, major success."

Bellisimo family members who launched the Buffalo chicken wing craze might have been generous with Flash, but that was then and this is now. Frank and Teressa Bellisimo died in the 1980s and Dominic died in 1991. Anchor Bar general manager Ivano Toscani—who says the bar sells 2,000 pounds of wings daily—kindly but absolutely declined my entreaty to release the recipe. He emphatically disputes Frank's Hot Sauce as a primary ingredient, insisting that the version marketed by the bar is the real deal. If you decide to do them at home, ask a butcher to cut the wings into sections but save the wing tips for making soup stock. If you want to try the hot sauce that the Anchor Bar markets, it's available online.

The Fleysher/Ivins friendship involved food on land and at sea. "Back in the early '80s Molly got this idea that we effete Eastern women had no appreciation for the West, so she cooked up this idea for a white-water rafting trip," Flash said. "It took us nearly a year and a half to put it together. We were going on the middle fork of Idaho's Salmon River, so of course we called ourselves the Salmonettes."

It took some doing, but by 1979 Molly had organized the rafting trip. At the time she was Rocky Mountain bureau chief for the *New York Times*. As an inveterate lover of wilderness, she wanted her city slicker pals to experience the great outdoors. The high-powered mixed bag of participants included women Molly knew from New York, while others were either childhood friends or college classmates. Some were friends of friends. Flash invited Rosanne Cahn because she knew how to pitch a tent.

To commemorate the event, a "class picture" was made in which all participants are wearing "Salmonettes" T-shirts. Murray Resnick, a friend of Flash's, had them made for the group. She had told him about the trip and he thought the shirts would be a fun idea. "On the back of each one it said, 'Sea front,' which was his idea of a little joke," Flash said, recalling the trip. "I think the only time we wore them was when we had the photo done. We were really looking forward to the trip, although the fact that it was called the 'River of No Return' wasn't all that encouraging."

Salmonettes included Carol Bellamy, Molly, Alice Rivlin, Flash, Lynne Abraham, Pat Cloherty, Marg Elliston, a Los Angeles–based West Coast editor for *Rolling Stone* whose name is lost to history, Ann Crittenden, Marcia Chambers, Nancy Dowd, Betsy Weiss, and Donna Shalala. Molly, Crittenden, and Chambers were *New York Times* reporters. Dowd wrote the screenplay for the film *Slap Shot* and won an Oscar for writing *Coming Home*.

Bellamy, the first woman elected to the New York City Council, later headed UNICEF for a decade. Abraham, who died from breast cancer in 2002, was Bellamy's press secretary and later became communications director for Planned Parenthood of America. Cloherty, former head of the Small Business Administration, later divided her time between Moscow and the United States as chairman and CEO of a company that manages venture capital funds and has more than $500 million invested in fifty-five Russian companies.

Shalala served eight years as secretary of health and human services during the Clinton administration before becoming president of the University of Miami. Weiss and Cahn are economists, as is Rivlin, an expert on urban issues and fiscal, monetary, and social policy for the Brookings Institution. At the time of the Salmonettes experience, Elliston was doing consciousness-raising work among Chicanas in New Mexico. She is married to Fred Harris, a former presidential candidate, US senator from Oklahoma, and diplomatic envoy in the Obama administration. It was a impressive convocation of formidable woman power.

"Here we were on the 'River of No Return,'" Flash recalled, "cooking over an open fire, chopping wood, and singing old rock lyrics from the '60s. We made French toast, which was probably pretty terrible, but anyone who has ever been camping knows everything tastes better when it's cooked outside over an open fire.

Participants in Molly's memorable white-water rafting trip on the Middle Fork of Idaho's Salmon River in 1979 were dubbed "Salmonettes." They included: (left to right, first row) Carol Bellamy, Molly, Alice Rivlin, Ellen "Flash" Fleysher, Lynne Abraham, and Pat Cloherty; (second row) Rosanne Cahn, Marg Elliston, a *Rolling Stone* editor whose name is lost to history, Ann Crittenden, Marcia Chambers, Nancy Dowd, Betsy Weiss, and Donna Shalala.

"For the most part our foods were pretty basic—stews and one-pot meals; no red wine reductions here. We even made quesadillas. Molly jerry-rigged this contraption and hooked it up so we could haul it behind us so that when we arrived at wherever we were going to camp, there was a cool one waiting. I don't know how she did it, but I don't think we ever lost a can of beer.

"Then there was the time Molly was invited to speak to the Anchorage ACLU—which I thought was pretty funny, like, where were they meeting, in a closet? But, hey, it was a trip to Alaska."

As it turned out, the meeting was in a filled-to-capacity auditorium and Flash did join Molly—who insisted on a side trip for a little salmon fishing.

"So I say to Molly, 'And what the hell do you know about salmon fishing?' And she says, 'I know that if we catch any, the skipper will kipper, smoke, poach, grill, or freeze it in individual packages so we can take it home and feed friends.' I felt further compelled to point out that when you add up the cost of getting to Alaska, hiring a boat and crew, paying the freight for shipping it home, the price tag comes out to about five hundred dollars a pound. Molly thought about it for a minute and said, 'Sounds perfectly reasonable to me.' And off we went."

Among the names in that atomic Rolodex of Molly's were those of what she liked to call her "gal pals," women of extraordinary distinction who, to her, were buddies. This trip was memorable for several reasons, not the least of them being in the company of Fran Ulmer, former mayor of Juneau, former lieutenant governor and environmentalist and now chancellor of the University of Alaska Anchorage. Coupled with the exquisite goodness of fresh-caught salmon drizzled with a touch of melted butter and a bit of citrus, it was Molly's concept of an ideal vacation.

"For some reason, folks were always coming up with one-liners," Flash continued. "So one day we're trolling for halibut in Glacier Bay National Park. Everybody's oohing and aahing over otters and these magnificent glaciers when Molly turns to me and says, 'Ya know, if they chopped up that ice for one Texas cocktail, the only thing you'd have left up here is something the size of Ohio.'"

In yet another highlight, a fisherman was holding up an enormous king crab destined to become dinner. Flash leapt to her camera to capture the moment uniting Molly, the fisherman, and the great big crab.

"All of a sudden the goddamn crab clamps down on one of Molly's fingers and draws blood. I thought we were gonna have to shoot it. Anyway, we showed it who was boss when we ate it that night with drawn butter and lemon. Molly said she had never tasted better crab in her whole life. Sitting on the deck of that boat taking in this fabulous vista was all it took for us to make another trip."

This time Flash insisted that the two of them try fly-fishing.

"Molly took to fly-fishing like a duck to water. She even caught a salmon in midair. The instructor said he had never seen anything like it in all his years. Meanwhile I'm hooking the boat and the deck and everything but a fish. And there's Molly catching a twenty-pound salmon in midair. Unfortunately it was catch-and-release and we don't have photographs, but that's the honest-to-God truth."

From left, former Alaska lieutenant governor Fran Ulmer, Ellen "Flash" Fleysher, Molly, and an unidentified guide show off a day's catch following a 2003 trip on the Agulowak River near Bristol Bay, which has been described as one of the salmon-rich fishing jewels of southwest Alaska. In addition to hooking the guide, Molly also caught salmon. Molly was in Alaska to address the Anchorage ACLU. Photo courtesy of Fran Ulmer.

After more than three decades in the news business, Emmy Award–winning Ellen Fleysher was named Frances Wolfson Chair in Broadcast Journalism at the University of Miami, settling down after a career that had crisscrossed the globe for CBS, CNN, and NBC.

BUFFALO'S CHICKEN WINGS

Since the Anchor Bar's general manager won't share the original recipe for Buffalo chicken wings, I devised my own. Go with Frank's Hot Sauce and you won't go wrong (as much as I love Tabasco, it isn't right for this particular dish). Molly and Flash made thirty pounds. I was frazzled making five! A deep fryer is ideal, but cast-iron works just fine.

INGREDIENTS

6 pounds chicken wings
    (separated at the joints)
6 cups vegetable oil
½ cup bacon grease

½ pound salted butter
½ cup Frank's Hot Sauce (or
    more, depending on taste)
2 tablespoons cider vinegar

DIRECTIONS

Rinse chicken wings and pat them dry. Cover with a dish towel and allow them to come to room temperature.

In a large (5- to 6-quart) cast-iron Dutch oven (or a heavy-bottomed stainless-steel stockpot) heat oil and bacon grease until a deep-fat thermometer registers 385°F or a drop of water pops when you flick it in. BE CAREFUL.

Carefully lower as many wings as will comfortably fit without touching one another into the oil and fry them, stirring occasionally, until they turn golden, 5 to 8 minutes. With a slotted spoon, transfer wings to paper towels to drain. Fry the remainder in the same manner, returning oil to 385°F after each batch.

In a large skillet melt butter over moderately low heat and stir in hot sauce, vinegar, and salt. Add wings and toss to coat. Serve with blue cheese dip and celery sticks. Serves 4 as a main course, 6 as an appetizer.

★ ★ ★

BLUE CHEESE DIP

(Make this a day ahead and keep covered and refrigerated.)

INGREDIENTS

1 cup mayonnaise

½ cup plain yogurt

¾ cup blue cheese crumbles

6 celery ribs, cut into 4-inch pieces

DIRECTIONS

In a bowl whisk together mayonnaise and yogurt. Stir in blue cheese (dressing will not be smooth). Cut celery into thin sticks. Soak celery in a bowl of ice water for about 30 to 45 minutes before serving.

★ ★ ★

TEXAS MUD PIE

There is a saying in Texas: "If it's worth doing, it's worth overdoing." So if you're gonna chow down on greasy, spicy chicken wings, might as well carry on with a good old-fashioned Texas Mud Pie. It's made with Oreo cookies and Cool Whip. How wrong can that be?

INGREDIENTS

22 Oreo cookies, crushed into crumbs

8 tablespoons unsalted butter, melted

1 quart Blue Bell chocolate ice cream, softened

4 tablespoons Taster's Choice instant coffee

2 tablespoons Remy Martin (or your favorite brandy)

2 tablespoons Kahlua

2 cups Cool Whip, divided use

Smucker's Fudge Topping (this is a '50s recipe, remember?)

4 strawberries, cut in half lengthwise

DIRECTIONS

Combine crushed cookies and melted butter, press into an 8-inch pie pan, and freeze. Stir together ice cream, coffee, brandy, and Kahlua. Add 4 T. whipped topping and spoon into pie shell. Freeze until very hard. Just before serving, place jar of fudge topping in hot water for 5 minutes to soften. Spread topping over pie, working as fast as possible. Spread remaining Cool Whip over the chocolate and arrange strawberry slices on top. Serves 6 to 8.

★ ★ ★

34

Burnt Offerings

MOLLY'S FRIEND MYRA MACPHERSON swears she and Molly planned to write a book about their respective kitchen disasters, but for whatever reasons that never happened. It was to be called *Burnt Offerings*. Myra figures she's the only friend Molly ever had who had absolutely no facility for, or interest in, cooking.

"It was as though she instinctively knew that cooking was for me a foreign language," Myra said. "We had always planned to write the book with me providing the 'burnt' and Molly the 'offerings.' We ate all over the country together—Miami, Tallahassee, DC, North Carolina, Dallas, Austin, New York, Boulder, Houston, San Francisco, Los Angeles—and I'll be damned if I can remember one thing we ate. Lots of times there were people in awe of Molly and she felt responsible for being the entertainment. All I can remember is great conviviality.

"Once, recognizing the supremely bad dinner I was preparing for guests in DC, Molly snuck out to the local fine-food emporium, found the smallest, sweetest haricots verts, and returned to the kitchen to steam them and added a wonderful fresh touch to the meal. That, plus her personality, saved the dinner."

Molly told of the time she decided to make her first duck with orange sauce. She got everything down pat, except the part about (a) putting the duck in a roaster instead of a shallow baking pan, (b) reducing the oven temperature from 450°F to 375°F, and (c) not taking a catnap while the bird is roasting. Ducks have lots of fat. When the fat spills over into a 450° oven, smoke—lots and lots of smoke—follows. If duck fat smokes for too long, fire is not far behind the smoke. Fortunately Molly woke up in time to avert flames, but as she liked to say with her characteristic flair for ironic humor, "Well, so much for the notion 'where there's smoke there's fire.' There was just smoke and more smoke. I had it under control."

Marg Elliston, Molly's high school chum and fellow Salmonette, might have merited mention in *Burnt Offerings* had the book materialized. She has her own smoky story.

"I was visiting Molly in New York sometime in 1980 or '81, after our trip on the Salmon River," Marg said. "Molly planned a dinner party for me and some of our river-trip buddies, including Ellen [Fleysher]. At the time Molly was really into a book about cooking with the seasons. She planned some sort of elegant and seasonal lamb stew. My assignment was to put the stew in the oven and have it bake while Molly went to her job at the *Times*.

"Something happened with me and her oven, and the stew ended up broiling and charring instead. I was mortified, but at Molly's suggestion we went to Zabar's for replacements. That fine New York City institution of epicurean delights, on Manhattan's Upper West Side at the northwest corner of Broadway and 80th Street, boasts foods from around the world in addition to an impressive cookware collection. The trip to the store's opulent delicatessen was quite an experience for someone from the boonies of Albuquerque. The resulting banquet was wonderful, with lots of laughter, good wine, and not-quite-so-seasonal food."

And yes, it was Marg Elliston who invited Molly to the Corrales community chicken slaughter, a tradition of ambiguous provenance. Oh, please. You're only allowed to recoil in horror if you've never eaten fried chicken.

Corrales is a hamlet in New Mexico situated on the Rio Grande between Albuquerque and Rio Rancho. Anyway, the Corrales chicken slaughter, regionally referred to as the "gang pluck," almost—but not quite—made it into one of Molly's news reports during her time as chief of the *Times*'s Rocky Mountain bureau.

Editors, weary of Molly's epigrammatic insouciance, hauled her before the big guys in an attempt to rein her in, but by then both Molly and the *Times* realized the Old Grey Lady was too dull for the Ivins way with words (although a senior *New York Times* editor is said to have had a wonderful time at one of Molly's parties at which a guest emerged from Molly's bedroom after dinner, dressed as, um, a female personal care product. Okay—a dancing tampon).

Rather than leave you with an image of dead, headless chickens, I encourage you to savor this instead: when Molly celebrated Hanukkah with Marg, frying latkes was not going too well. Ivins to the rescue, passing on a recipe that had been passed on to her, which Marg now passes on to y'all, as Molly might say in one of her all-Texas, most-of-the-time moments.

A FOOLPROOF LATKE RECIPE

Marg says she's made this recipe with a few amendments based on the 5,023-foot elevation of her New Mexico home. Use Yukon Gold potatoes, well scrubbed but not peeled. (And thank you, Carl Sontheimer, for inventing the food processor!) Because of Albuquerque's altitude, she omits baking powder and flour sifting as well. For you at sea level, carry on.

INGREDIENTS

3 large potatoes
1 large onion
2 eggs
2 tablespoons flour

1 teaspoon baking powder
Kosher salt
2 cups vegetable or grapeseed oil

DIRECTIONS

Using the grater attachment of the food processor, put potatoes through in manageable sections. DO NOT RINSE. Wring out moisture using a linen kitchen towel and place potatoes in a large mixing bowl. Run onions through the grater and stir into potatoes. Stir in eggs. Sift flour and baking powder together into the mixture to make a batter. Add salt to taste.

Heat oil until it is almost smoking. One by one, carefully lower generous tablespoons of batter into the skillet, but do not crowd. Fry on both sides until golden brown and crisp. Drain on double thickness of paper towels and serve immediately. Serves 4.

★ ★ ★

<h1 style="text-align:center">35</h1>

Dinner and the Dancing Tampon

SINCE WE LIVE IN A LUDICROUSLY LITIGIOUS SOCIETY, names will be omitted here, but two sources have verified the event attended by a *New York Times* editor, hereafter known as NYTED. So since there are differing memories of which *New York Times* editor was present, I'll just skip the name and tell the story. In Texas only the story and the telling of it matter. Story first, details later. What is not at issue is that the event did indeed transpire. Time, scotch, bourbon, beer, and wine have a way of clouding details. So here's what can be agreed upon:

One evening Molly and several friends attended a dinner party for NYTED, who was doing a grand-rounds tour for his newly released book. It is not clear whether he asked Molly to make introductions for him or she offered—by that time Molly was long past holding a grudge against the *Times* for firing her. After all, she had become successful beyond her wildest dreams. Probably theirs too, but never mind.

Molly consulted Ann Richards about organizing a dinner for NYTED that would be an authentic Austin social gathering. She wanted him to meet "true" Austinites. Ann, who was still married to Dave Richards at the time, had just been elected a Travis County commissioner.

"We decided we should invite Jap Cartwright, Bud Shrake, and Mike and Sue Sharlot," Dave Richards said. "He was dean of the UT law school and she was just plain cool. They were Jewish and had grown up in New York, so we figured we'd have a nice balance."

A bit of background is called for here. Shrake, Dave Richards, and Cartwright were part of Mad Dog, a mostly male group of writers, musicians, artists, and sundry rebellious types who lived and worked in Austin in the '60s and '70s. Its unofficial anthem was Jerry Jeff Walker's interpretation of Ray Wylie Hubbard's "Up Against the Wall, Redneck Mother." Membership in this exclusive oddball organization included Willie Nelson, actors Dennis Hopper and Peter Boyle, sculptor Fletcher Boone, and Dave Richards, whose wife managed to get elected governor in spite of it all.

Mad Dog actually became an incorporated entity, with a start-up "investment" from Shrake. Mad Dog's corporate divisions included Mad Doggeral Vanity Press, the Institute for Augmented Reality, the All-Night General Store, the Mad Dog Foundation for Depressed Greyhounds, and the Freak Nursery. Cartwright and Shrake, an Austin literary lion who died in 2009, were cofounders.

Back to the dinner.

According to Dave Richards's recollection of NYTED's dinner party, Shrake and Cartwright arrived, having clearly been doing a lot of something illegal, and they were absolutely off the wall. At some point, Dave, who stands six foot three, ended up wearing a big purple Afro wig.

"Then Shrake put it on and Jap starts treating Shrake like he's Dr. J, the basketball player," Dave said. "Jap holds up a big spoon to Bud like it's a microphone and NYTED jumps in, also pretending to hold a microphone and says, 'So, Dr. J, what can I do to be like you?' and without missing a beat, Shrake says, 'Learn to jump, white boy!' NYTED was really getting into it. It was the funniest damn thing, this buttoned-down New York Times editor being part of this craziness.

"By now things are getting completely out of control, and—I can't remember who was wearing it now—but somebody emerged wearing a costume that was a giant tampon. It was an evening beyond all measure. A couple of years later, I swear, he wrote an op-ed column in the Times about how people with imagination can have a great time without spending a lot of money. He even alluded to the possibility that recreational drug use might have played a part in the success of the evening."

There were, of course, a number of more sedate Molly meals: simple, elegant, and skillfully assembled. A simple lunch of salad, a baguette, and carrot soup could be more than just satisfactory. Just ask Juli Bunting and Marie

McCaffrey. Juli formerly worked in radio news and Marie was the widow of Seattle's Walt Crowley—a Democrat activist and the cofounder of HistoryLink .org. The two women came to Austin to join the Mouton Hunt.

The provenance for this particular event resides in Kaye Northcott's well-stocked memory bank. It is a curious moniker for a gathering with even curiouser beginnings; it came into being almost forty years ago as a diversion for wives of journalists whose husbands were off gallivanting with lobbyists who wined and dined them on hunting and fishing expeditions.

Over time the gathering came to include only a handful of female reporters. Molly and Kaye were early participants as the only female Capitol reporters. As more women infiltrated the Capitol Press Corps, the group morphed into an informal gathering of women reporters who assembled at Gumbert's Ranch near Wimberley, Texas. This testosterone-free zone had no purpose other than conversation and camaraderie.

The Hunt began in the early '70s as Wives Weekend. Former huntresses still remember the weekend a husband was so overwhelmed with the burdens of child care for two whole days that he brought the kids to the retreat—and never lived it down.

Gradually the group expanded to include new young reporters around the state. One evening, conversation turned to who had done what before going off to college. It transpired that the group included a Guinness World Record hula hoop performer, a national junior twirling champion, and a former governor of Girls State.

At some point talk shifted to clothes and what participants had worn as adolescents. When Kaye, who stands barely five feet tall and weighs in at maybe 120 pounds soaking wet, said she never had a mouton coat because they didn't come in her size, reporter Jackie Calmes, now a congressional reporter for the *New York Times*, asked what a mouton was. Older retreaters were able to fill her in on the luxurious shaved sheep coats that were all the rage in the '40s and '50s.

Kaye continued: "Those of us who still had them or who could find them at garage or estate sales would wear them every year. People in the Cypress Creek Cafe in Wimberley probably muttered to each other as we ambled in, 'Who are the broads in the tatty furs?' For the most part we dined in Wimberley or just snacked on an amazing variety of unhealthy food and, of course, beer. I mainly remember Molly for her cases of beer. She never cooked anything remarkable at the Mouton Hunt. She was too busy drinking and talking."

The annual Mouton Hunt continued until women became an increasing presence in both the legislature and the media. Only on the last few retreats did the group go gourmet, when one of the members, Saralee Tiede, orchestrated a great paella supper. Appetizers featured smoked salmon that Juli brought from Seattle. In fact, it was Juli's husband, Ken Bunting, former senior editor at the *Star-Telegram*, who hired Molly to write for his publication.

Before its unfortunate demise, Molly's previous employer, the *Dallas Times Herald*, gave Molly free rein to write. One of her more memorable political characterizations focused on ultraconservative US representative James Collins (R-Dallas), who suggested that the energy crisis could be avoided if the nation didn't spend so much money on gasoline for school busing. Molly's response included a suspicion that "if his IQ slips any lower we'll have to water him twice a day." The notion that his intellectual capabilities might be found somewhere between asparagus and zinnias provoked a storm of protests from Collins supporters, one of whom plaintively asked, "Molly Ivins can't say that, can she?" It was the perfect title for a compilation of her columns, which eventually spent twenty-nine weeks on the *New York Times*'s best-seller list.

Juli remembered one particular Mouton Hunt conversation with Molly. "The wine-infused discussion had drifted into talk in which someone said Bush was likable, somewhat charming and much more approachable than the former governor, Ann Richards, whom Ivins admired and even considered a personal friend," Juli said. "Although Molly had started the discussion, the praise of Bush eventually became more effusive than she could stand and she brought it to a close by simply saying, 'He may be charming, but, ladies, it's the wrong program.'"

It was a view of Bush that didn't change during his White House years. Ken Bunting recalled Molly's unswerving commitment to tracking Bush's political career. "As his troubles grew and his popularity plummeted," Ken observed, "Ivins liked to use the president as an object lesson she would forcefully share with readers, TV viewers, and social companions. The gist was, 'You oughta listen when I tell you something about a Texas politician.'"

When the Mouton gathering ended, Juli and Marie stayed on to hang out with Molly, where they cooked together. Marie's memories of the experience remain vivid. "I couldn't have been more excited when [participation in the retreat] led to an invitation to have dinner the next night at the house of one of my all-time heroes," she said. "Shortly after we arrived, Molly went out and returned with bags and bags of groceries. She announced that we were making carrot soup and off to the kitchen we went. Much chopping, peeling, mincing, grating, and slicing were required.

"Molly pointed to a wall of cupboards and said that she had commissioned them to hold her collection of kitchen tools. For what seemed like hours, we chopped, skinned, mashed, and sliced. We told stories and laughed and laughed. So whenever Molly's name comes up in conversation, I always say, 'I'll tell you something about Molly Ivins you don't know: she was a great cook.'"

CARROT SOUP

Adapted from *The Art of Simple Food* by Alice Waters. Molly's notations on the recipe indicate she used unsalted butter, organic chicken stock, and sea salt (which should be used sparingly), and she chopped the shallots. Finally, she put the finished product through a food mill to puree before reheating and serving (you can also use a food processor as long as the soup is not too hot).

INGREDIENTS

½ stick unsalted butter
2 large shallots, chopped
2½ pounds carrots, peeled and
    sliced (about 6 cups)
1 teaspoon dried thyme
6 cups chicken or vegetable stock
Salt to taste

Crème fraîche
Chopped fresh herbes de Provence
    (a blend of a tablespoon each
    of oregano, thyme, savory,
    lavender, basil, sage, and
    rosemary) or 1 tablespoon
    dried

DIRECTIONS

In a heavy-bottomed saucepan, melt butter and sauté shallots, carrots, and thyme for about 5 minutes. Cooking the carrots with the onions for a while builds flavor. Add chicken stock, bring mixture to a boil, then lower heat and simmer until the carrots are tender, about 30 minutes. When done, season with salt to taste and puree if desired.

Serve with a dollop of crème fraîche and a sprinkling of herbes de Provence. Serves 8.

★ ★ ★

36

Biscuits, Anyone?

I HAD NEVER HEARD OF SHIRLEY CORRIHER until I became a food writer at the *Dallas Morning News*. So when she came to town and I was assigned to cover her cooking class at Sur la Table, I dutifully trundled along. I had been given a major heads-up about her "Touch of Grace" biscuits. Molly had never heard of Corriher either until I told her the surefire dinner menu of extraordinary proportions that I experienced on that assignment.

Before there was Alton Brown on TV talking food science, there was jovial Shirley Corriher making sense of the chemical and physical properties that determine why, how, and whether a particular preparation method works.

In my job covering the food beat, I was often forced to endure meeting world-class chefs and sampling their wares. It was a rotten job, but somebody had to do it. Corriher's Touch of Grace biscuits are called that for a reason.

This particular assignment demanded that I sit through the preparation and sampling of a three-course meal: green salad tossed with ramen noodles, walnuts, cauliflower, three kinds of lettuce, and shallot dressing; slow-roasted pork prepared with Worcestershire sauce, apple juice, and brown sugar; steamed broccoli with chile oil; biscuits with Chambord butter; and peach cobbler for dessert.

By the time the biscuits were served, I was perched precariously on the brink of a food orgasm. I'd like to think I didn't put it exactly that way when I called to tell Molly about the meal, but I didn't have to get graphic. As soon as I got to the part about the pork roast, she stopped me.

"Fax it," she said.

"The pork butt recipe?"

"All of it."

A day later I got a call.

"Sweetsie? Ivins." I could hear the sound of calendar pages rustling. "We're doing that dinner you sent me."

"Which one?"

"The one with the pork butt, broccoli, biscuits, and cobbler. I've parceled out each course, but we need someone to do the biscuits. Who haven't we seen lately?"

"We've never seen Angela Shelf Medearis."

"Who?"

"Angela Shelf Medearis. The Kitchen Diva. She's written a couple of cookbooks, and I interviewed her for the *News* and said the next time I was in Austin I'd give her a call."

"Okay."

A week or two after that conversation, six of us assembled. Shelia Cheaney got the simplest task because, well, cooking is not her strong suit. Anyway, preparing cherry-Chambord butter required only squishing together some butter, cream cheese, liqueur, sugar, and preserves. Since the grated orange zest was optional, this was a non-cook's slam dunk.

Molly made the salad. I had assumed responsibility for getting the slow-roasted pork show going that morning, because it needed eight hours to cook. Del Garcia steamed the broccoli and made the chile oil; Courtney Anderson, who still loves to bake, took on cobbler. Angela was on biscuit duty because they had to be done at the last minute. We even went so far as to buy Shirley's preference, White Lily Flour, a low-protein self-rising flour. Everything had to be done the way Shirley had done it, or, in my little pea brain, the meal was doomed.

There was no doomsday scenario. Everything was perfect, especially the biscuits. The dinner was the usual rowdy, ribald, hooting success. I think Angela was a little overwhelmed. I don't think it was the image of Molly she had envisioned. But her interpretation of the biscuits was spot-on. They are the most perfect, the lightest, the most heavenly biscuits ever, even better than the ones at Lucile's, a popular Colorado restaurant in Boulder and Denver—and Lucile's biscuits are killer.

Shirley Corriher alternately described the dough as "grown-up mud pies" and "Grandmother's wet mess"—primarily because unlike the dough usually associated with biscuits, it is sticky-gooey. Apparently wet dough makes more steam in a hot oven and that accounts for the lightness.

The other secret—other than cream, buttermilk, and shortening—is the methodology. The cottage cheese–like dough gets shaped with an ice cream scoop, dusted with flour, and packed into a baking pan. The flavored butter is a nice touch, but the first two or three biscuits don't need anything. You might want butter on the next two or three. When you regain consciousness you can finish the meal if you've got room for cobbler. Guests eyeing the remaining biscuits were allowed to take two home. We saved two biscuits for Hope, Molly's indefatigable housekeeper, who almost croaked when she saw the flour-dusted kitchen that awaited her the following morning.

SHIRLEY CORRIHER'S "TOUCH OF GRACE" BISCUITS

From Shirley Corriher's notes: "As a little girl, I followed my grandmother around the kitchen. . . . I used her bread bowl, her flour, her buttermilk—I did everything the same, and I shaped the biscuits just like she did. But mine always turned out a dry mealy mess. I would cry and say, 'Nannie, what did I do wrong?' She was a very busy woman with all my uncles and grandfather to feed three meals a day, but she would lean down and give me a big hug and say, 'honey, I guess you forgot to add a touch of grace.'

"It took me twenty years to figure out what my grandmother was doing that I was missing. I thought the dough had to be dry enough to shape by hand. She actually had a very wet dough. She sprinkled flour on it, pinched off a biscuit-sized piece of wet dough, and dipped it in the flour. She floured the outside of this wet dough so that she could handle it.

"This wet dough in a hot oven creates steam to puff and make feather-light biscuits. Wet dough was the big secret. Now I make biscuits almost as good as my grandmother's, and so can you, with a good wet dough and a touch of grace."

INGREDIENTS

Nonstick cooking spray
2 cups self-rising flour (preferably a low-protein flour like White Lily)
¼ cup sugar
½ teaspoon salt
4 tablespoons shortening
⅔ cup cream

1 cup buttermilk (or enough to make dough resemble cottage cheese; if you're not using a low-protein Southern flour it will take more than 1 cup)
1 cup plain (all-purpose) flour
2 tablespoons butter, melted

DIRECTIONS

Preheat oven to 425°F and arrange shelf slightly below the center. Spray an 8- or 9-inch cake pan with nonstick cooking spray.

In a large mixing bowl, stir together the self-rising flour, sugar, and salt. Work shortening in with your fingers until there are no large lumps. Gently stir in cream, then buttermilk. Stir in buttermilk until dough resembles cottage cheese. It should be a wet mess—not soup, but cottage-cheese texture.

Spread *plain* flour out on a plate or pie pan. With a medium ice cream scoop (about 2 inches) or a spoon, place three scoops of dough well apart in the flour. Sprinkle flour over each. Flour your hands. Turn a dough ball in the flour to coat. Pick it up and gently shape it into a round, shaking off the excess flour as you work. Place the biscuit in the prepared pan. Coat each dough ball and place the shaped biscuit smooshed up against its neighbor. Continue scooping and shaping until all dough is used.

Place in the oven and bake until biscuits are lightly browned, about 20 to 25 minutes. Brush with melted butter. Invert onto one plate, then back onto another. With a knife or spatula, cut quickly between biscuits to make them easy to remove. Serve immediately. Makes 12 to 14 biscuits.

★ ★ ★

FALL-APART-TENDER SLOW-ROAST PORK

This recipe from the cooking class Shirley Corriher taught in Dallas is the most outstandingly delicious hunk of pork I've ever roasted. Cooking meat slowly at a low temperature produces a tender, juicy dish. Pork butt, a less expensive cut of meat, is often avoided because of the fat and connective tissue, but here it's ideal because slow cooking dissolves both. All of the following recipes are from the cooking class handouts and are reprinted with permission. Shirley is a serious Molly fan.

INGREDIENTS

1 pork butt, 4 to 5 pounds
⅓ cup Lea & Perrins
   Worcestershire Sauce

¼ cup light brown sugar
1 cup apple juice
½ teaspoon kosher salt

DIRECTIONS

Position an oven shelf slightly below the center and preheat oven to 400°F.

Place pork in a casserole that has a lid and is just large enough to hold it. Sprinkle pork on all sides with Worcestershire sauce. Press brown sugar coating on all sides of the pork. Pour apple juice down the side to the bottom of the casserole, NOT over the crusted meat. Cover tightly.

Place in oven and reduce oven heat to 200°F. Roast without opening the oven for about 5 hours, or until the meat is so tender it pulls apart easily. If it doesn't, cover, return to the oven, and continue roasting 30 minutes more. Check again and roast 30 minutes more as needed. Depending on your oven, the roast might take 7 hours to arrive at the pull-apart stage. When it gets there, transfer it to a large platter, pull it apart, and remove the bone. Stir salt into the sauce and return meat to the casserole. Serve pork hot or cold. Serves 6 to 8.

★ ★ ★

=== 37 ===

Without Hope, All Is Lost

HOPE REYNA.

Where to start?

What to say?

Hope was probably as close to Molly as anyone—maybe closer than most. By the time Molly died, Hope had been with her for almost a quarter century. Hope was there during Nadine Eckhardt's tenure as Molly's first official assistant and through all successive ones.

Over the years Molly realized she needed help managing her schedule, which, with the success of her first book, became ridiculously demanding. Riding to her rescue was a series of steady assistants—Nadine, Liz Faulk, Betsy Moon, and Mike Smith (who in 2009, with author Bill Minutaglio, coauthored *Molly Ivins: A Rebel Life*), all of whom miraculously got Molly to the airport almost always on time. Getting Molly to the airport, or anywhere else, on time merited hazardous duty pay.

Betsy's six-year tenure was the last—and longest—unbroken stretch of Molly management and the most taxing. Keeping Molly on track, as old-timers say, was more than a notion. Betsy's responsibilities included navigating Molly's propensity for making flights just as the doors were closing; making sure Molly had the appropriate text for her multiple and varied speaking engagements, whether in or out of town; organizing breakfast, lunch, brunch, and dinner schedules; holding Molly to deadlines for syndicated and other columns she wrote for various publications; and later, managing her rigorous medical regimen. When neuropathy made it almost impossible for Molly to type, she dictated and Betsy typed. We looked on and marveled at Moon Management.

When Molly insisted on honoring a speaking engagement despite faltering stamina, it was Betsy who quietly rearranged her life to factor in as much rest as possible. When Molly became too weak to travel alone, Betsy rode shotgun. There was decreasing light at the end of the tunnel, yet Betsy continually dodged the oncoming train.

But Hope. God Almighty. Hope didn't just keep Molly's house in order; she was the Mussolini of housekeeping. She had an almost mystical ability to enter a kitchen that was in astounding disarray and, within minutes, transform it into a room suitable for making a brand-new mess.

Neither Molly nor I thought anything of having a dinner party for eight on Friday evening, a barbecue for twelve on Saturday, and late breakfast on Sunday for six or so. We had Hope. This mad round of cook-and-eat-and-cook-and-eat-and-cook-and-eat-some-more didn't always make sense, but it made as much sense as trying to make me believe a giant fish leapt up and gobbled a lure in midair.

Hope would walk into the house, look at the kitchen, look at me, heave a sigh, and work Reyna magic. I'd retreat to my room with a book until the kitchen was quiet. Molly hid from her, too. We never realized how much mess we'd made until cooking and eating were over and done with.

On her way out the door Hope would shout, "Try to keep it that way until I get home!" She lived a block away. Then she'd look toward Molly's room. "Have you lost anything you need me to find before I go?"

Hope knew when Molly would need to find keys before Molly knew they were missing. "Hopester," Molly would intone, in that voice that signaled something was not findable. That was all she had to say.

"On the kitchen counter, near where you left your coffee."

"How'd it get there?"

"You were about to order something online when the phone rang and you put the credit card down to answer the phone in the kitchen. You were in the kitchen to check the spice rack you wanted to buy as a housewarming gift for somebody. The phone rang. You put the card down."

Molly loved to shop online, and she especially loved shopping for kitchen-related exotica of any kind. Anyone who knew her also knew the perfect gift for her was something with either practical or no utilitarian value.

Scales? She baked. Reasonable.

Digital thermometer? She roasted great hunks of meat. Okay.

Cherry pitter? Okay. For the *clafouti*. Got it.

Zesters? Whisks? Graters? Peelers? Fine. But an avocado masher? Tomato holder? Shrimp deveiner? Corn stripper? Onion goggles? Electric salt and pepper mills?

The crème brûlée torch made sense; Molly actually made a lovely crème brûlée. And I must admit to getting a kick out of the egg topper—a truncated scissors-like device used for clipping off and removing the pointy end of a soft-boiled egg. I sometimes think Molly served soft-boiled eggs just so she could do the snip-'n'-spoon-the-egg thing. Of course, she had a set of small spoons for scooping out the egg—all of which struck me as some form of Houston-induced affectation, which of course, it was—but at least it was for fun.

I still think she fabricated the business about planning to buy a combination bread- and coffeemaker just to hear my tirade about what a totally dumb idea it was.

Molly loved an honest-to-goodness chili supper beer blast, but she had just as much fun with the silliness that others took seriously. Those of us who went along for the ride learned what an oyster plate (which more often doubled as a deviled-egg plate) was for, whether we liked it or not.

Once she tried to incorporate as much over-the-top stuff as she could into a single dinner party: individual salt cellars with itty-bitty sterling silver salt spoons (one of which became an itty-bitty spoon sculpture after it fell into the garbage disposal); asparagus tongs that left all but one guest completely bumfuddled (when you see these by your plate—and may you never—wait for someone else to use them, then nonchalantly follow suit); finger bowls (that no one drank from); and demitasse spoons, none of which went into the disposal and none of which were confused with dessert spoons.

More often than not, she'd start out buying some novel piece of kitchen paraphernalia for someone, but end up buying one for herself as well. Why else would she have the Dean & Deluca French *and* Italian spice collection in addition to rows of alphabetized herbs and spices sequestered in her kitchen pantry?

Hope met Molly through Shelia Cheaney. Like a lot of professional women, Shelia doesn't have the time (or, let's face it, the inclination) to work seventy to eighty hours a week, cook, and clean house. At one point, however, she was between jobs and had to reduce Hope's working hours. Hope, a single mother with four children, one of whom is disabled, needed all the income she could earn.

At the time Molly was living with Shit—the dog, not a hygienic abomination. Molly, who has never been known as anybody's domestic goddess, would later insist that "everyone needs a wife, or at least Hope."

Hope went to work for Molly when Molly was living a tiny two-story townhouse in South Austin and writing for the *Dallas Times Herald*. When it folded, Hope stayed on, first as an every-other-week housekeeper.

When Molly signed her contract for *Molly Ivins Can't Say That, Can She?*, she got enough of an advance that she could make a down payment on the bungalow in Travis Heights. "When she first looked at the house the price was too high and she wouldn't buy it," Hope said. "Then it vanished from the listings. Molly assumed it had been sold. Later, she saw it was on the market again at almost half the original price. I remember Molly saying, 'I'm gonna pack up all my stuff.' I looked at her and said, 'What stuff? You don't have anything worth moving.'

"Once the requisite papers were signed, movers were supposed to come on Monday and didn't," Hope continued. "I went back the next day and the movers didn't come again. On the third day, I called Molly, who was out of town, and said, 'They still aren't here; what am I supposed to do?'

"That's when she told me: she had bought a bunch of furniture and it was coming from Italy. It was a kinda like 'oh and by the way, the furniture's coming from Italy,' you know, like it was no big deal. Like everybody bought furniture from Italy.

"So every day for five days I went to her house and sat and waited for this leather couch and fancy cobalt blue buffet. Then for all that, when it arrived it was broken in two or three places."

It wasn't just that Hope maintained order. Until I got to know Hope, I wondered how Molly managed to produce columns for *Mother Jones* and the *Nation*, write books, travel to give speeches, and still find time for grocery shopping.

She didn't. Hope did. In time the Hopester had her own credit card to Molly-shop.

"Molly would make a list and I'd go to Central Market and tell the guy behind the counter what I needed, that it was for Molly, and he'd say, 'Oh, okay.' They knew how to pair the meal she was cooking with the right wines. All I had to do was bring it home."

Molly easily spent three times as much on food and wine as she did on clothes. But Shelia Cheaney fixed that by introducing her to Chico's. After some discussion and debate among friends, it had been determined that the wardrobe of this now-Famous Arthur wanted some sprucing up—as in no more duct tape on the underside of a tear in a favorite pair of slacks. It was okay to buy new ones. Molly accepted Chico's into her life as her wardrobe's personal savior. My friend Del Garcia—also a close friend of Molly's—and I also introduced her to Blue Fish clothing when Blue Fish still had a store in Austin. Molly's style-savvy sensibilities got kicked up another notch in New York, where she was frequently called to speak or read, sign books or just glad-hand. But it still fell to Hope to pair pants with shirts, sweaters, and such.

Molly's new style consciousness drew notice from her friend Ann Richards, prompting Molly, in one of her characteristic displays of generosity, to instruct Hope to have an identical outfit sent to Ann.

It was Hope who bore the brunt of Molly's (mercifully) momentary infatuation with all things Martha—as when Molly once again decided herbs and spices should be alphabetized. Bottles of various geometric shapes were assigned containers for kitchen soap and dishwashing detergent.

It was also Hope, when Molly insisted she could manage alone, who refused to leave her on bad nights—no small feat, given Molly's remarkable stubborn streak. And she did have a stubborn streak. She also had a real low tolerance for women who, in her opinion, let the team down. Special laser-guided brickbats flew their way. They were few and far between, but when the boom was lowered, the aim was true. For a sample, visit Molly's lengthy 1991 book review for *Mother Jones*, ripping into the "I Am the Cosmos" manifesto by controversial self-styled feminist and author Camille Paglia. Molly wrote:

> I have myself quite cheerfully been both a country-music fan and a feminist for years—if Camille Paglia is the cosmos, so am I. When some fellow feminist doesn't like my music (How could you not like "You are just another sticky wheel on the grocery cart of life"?), I have always felt free to say, in my politically correct feminist fashion, "Fuck off." . . . What we have here, fellow citizens, is a crassly egocentric, raving twit. . . . That this woman is actually taken seriously as a thinker in New York intellectual circles is a clear sign of decadence, decay, and hopeless pinheadedness.

Yes, but how do you really feel, Ms. Ivins?

This 1993 photo captures Molly in one of her infamous playful moods as she removes a, um, speck, from the nose of Darwin, the massive concrete gorilla a Waco homeowner decorates seasonally. At left is Linda Lewis, and in the center is her friend Gwen Williams. Ellen Sweets collection.

Molly visits the gravesite, in 1993, of former Baylor University president and Waco law professor Abner McCall, who gave Bob Bullock a D in ethics when Bullock was one of McCall's law students. Bullock, a powerful political figure in Democratic politics, ultimately incurred the wrath of progressives when he supported the reelection of then-governor George W. Bush. Photo by Ellen Sweets.

38

Let's Diversify This Popsicle Stand

MOLLY, HERSELF A CHARACTER IN NO SMALL MEASURE, was always surrounded by interesting and unusual people. One candidate for both categories is Waco's Linda Jann Lewis, who first met Molly in the summer of 1973. Linda had a part-time job at the state capitol and Molly was reporting for the *Observer*. Molly's reputation for having a sharp way with words was en route to being well established around the Lege, and Linda had a friend who wanted to meet this rising star. Linda had never heard of Molly.

"So we just went over to the *Observer* office and announced that we wanted to meet Molly Ivins," Linda recalled. "About that time, here comes Molly paddling down the hall, followed by her dog, Shit. We said, 'We heard you didn't write about anyone unless they're rich and famous, so we're here to tell you we're gonna be rich and famous and we're here to save you the time.'

"I know she thought we were nuts, but we ended up talking for a couple of hours. I was making a grand total of something like four hundred dollars a month. We used to call ourselves the pet rock Negroes because if we didn't show up there weren't any black folks at any of those Democratic Party rallies.

"But the *Observer* crew were talking about things I wanted to talk about; at the time we had the local NBC affiliate jacked up because we were gonna challenge their license. Then in the middle of negotiations they offered me a job. I turned them down. I said, 'This isn't about me getting a job, it's about you making commitments.' And Molly wrote about it."

Linda's spirit and quirky character endeared her to Molly, and despite her reservations about sleeping under the stars, Linda actually went camping for Molly's thirtieth birthday.

Sort of.

"We were going camping, or should I say *they* were going camping on San Gabriel River property that belonged to Dave and Ann Richards, who were married at the time. I had to explain that my idea of roughing it is a Holiday Inn with bad room service. I had a raggedy Nash Rambler with a door held together by a coat hanger. So while they pitched tents and slept on the ground, I slept in the back of the car—I tried to explain that black people don't sleep on the ground. In the end it really didn't matter because we sat up all night drinking beer and telling lies."

Linda's birthday gift to Molly was a case of Coors, which was consumed for breakfast the next day. Through a series of adventures—and misadventures— Linda wound up also endearing herself to the legendary Bob Bullock, who was state comptroller at the time and who eventually hired her. Linda hung out at Molly's house, dubbed "the chicken coop."

Even then Molly alphabetized herbs and cooked from a Junior League cookbook that belonged to her sister, Sara. When Molly moved into Travis Heights she began her dinners for widows, orphans, and strays. They started out as potlucks but morphed into annual holiday events. If you didn't have anyone to be with at Christmas, you came to Molly's.

"We'd have this big-ass meal, then her big sing-along," Linda says. "I used to tell her she was just a frustrated camp counselor. But she loved to cook for people and feed them. If anyone knew political progressives were in town, her house became the place to take them, like the time Molly called me on a Sunday morning because this editor from Australia was coming for brunch and I had to bring eggs and Bisquick and be at her house in forty-five minutes. She whipped together the most fabulous cheese grits soufflé thing. We had champagne, fresh fruit, and an egg casserole with chiles and lots of bacon. She also made a spinach salad with fruit—I think it had dried cranberries, mandarin oranges, and red onion. We were making it thirty years ago, and twenty years later it was in all the fancy restaurants."

Molly and Linda, who forged a friendship that spanned three decades, had a great time playing together. On one particularly memorable 1993 visit to "SoWaco," as Linda loved to called her hometown, Molly drove up from Austin because I drove down from Dallas on an assignment that intrigued her. A Waco family had become known for seasonally decorating the giant concrete gorilla that stood on a spacious front lawn in a very nice part of town—and certainly not a neighborhood where you'd expect to see a giant concrete gorilla in a painted-on orange and black Halloween outfit.

My assignment was to write a story about this goofy gorilla. Always one to make the best of a road trip, Molly decided that since none of us had ever visited the Dr Pepper Museum, we should do so. She got so carried away with the tour that she bought a T-shirt on the spot, ducked into the ladies' room, and changed out of what she had worn—an outfit that, unsurprisingly, no one can remember. What we do remember is that upon seeing Darwin the Gorilla, dressed in his finest black and orange Halloween glory, Molly was like a child in a toy shop.

She insisted on having her picture taken with him—but not hugging him or leaning in and displaying the toothy smile that invariably lit up her face. No, Molly opted for a photograph of her picking Darwin's nose. I am not making this up. The photograph tells the tale. And with the kind of wicked glee that one would never associate with a noted columnist, Famous Arthur, and established member of the literati, she intoned, "You can pick your friends, and you can pick your nose, but you can't pick your friends' noses. But that's not true, is it, Darwin?"

We laughed like ten-year-olds, which is roughly the age we were functioning at at the time. If only Molly's sophisticated East Coast friends could have seen her then, we giggled. Molly making gorilla booger jokes!

We also made a pilgrimage to Waco's Oakwood Cemetery because Molly wanted to visit the grave of William Cowper Brann. He was a nineteenth-century journalist, playwright, and iconoclast who in fact founded a publication called *The Iconoclast*. As the story goes, his writings incensed one reader, Tom E. Davis, enough that in 1898 the man was provoked to homicide. Irate over a Brann attack on Baylor University, Davis shot Brann in the back, and Brann, before dying, shot and killed Davis. Mind you, this was a year *after* another Brann-related shoot-out. That one involved G. B. Gerald, a county judge and Brann supporter; J. W. Harris, the pro-Baylor editor of the *Waco Times-Herald*; and his brother W. A. Harris. Both brothers died and the judge lost an arm.

And we wonder where people get the idea that Texas was part of the Wild West.

From there we traipsed around until we found the gravestone of Abner McCall. Texans would recognize his name because he was president of Baylor University from 1961 to 1981 and then became chancellor. But Molly wanted to pay her respects for another reason: when McCall was a law professor, he once gave Bob Bullock a D in ethics. Molly wanted to assure McCall's spirit that he had done the right thing. After according McCall and Brann their due, the three of us repaired to the old Elite Circle Cafe for a late-afternoon lunch of bacon cheeseburgers, fries, and Dr Pepper. From there I hit Interstate 35 north to Dallas, Molly took it south to Austin, and Linda went home.

As gorilla stories go, it was a good day.

= 39 =

Talking Turkey

MOLLY WAS ALWAYS WILLING TO EXPERIMENT with ethnic foods, so when I suggested we do a Cajun Thanksgiving, she was all for it.

As usual, the first order of business was mood-setting music, which required a search through Molly's extensive, intermittently alphabetized CD collection. Buckwheat Zydeco. Beausoleil. Wayne Toups. C. J. Chenier. The Neville Brothers—all requisite listening for a holiday meal replete with, in the finest Louisiana tradition, entirely too much food.

The meal revolved around turducken, a-boned-chicken-in-a-boned-duck-in-a-boned-turkey concoction that has remained popular ever since Paul Prudhomme popularized it in the 1980s. Each successive bird is encased in its own layer of dressing—each different from the next.

Molly insisted we should make our own. I agreed, provided she read the six-and-a-half-page set of instructions from *The Prudhomme Family Cookbook*—calling particular attention to the fact that the recipe's prologue cautions right there on page 110: "Since the turducken takes 12 to 13 hours to cook, and it needs to cool at least one hour . . ." That doesn't include the time it takes to bone the birds and assemble it—or the hours invested in making the three dressings and packing them around each bird.

Common sense prevailed and we ordered online from Louisiana. Cajungrocer.com became our new best friend.

We e-mailed plans back and forth, establishing a timetable for either making or assigning the sweet potato casserole, carrots sautéed in brown butter and shallots, oyster dressing, sautéed spinach, macaroni and cheese, baby

Brussels sprouts in Dijon cream sauce, mashed potatoes, and a salad of baby lettuces, red onion, artichoke hearts, and hearts of palm.

The frozen fifteen-pound package arrived a week before Thanksgiving, allowing plenty of time to thaw it in the fridge.

We haggled over whether to buy additional dressing or make it ourselves and finally compromised: we bought the andouille-cornbread stuffing but made the oyster dressing ourselves. Side dishes were parceled out.

Linda Lewis was part of the preparation action. "Everybody was curious about turducken; nobody had ever eaten one," she recalled. "I just remember going out on the patio to chop onions and celery because there were too many bodies in the kitchen. We did mashed potatoes with butter and sour cream, which was pretty funny because everybody was oh-so-diet-conscious until they glimpsed the spread."

Iowa farm boy Doug Zabel brought a rich, creamy macaroni and cheese. Molly was always in charge of anything involving shallots, in this instance her precious haricots verts, briefly steamed and tossed with buttered shallots. I was responsible for making gravy and the baby Brussels sprouts. This three-hour bacchanalian revel concluded with three kinds of pie—cherry, pecan, and pumpkin. Real whipped cream and vanilla ice cream were also in the mix. Those able to rise from their seats draped themselves across wingback chairs, lay supine on the couch, or spread-eagled on the floor, experiencing the consequences of debauchery worthy of second-century Romans, who, sad for them, had no mac 'n' cheese, turducken, oyster dressing, or giblet gravy.

= 40 =

Bacon Has Calories?

LOOKING BACK CALLS TO MIND so many memorable meals. Old, new, borrowed—none, mercifully, blue. One of the borrowed hits originated in a kitchen next door to the Dallas home of Betsy Julian and her husband, Ed Cloutman. Their neighbor, microbiologist Harrell Gill-King, works primarily as a forensic anthropologist. And if you don't think he's got some tales to tell, think again. Let's just say he's frequently called upon to identify the dearly departed after they've been departed for a while. Only the strong survive detailed dinner discussions of his assignments, especially if it's a dinner where red sauce and noodles are involved.

The first time I had a bacon-spaghetti casserole at his house, I thought I'd died and gone to bacon heaven. It only seemed right to bring it immediately to Molly's attention. As was often the case, her response was cryptic—she really didn't like talking on the telephone. I learned over time to keep it short and to the point. So I started by saying, "I gotta tell you about this meal I had tonight." I could hear her "make it quick" sigh at the other end until I said, "First you chop up and fry a pound of bacon, then you chop three onions and sauté them in the bacon grease. Meanwhile you grate two pounds of sharp cheddar—"

Whereupon she interrupted.

"When're you comin' down again?"

"I don't know. Whenever you're in town and feel like a bacon-spaghetti casserole."

Suddenly there is silence save for the sound of pages rustling. Molly came back on the line.

"I got a bunch of stuff to do this weekend and I'm out of town the next. How about the weekend after that? Tell me what to buy and we'll make it that night. You comin' on a Friday? Let's make it Friday night."

Once again I manufactured a reason to not return to the newsroom after Friday lunch and hit I-35 heading south. By 5:30 p.m. we were slow-frying bacon in a heavy cast-iron skillet—this is the South; we don't cook bacon in "frying pans": we fry bacon in skillets, usually of the cast-iron persuasion.

There is an art to frying bacon low and slow enough to force maximum crispness—that point at which it surrenders as much cholesterol-laden fat as possible. Achieving this state of fried-bacon perfection requires patience. We took turns removing bacon bits as each piece crisped up, leaving behind those precious drippings—no, *grease*—in which we would sauté mounds of pungent onion, chopped not too coarse, not too fine.

Meanwhile the kitchen was getting steamy from boiling water that would bring spaghetti just to the al dente state. By the time Molly grated the sharp Cheddar (none of that prepackaged stuff for us—although it's perfectly acceptable for the person who lacks time, patience, or both), it was time for the finishing touches: a 28-ounce can of San Marzano tomatoes (although any brand will do), dumped into a big bowl and cut up as much as possible, then added to the onions. At last the ingredients were ready. With flourishes worthy of Leonard Bernstein whipping a downbeat on the opening bars of Beethoven's Fifth, assembly began.

Molly would lay down a ladleful of tomatoes and smoosh them around the bottom of the casserole just enough to cover it, then add a sprinkle of black pepper. I'd scoop up a honking forkful of spaghetti and spread that around. She'd spread several spoonfuls of onion on top of that and I'd sprinkle bacon over the onions. She'd finish it off with a generous layer of cheese and a little more black pepper.

I always wished someone had been around to take a photograph of us from behind. It would show this very tall white-haired white woman assembling a casserole with this very short gray-haired black woman, both barefoot, both wearing T-shirts and matching shiny-butt black Travelers pants from Chico's.

The layering continued—tomatoes, spaghetti, onion, bacon, cheese, pepper—until the casserole topped out with the remaining cheese (warning: there's enough salt in the bacon and cheese that it's better for diners to add their own).

We popped that puppy into a preheated 350°F oven for 30 to 45 minutes, or until the cheese melted and the contents swelled and spilled over and darned near ruined the oven because we forgot to put aluminum foil or a baking sheet under the casserole. The luscious aroma of onion, bacon, and cheese was almost overwhelmed by the odor of incinerated spillover, but the flavor was fine.

We deliberately kept the number of guests to six, knowing there would be a substantial uneaten portion. There almost wasn't after folks went for seconds and we fashioned a to-go container for Elliott. The next morning we nuked casserole vestiges and topped each serving with an over-easy egg. It was one of the few times Molly sat me down and made me write out the recipe before I went home.

A 1980s photo captures Molly (second from left) and Denver friends Zeik Saidman, Betsy Cox, Alana Saidman, and Jack Cox at the Buckhorn Exchange. Founded in 1893, it holds Colorado's oldest liquor license. Photo courtesy of Zeik Saidman.

═ 41 ═

Colorado Adopts Molly

> When I try to describe Molly to others, the best way I know
> is to characterize her as the Mark Twain of our time.
>
> MAURA CLARE, *Director of Public Affairs, Council on*
> *World Affairs, Boulder, Colorado*

IN THE LATE 1970S MOLLY became the *New York Times*'s Rocky Mountain bureau chief, an assignment possibly designed to get her out of the Manhattan office, but in the best Molly Ivins tradition, she turned that to her advantage. A staunch lover of chili, she organized chili suppers at her home and entered chili cook-offs.

Zeik Saidman, associate director of The Centers at the School of Public Affairs at the University of Colorado at Denver, has his roots in the communications and organizing tradition of Saul Alinsky, generally acknowledged to be the father of community organizing—which promptly qualified Zeik as an Ivins kindred spirit. Zeik met Molly when she hosted Ernie Cortes at her Dallas home. Cortes, also an Alinsky disciple, received a MacArthur Fellowship in 1984 for his innovative work on behalf of social justice initiatives, including efforts to bring drinking water, sewers, and flood management to poor communities in South Texas. Zeik fit right in with that milieu. He was sufficiently impressed with Molly that when he needed a powerhouse keynote speaker for a fund-raiser, Molly was a natural choice.

Fast-forward to the 1990s.

"The school of public affairs had a dinner—I have no idea what was served, but John Hickenlooper, who owned Wynkoop Brewery before he went on to become Denver's mayor [and now Colorado's governor], wanted to do something special," Zeik said. "So we decided on a Texas theme and he created a special beer bottle for Molly as a favor to me. It was probably a regular twelve-ounce, but it had a label featuring a caricature of Molly in the center, with a wraparound that said, 'Molly Ivins Can't Drink This, Can She?' a takeoff of the success of her book by a similar name. Then, on the bottom it said, 'What *ales* this lady?' There were about two hundred people and they all got to take a bottle home. I still have mine. Of course everyone was dressed in jeans and boots and Molly came waltzing in in a fancy ball gown. It was hilarious."

It was Molly's mix of fearless wit and razor-sharp intellect that combined to make her way with words so dynamic. It especially endeared her to the Conference on World Affairs (CWA), held annually on the campus of the University of Colorado in Boulder.

Molly held a handful of organizations near and dear. One, as we all by now know, was the *Texas Observer*. Another was the American Civil Liberties Union. But the third was CWA, a festival of ideas not unlike Aspen's annual convocation of critical thinkers—except that Boulder's is free at 5,430 feet, and 2,700 feet closer to sea level.

Each April more than one hundred participants representing an eclectic range of backgrounds gather in Boulder for what the *New York Times* once characterized as a "week-long extravaganza of discussion and debate" with more than two hundred panels, plenaries, and performances. Conference participants discuss issues on an impromptu basis—a refreshing alternative to the high-priced gatherings of academia and the business world. Davos it ain't.

Past participants have included author Studs Terkel, poet Andrei Codrescu, '60s radical Bernardine Dohrn, architect Buckminster Fuller, film critic Roger Ebert, Israeli diplomat Abba Eban, photographer Annie Leibovitz, Secretary of State Henry Kissinger, Pulitzer Prize–winning economist Paul Krugman, First Lady Eleanor Roosevelt, publisher I. F. Stone, former Black Panther Huey Newton, artist Louise Nevelson, news commentator Rachel Maddow, and—well, you get the picture.

Roger Ebert, who participated in the CWA for almost forty consecutive years, once characterized the five-day event as "the Conference on Everything Conceivable."

Every other year one person was an assured presence: Molly. She first learned of the campuswide event during her Colorado tour of duty. She wrote about the conference, having already buddied up to founder Howard Higman, himself a character of no small note. He liked Molly's spunk and admired her writing skills. She was just the kind of spirited iconoclast the conference welcomed. There was a hitch, however; residents of Colorado can participate in the conference only peripherally, as moderators or volunteers. But when Molly left the *Times*, returned to Texas, and was no longer covering it, she became immediately eligible for full-fledged participation. She was an instant hit.

For almost twenty-five years she drew standing-room-only audiences who flocked to hear her compelling stories and informed commentary. She loved meet-and-greets with students; she took as much time as she could with

Molly harvests raspberries for breakfast from the prolific backyard vines of Michael and Tracy Ehlers of Boulder, Colorado. Molly was their guest for several convocations of the annual Conference on World Affairs at the University of Colorado.

anyone who wanted to talk to her, especially young people. She once characterized CWA offerings as a "whole new way of looking at old questions . . . that can transform the way you look at everything else."

Every year Jane Butcher, a moving force behind *Mother Jones* magazine and CWA's success, hosts a blowout party for participants and their guests.

Envision a room crowded with people from all over the world—documentary filmmaker Alice Elliott chatting with Laurent Guérin, a photojournalist from Taos; Simon Hoggart, Parliamentary correspondent for the *Guardian* of London, sharing a point of view with Washington, DC–based Jurek Martin, a columnist for London's *Financial Times*; an ebullient Kenneth David Kaunda, former president of Zambia, chatting with a circle of admirers; and former Pentagon analyst-turned-pacifist Daniel Ellsberg (who released the Pentagon Papers) talking to Pulitzer Prize winner Richard Aregood, former editorial page editor of the *Newark Star-Ledger*.

Several participants had a remembrance or two revolving around Molly and food, especially Aregood, who, while not quite a foie-gras-and-truffle aficionado, would pal around with Molly for food from another dimension.

"Molly must have intuited that I wasn't exactly a haute cuisine type," he said. "That led to an Ivins profundity that I've always relied on. One night at Threadgill's, she insisted that I have a chicken-fried steak. I demurred until she changed my mind with impeccable Ivins logic: 'If you do it now, you don't have to ever eat another one.' That's exactly how it worked out, and it's a great mantra to use whenever you have to do something about which you're dubious. She and I and the poodle would drive for an hour or more in the pickup for barbecue, another of my passions, ending up at a place I've long since forgotten the name of, with barbecue so wondrous it turned the butcher paper underneath translucent and me somewhere beyond transcendent."

Fellow Texans participated in CWA as well: author, commentator, humorist, and political progressive Jim Hightower; Michael Stoff, author and a distinguished associate professor of history at UT; author Lou Dubose; and—whaddya know—Elliott Naishtat.

One year I moderated a media panel, a welcome task that was accompanied by an invitation to the post-conference party, hosted by ardent supporters Jane and Charlie Butcher. After Charlie died in 2004 Jane soldiered on, although there was some concern that his death might cause this annual celebratory evening to be deferred. But no. The conversations, music, and dancing were back the following year—albeit tinged with a touch of melancholy.

The centerpiece for the annual spread featured an absolutely killer baked salmon, huge fillets that dominated each side of a seven-foot-long dining table. It had a richness of flavor derived from a luscious blend of white wine, fresh thyme, basil, tarragon, rosemary, shallots, celery leaves, and lemon. Accompaniments for this luxe offering featured curried peas, as well as noodles tossed with sour cream, blue cheese, butter, parsley, onion, and garlic. The spread was the embodiment of elegant simplicity. It seemed rude not to have seconds. You hoped no one saw you return for thirds. After all, volunteers had been planning this food for weeks in advance. It wasn't right not to eat it. It was one of Molly's favorite meals. Jane says the planning committee tried to change the party's menu over the years, but to no avail. Small wonder.

In rummaging through Molly's random recipe collection—that series of folders labeled "Soups," "Salads," "Meat," "Fish," "Appetizers," and "Desserts," I stumbled on a handwritten note from Jane with recipes for that CWA dinner—sent at Molly's request. So even if you don't live in Boulder and you're never asked to moderate a CWA panel, host a family, address a plenary, or serve on a committee, you can still have your own if-I-had-been-there-this-is-what-I-would-have-eaten meal, thanks to Jane's generosity and Molly's insatiable appreciation for good food.

CURRIED PEAS

The truly amazing thing about this dish is you'd never suspect that the featured ingredient is canned.

INGREDIENTS

2 cans Le Sieur peas, drained (what a shock!)
1 4-ounce can sliced water chestnuts
1 tomato, chopped

½ red onion, chopped fine
½ cup mayonnaise
1 teaspoon curry powder (or to taste)

DIRECTIONS

Gently combine ingredients with a wooden spoon or a silicon spatula. Chill for 45 minutes. Serve at room temperature. Serves 4 to 6.

★ ★ ★

WHOLE SALMON BAKED IN FOIL

INGREDIENTS

¾ cup dry white wine
¼ teaspoon dried thyme leaves
8 fresh basil leaves or ½ teaspoon
　dried
3 sprigs fresh tarragon or ¼
　teaspoon dried
2 sprigs rosemary or ¼ teaspoon
　dried
1 cup celery leaves
3 minced shallots or 1 small onion

7-pound salmon fillet (have the
　fishmonger clean and remove
　pin bones; just remember,
　some are likely to remain
　despite his/her best efforts)
2 slices lemon (with peel)
Parsley sprigs, cherry tomatoes,
　and additional lemon slices for
　garnish

DIRECTIONS

In a saucepan, combine wine, thyme, basil, tarragon, rosemary, celery leaves, and shallots or onion. Simmer on low for about 30 minutes. *Do not boil.*

Preheat oven to 350°F.

Place fish lengthwise on a sheet of foil in a baking dish. Pour wine mixture over fish and place lemon slices on top. Place second sheet of foil on top of fish and tightly crimp foil sides together. Bake for 1½ to 2 hours. Remove from oven and allow the fish to come to room temperature. Slide fish onto a serving platter or board and garnish with parsley, cherry tomatoes, and extra lemon slices. Serves 6.

★ ★ ★

BAKED NOODLES

8 ounces wide egg noodles
1 small clove garlic, crushed
1 cup sour cream
½ cup blue cheese

¼ cup melted butter
¼ cup chopped parsley
¼ cup minced onion
3 eggs, beaten

Prepare noodles according to instructions and drain well.

Preheat oven to 350°F.

Combine garlic, sour cream, blue cheese, butter, parsley, minced onion, and eggs. Gently fold in noodles.

Transfer noodle mixture to a 1½-quart casserole and bake for 30 minutes. Serves 6 to 8.

★ ★ ★

In 2006, not quite a year before she died, Molly insisted on taking a trip on the Colorado River through the Grand Canyon. Between stops during the ten-day journey, she found moments to relax and regroup. Photo courtesy of Sandy Richards.

=== 42 ===

Où Est Mon Sein?

MOLLY ATTENDED HER LAST CWA CONFERENCE IN 2005.

As she became increasingly frail she nonetheless remained determined to do as many of the things she had been deferring for when she had more time as she could—and, of course, to do them on her terms.

She could be remarkably intransigent once she resolved to do—or not do—something. Two trips in particular loomed large. She very much wanted to return to France. The other wish was to take a ten-day Colorado River rafting trip through the Grand Canyon.

A little more than a year after 9/11 Molly went back to Paris for Thanksgiving. It was her position that 2002 was the safest time to travel. It broke my heart to decline her invitation to join her and friends from New York, Austin, and New Orleans, but by then my ninety-seven-year-old mother's health was steadily deteriorating and I could not be away.

The Thanksgiving crew was joined by Nicole Concordet, Molly's godchild and daughter of Molly's former classmate Susan. Susan married French architect Jean Concordet and has remained in France for more than twenty-five years. She couldn't participate in the party because she had to tend to Jean, who was dying of cancer.

Molly was once again in the city she so loved. On this trip she regaled the assembled crew with what has to be one of the funniest post-mastectomy stories ever. In it she described her 2001 quest to buy a prosthetic breast, since the only one she had was in her luggage, which had failed to arrive with her (a note: always take a change of underwear in your carry-on, even if it has to get stuffed in the bottom of a big purse).

She had me peeing my pants laughing when she recounted her efforts to buy a replacement for her prosthesis. At first she decided to just do without until her luggage arrived, but Susan assured her that in France no one would understand a woman whose breasts weren't properly balanced and insisted that she buy a replacement forthwith.

Susan located a store where this particular item could be found and Molly set out. But her familiarity with the language had not kept pace with the evolution of vernacular French, and the clerk, completely misunderstanding her needs, presented a padded bra. Not quite. Molly tried again, stumbling for the words, gesturing, pointing dramatically at her flat chest, thereby creating an "aha" moment for the slightly frazzled saleswoman, who rushed back to the storeroom and returned with nipples and a baby bottle. By now both were just about wired for sound.

At last Molly summoned up something that sounded enough like "reconstruction *anatomique; prothèse*" to drive her message home. "Eh bien," the clerk said with a smile. And several francs later, off Molly went with her new breast-in-a-bra. Of course by the time she returned to the Ile St.-Louis flat where she was staying, her luggage had arrived.

= **43** =

The Beginning of the End

IT IS SAID THAT IF YOU PAY ATTENTION you can learn from your children. Since I had only one, I learned to listen perhaps more carefully than others. As a result, I'm incredibly indebted to my daughter and chief cheerleader, who wept with me and thousands of others as they learned of Molly's way-too-early god-awful death.

The news took me back to the weekend I visited in 1999. Molly had been fighting what she diagnosed as a rotten sinus infection, but it was clear from a wickedly relentless cough that whatever was plaguing her had gone to her chest. I suspected a really bad case of bronchitis.

Unable to get her to see a doctor, Hope Reyna made a stealth call. I was living in Dallas at the time. Hope suggested that I do one of my spontaneous weekend drop-ins and try to persuade Molly to stop treating herself. She was a heavy smoker, and there was no way that cough was doing her lungs any good.

The problem: as those who knew her realize, Molly didn't do anything unless she wanted to. Nagging could never work, and she would have been royally pissed had she sensed a conspiracy brewing behind her back. As a charter member of the nothing-ventured-nothing-gained society, I hopped in my little Nissan and made the three-and-a-half-hour drive south to the People's Republic of Austin.

When I arrived she sat slumped at one end of the leather sofa in her living room, shades uncharacteristically drawn, room darkened. The coughing was awful. She looked up long enough to say I should have called first, something she'd never suggested before, and that she didn't want anyone in the house, that she just wanted to be alone—also something that in all the years we had known one another she had never said to me.

Employing the time-honored technique of 20/20 hindsight, I suspect she knew she had something serious but didn't want the doctor to confirm her suspicions. So I went to Malcolm Greenstein's house, dropped my bag, and headed for the grocery store to buy ingredients for chicken soup.

Surely *my* chicken soup would help her turn the corner.

Surely.

While shopping I also bought a mess of those two-cup microwavable plastic containers, the better to freeze manageable portions. That way she'd have a bit available until whenever whatever she had was vanquished.

But there was no casting out this demon.

When she finally saw a physician, the news was as bad as it gets: a highly aggressive stage 3 inflammatory carcinoma of the left breast. After the initial diagnosis, there followed the appropriate gnashing of teeth, cursing the gods, shedding of tears, and hoping for the best. Although a number of engagements had to be canceled, Molly, being Molly, endured surgery and treatment and steered her life back to relative normalcy within a year, eventually returning to writing, traveling, and speaking. We thought she'd wrestled that booger into submission.

So we thought. But damned if it didn't return in 2003. And because she figured she was a better judge of her limitations than her doctors were, she decided to go fishing. Fishing led to swimming. Swimming led to torn stitches and an infection around her implants, thereby requiring more surgery to, at her instruction, remove them altogether.

Mol had already opted to, as she so delicately put it, "lop off the other tit" to maintain better equilibrium. "Who wants to be lopsided?" she asked in a moment of rhetorical whimsy. "Not me. Make that 'not I.' I'm a Published Arthur. I should know grammar better."

The third recurrence, in 2005, was anything but a charm. It took two years to take her out, though, and she went fighting to the end, finally dispensing altogether with the very expensive wig occasionally worn at curiously odd angles.

In the end, Molly got both wishes. She saw Paris one last time and she did the Colorado River Grand Canyon tour in 2006. For that grand event she gathered friends of long standing, many of whom had shared river adventures with

On her last river run on the Colorado River, Molly relaxed in late-afternoon shade while others explored their stopping point. Photo courtesy of Sandy Richards.

her for twenty-five years—from five-day floats on the Rio Grande to lesser sojourns on the San Gabriel. These were not just river floats; they were historical reviews as well.

Participants would make a point of identifying the place near where Cortés landed in the sixteenth century and began his conquest of Mexico, or where Pancho Villa made his last raid into the United States. River rats could regale you with unanticipated adventures—like the night the camp was awakened by a herd of wild burros thundering through, near enough to the campsite to get everyone's undivided attention.

If only Molly were here now, she could tell the story of how she, highly accomplished at the oars, once volunteered to take Frank Cooksey, Austin's mayor at the time, on a canoe ride through the Barton Creek watershed to make the point that the watershed was worth preserving. The water was unusually high and in an unfortunate miscalculation, a low-hanging branch promptly knocked the mayor unconscious.

She could tell you about far-flung adventures through Santa Elena Canyon, where you could decamp and watch a full moon rise over the canyon's sheer walls, with only the sounds of rushing water, coyote howls, and tops popping off longnecks to disrupt the quiet.

I couldn't afford the Grand Canyon trip—the only camping expedition I really wanted to go on. I knew it would be Molly's last. She knew it too. There was much concern over her even considering such a strenuous adventure. Her health had become increasingly fragile.

Once again, I was asked if I thought I could dissuade her. No way, I insisted. It meant too much to her. I figured if they had a Make-A-Wish program for children, adults should be able to create their own. This was Molly's Make-A-Wish river trip.

Votes among her friends were all over the place. Some said yes, some said no. Molly's rejoinder was, "What's it gonna do, kill me?"

Here's how Dave Richards remembers it.

"I got a call from Molly. She had been in the hospital around the first of the year. We had talked off and on about doing a trip through the Grand Canyon—in fact, she had previously applied for and received a permit to raft it. She'd bought about eight cases of beer and eight quarts of brandy, but for some reason never pulled it off.

"Anyway, she was determined to make it this time. She called Fran Ulmer, who had been on another rafting trip with her, and some other folks and Sandy and me. When she said, 'If I'm still alive, will you promise to go?' I said, 'Of course.' I saw Molly shortly after that conversation and began to debate whether it was realistic for us to plan this trip.

"Sandy had the good sense to contact Brady Coleman [Austin lawyer-turned-actor-and-musician], and he readily agreed to be Molly's chaperone. They flew out to Flagstaff [Arizona] together. But by the time it got close we had huge misgivings about whether it was doable."

Despite the misgivings, friends who understood the importance to Molly came. Dave and Sandy Richards, who were living in Mill Valley, California, by then, were among those determined to convert Molly's wish to reality. Others were longtime friends and fellow campers, like Brady, who had made many of these trips in Molly's company. For this last grand run on the Colorado the entire group included some who didn't know Molly at all. Bill Council and Fran Ulmer joined the group from Alaska.

All flew into Flagstaff, where the rafting leaders picked them up and drove them to the river's entry point. There she was, finally, aboard a raft that comfortably accommodated three crew members and twelve passengers.

Just packing and unpacking all that gear was an achievement unto itself, as Dave Richards recalls. The crew's leader was photographer David Huff, who put himself through college running the river and figured he'd done it maybe a hundred times. Unsurprisingly, he remembers Molly well.

"I knew there were some concerns about her because of her health, but she did great," he said. "In fact, I used that trip as an example of how group attitude can influence the enjoyment people can get out of a trip like that. She never complained—but neither did any of the people with her. I remember thinking, 'Wow, we never had anyone complain on that whole trip, and the one person who had the right to complain never did.' She didn't want help, but if she did, it was there for her. I mean, for healthy people who camp a lot, it's a hardship, so I was very impressed with her. She seemed to bring joy to the other passengers."

Although Molly mainly hung out at the river's edge while others went on hikes, she also helped out in the kitchen, chopping ingredients and telling stories about her early years as a reporter. True to Molly form, she organized a sing-along and talent show. As sick as she was, she still had the energy to invigorate others.

For all that, getting her in and out of the raft was a major undertaking, but, typically, she insisted on doing everything on her own. As Dave Richards put it, "We for damn sure weren't going to let anything happen to her, not on our watch. For the most part it was pretty quiet water except for a few places like Rattlesnake Rapids. Molly, being Molly, insisted on sitting up front, where you take the brunt of the shocks when you hit the rapids. You really have to hold on. Well, Molly lost her grip and went airborne. Somehow she came down partially straddling the boat. I got hold of her and we're still in the middle of the goddamn rapids. Brady held on to one leg and I held on to her until we got to calm water. I think that chastened her for the time being, but it sure as hell scared the shit out of me."

Hearing Dave recount Molly's apparent energy surge resurrected memories of a benefit concert for the Dallas Black Dance Theater that Ella Fitzgerald did just months before she died. As this jazz icon walked onstage, murmurs stuttered through the audience. She looked frighteningly fragile. I'm sure I wasn't the only one who wondered how on earth she was going to make it through a performance, scatting and running those trills for which she was so famous. A chair had been placed on the stage for her. She sat down after coming onstage, and stayed seated for maybe one and a half songs, and then she stood. Once the downbeat was struck she opened with familiar numbers from the Cole Porter songbook that she'd made famous.

She sang another song. Then another. She rose from the chair and moved across the stage in little steps. And as she sang, the frail, bespectacled septuagenarian magically morphed into someone twenty years younger. This was the kind of transformation Dave's wife, Sandy, recalls.

"Molly seemed to get stronger as we went along," she said. "In the end it was the right thing to do and she was a wonderful companion. Much of the trip was hiking trails, so either Dave or I stayed with her while others went on walks. We talked, and of course we sang. We were ten days on the river, and at the end Molly insisted on taking everyone to dinner. I was so glad she had made the trip and enjoyed it so much, I don't remember anything anybody ate. I just remember that there were some people on the trip that we didn't know and by the time we parted company Molly had them all singing along."

To me that trip was a sign of acceptance. The cancer had metastasized. Still, Molly's sense of humor rarely flagged. Betsy Moon remembers that around this time Molly was determined to make brownies and several kinds of Christmas cookies for her neighbors. She was sufficiently pleased with the outcome that she ate them all—and instead sent notes to her neighbors, confessing her transgression and nevertheless wishing them a Very Happy Holiday.

For several years Molly had sent an e-mail to friends and fans at the end of the year. Christmas 2006 was no exception, just about a month before she died. I couldn't attend her last tree-trimming party and Elvis sing-along because at the time, my mother was also dying, in St. Louis. In her last holiday missive Molly wrote:

> Dearly Beloveds,
>
> Two zero zero seven and I'm stayin' alive, and that's the main thing. The doctors continue to find new ways to torture me. I'm in pretty weak shape now but planning to get better. A round of physical therapy may help me get my strength back. I've certainly kept up my weight. For that I owe a considerable debt and countless pounds to Blue Bell Cookies and Cream and a better-than-average appetite.

Being an invalid means you can almost always have your way when it comes to daily desires. That's why I invited almost 50 people to help trim my Christmas tree in early December.

For Christmas I hauled out many cookbooks and made a menu with Sara Speights, her son, Dylin Howze, and Marilyn Schultz. This included Marilyn's prime rib and Yorkshire pudding; Sara's ginger-carrot soup; Kaye Northcott's potatoes with heavy cream and gruyere; Courtney Anderson's spinach with artichoke caps; and my sister-in-law Carla's unsurpassed pecan pie. In addition to the above there were my sister Sara, brother Andy, niece Darby and nephew Drew on hand—a lovely seated dinner for twelve.

That might not seen like a whup until you understand that my stove was on the blink and couldn't be fixed in time because all of NASA's engineers were otherwise occupied for the holiday.

Lo, came the miracle of Alta Vista Avenue. Ovens to the left of me, ovens across the street, as well as their owners, opened their doors to the elves. Andy said he liked carting things from house to house. It put him in the holiday spirit.

I visited some and rested some as the preparers prepared. It was lovely hearing the bustle of my friends and family getting a great meal together. My only regret is that I couldn't smell the prime rib as it roasted across the street.

Meanwhile I've taken up a new sport—shooting BBs from my lounge chair at the squirrels trying to rob the bird feeders in my back yard.

So now it's the new year and I want to give each and every one of you a hug and wishes for more good news on the political front. May the Ds avoid making bigger fools of themselves than the Rs, which seems like a doable task.

From your as yet unsinkable Molly.

It is that Christmas that nephew Drew remembers best. Molly would have been as proud of him as his sister, Darby. He makes his home in Chile, where he works with an educational program jointly operated by the US State Department and the Chilean government. It helps Chilean graduate students earn a master's degree. He's also in sync with Molly pals who knew her food side. He spent many holiday meals with her and was an appreciative recipient of meals during his time as a Tulane undergrad.

He remembers many a meal around her table, as well as breakfasts and brunches at Austin restaurants large and small; the lunch in his honor when he graduated from Tulane and Molly took the family to Commander's Palace. Still, his favorite memory of eating with her was that last Christmas when the oven went south.

"It was a scramble all day long," he said. "She sat comfortably in her big chair loving all the commotion swirling around her. After the food was prepared, everybody had a great time around the table talking with Molly and hearing her famous laugh."

There was almost always too much food and drink at these Christmas shindigs, and the party wasn't over until those assembled participated in "The Twelve Days of Christmas." I say "participated" because one not only sang, one acted out each of the lords a-leaping, maids a-milking, and swans a-swimming. Of course, by the time singing commenced, the only thing everyone could remember for sure was a robust intonation of ". . . two turtledoves, and a partridge in a pear tree!"

By then the spirit of these Christmas shindigs took hold with such a vengeance that some had lords milking, pipers swimming, swans dancing, and two turtledoves wearing five gold rings with that ever-loving partridge in the damned pear tree. Fractured singing and much laughter signaled the party's end.

The usual stalwarts were there, as well as friends who knew this would be her last. Anthony Zurcher, Molly's editor at Creators Syndicate, was among them. "I had been a fan for years," he said, "so it was a kind of dream come true to be working for the same syndicate. Her editor left and she was handed off to me; I took her quite eagerly. That Christmas I could see she was failing, but she soldiered on. It seemed so strange, saying good-bye, knowing it was for good."

OUTRAGEOUS BROWNIES

In her introduction to this recipe, author Ina Garten says: "Inspiration for this recipe came from the Chocolate Glob I recipe in the *Charcuterie Cookbook,* published by William Morrow in 1983. In its heyday the SoHo Charcuterie was the cutting edge of New York restaurants. The giant confection was a blob of chocolate dough filled with chocolate chips and nuts. I thought I could make a brownie using almost the same formula. They've been flying out the door ever since!"

The recipe comes from Garten's award-winning *Barefoot Contessa Cookbook.* The brownies can be baked up to a week in advance, wrapped in plastic, and refrigerated. Molly made them from scratch, so you can either go for the mix now available in a box or go Molly's route and crack out the ingredients and get to work.

INGREDIENTS

1 pound unsalted butter

1 pound *plus* 12 ounces semisweet chocolate chips

6 ounces unsweetened chocolate

6 extra-large eggs

3 tablespoons instant coffee granules

2 tablespoons pure vanilla extract

2¼ cups sugar

1¼ cups all-purpose flour, divided use

1 tablespoon baking powder

1 teaspoon salt

3 cups chopped walnuts

DIRECTIONS

Preheat oven to 350°F.

Butter and flour a 12 × 18 × 1-inch baking sheet.

Melt together butter, 1 pound of chocolate chips, and unsweetened chocolate in a medium bowl over simmering water. Allow to cool slightly. In a large bowl, stir (do not beat) together eggs, coffee granules, vanilla, and sugar. Stir warm chocolate mixture into the egg mixture and allow to cool to room temperature.

In a medium bowl, sift together 1 cup of flour, the baking powder, and the salt. Add to the cooled chocolate mixture. Toss the walnuts and the remaining 12 ounces of chocolate chips in a medium bowl with ¼ cup flour, then add them to the chocolate batter (flouring the chips and walnuts keeps them from sinking to the bottom). Pour onto the baking sheet.

Bake for 20 minutes, then rap the baking sheet against the oven shelf to force the air to escape from between the pan and the brownie dough. Bake for about 15 minutes more, until a toothpick comes out clean. Do not overbake! Allow to cool thoroughly, refrigerate, and cut into 20 large squares. Makes 20 large brownies.

★ ★ ★

$=44=$

Adieu and Adios

THE YEARS 2006 AND 2007 WERE TWO I'D JUST AS SOON FORGET,
although I will always remember Molly's laugh. Three months before Molly
died, my mother died. Shuttling between Denver and Austin and Denver and
St. Louis had brought me as close to certifiable as I ever need to be.

It had been two years since Molly's worst diagnosis. Her friend Ann Richards, another authentic spitfire and the first woman to be elected governor in
her own right, had died in 2006. I hate that I never talked with Ann about meals
she had shared with Molly. When we last encountered one another in Austin,
we engaged in the kind of chitchat that people do when they're at a huge dinner
with too many people and too much noise. Few knew that Ann was dying too.
I didn't. But then, I didn't know I'd ever write about cooking with Molly beyond
the brief tribute I wrote for the *Texas Observer*.

I last saw Eden Lipson at a small dinner party in New York several years before cancer claimed her in 2009. Eden, Molly's "New York Mom," cooked with
her, fed her, hauled her off to smart shops for good clothes, and nurtured her
spirit even when it became apparent that Molly was not quite right for the Old
Grey Lady.

I never met the writer John Henry Faulk, Molly's truest hero, although I did
get to know his widow, Liz. And by the time I knew there was a food connec-
tion between Molly and Bud Shrake, he too had died.

Molly and I shared one of those long, lingering Mexican meals at Manuel's
in Austin with R. W. "Johnny" Apple, a friend from Molly's tenure at the *Times*.
After a few gossipy exchanges, they reminisced at some length about good and

bad meals taken in various restaurants in various cities around the world, but he too died in 2006—again, way before a Molly book was a probability.

Former Texas secretary of state, comptroller, and lieutenant governor Bob Bullock was also gone, and with him went a treasure trove of Molly-based meals-around-the-campfire tales.

(Bob Bullock tales abound, not the least of which is almost everyone's favorite; it is the kind of story Texans like to tell, so I'll repeat it here because it not only appears in *Bob Bullock: God Bless Texas*, by political writer Dave McNeely and journalist and author Jim Henderson, but it surfaced again in a column by *Austin American-Statesman* columnist John Kelso, following Bullock's death.

It concerns the time Bullock got kicked out of the house by one of his several wives during a heated, bourbon-fueled domestic dispute. He somehow managed to drive to his friend Carlton Carl's house. Getting no response after knocking on the door, he crawled into the back of what he thought was his friend's car to sleep it off.

The next morning, our erstwhile public servant woke up in the backseat of the car as it headed up Interstate 35. The driver thought he was alone. Bullock sat up and scared the bejeebers out of the poor man by cheerfully announcing, "Hi, there. I'm Bob Bullock, your secretary of state.")

I know Molly prepared *saumon en papillote* for Judge William Wayne Justice, another of her heroes. There was more than a little irony in his surname. He is credited with reconfiguring the landscape of civil rights law by handing down some of the largest institutional reform decisions in the country, affecting juvenile justice, prisons, education for the children of undocumented workers, and the right of men with long hair to attend college. Yes, this took a federal court decision. Those decisions, invariably in support of plaintiffs least able to defend themselves, earned him death threats and the undying appreciation of those who believed in, well, justice. He was on my list of people to interview, but that was not to be. He died in 2009.

As I rooted through Molly's archived material, a variation on an old bromide kept rattling around in my head. It says, "If I'd known I was going to live this long, I'd have taken better care of myself." My version: "If I'd known I was going to write a book about Ellen/Molly cooking adventures, I'd have talked to people sooner. I'd have kept notes as meticulously as she did." Some time ago someone said, "We know Molly got a lot of enjoyment out of your visits; but what did you get from her?" I had never asked myself that.

I certainly paid more attention to politics, going beyond just reading up on candidates on election eve; I learned that invective laced with humor is less likely to lead to an upset stomach; I had never read Howard Zinn, but I once spent a lovely evening with Studs Terkel, whom I had admired for many years. Molly loved that I met him at a dinner party in Chicago where, believe it or not, the main course was seafood and sausage gumbo.

Gumbo lore aside, I now have a dog-eared copy of *A People's History of the United States*, by Zinn, who died in 2010. I write letters to my representatives in Washington. I'm not afraid to criticize even Democrats when I think they're screwing up. I write to corporations who abdicate their corporate responsibilities to the consumers who make their cushy lives possible. I rail against entities like BP and Exxon. Got a petition castigating them? Gimme. I remember a favorite Molly quote that she used to define populism. It's from long-gone Texas senator Ralph Yarborough: "Populism is putting the jam on the lower shelf so everyone can reach it."

Over the years Molly and I forged a relationship that was more like a sisterhood. I'd always wanted a sister, but got two brothers. I love them both, but it's not the same. Molly and I shared details about our lives. We talked about men we'd, ahem, known, those we wished we had, and those we wished we hadn't. I also learned to employ the phrase "Bless his/her heart" properly.

We shared confidences I could never bring myself to write about. It's not that she ever asked that anything *not* be repeated; she didn't have to. At some point you gotta engage a personal braking mechanism when it comes to revealing a friend's private conversations. Bringing people together on a regular basis creates a bond, and as that bond grows stronger, trust levels evolve. You only invite into your home those you care about, and you only cook for those you love. Time and again, friends cited the way Molly used food to bring people together.

And what better way to commemorate that assessment than to share a cookbook for all seasons. Many of the same cookbooks that lined Molly's shelves also sat on shelves wherever I happened to land. So for my sixtieth birthday she gave me a copy of something I surely lacked: *In the Kitchen with the Chippendales*, 100-plus pages of recipes illustrated by a multiculti collection of photographs that almost have something to do with food but nothing, I assure you, to do with antiques.

The recipe for Chick on a Bed of Roses (chicken breast with rose petal mole) ain't half bad, nor is the one for Saffron Potatoes. I'm not as interested as I once was in such recipes as the one for Orange Orbit edible body paint—concentrated orange juice mixed with vanilla pudding—but I've bookmarked it just in case.

On the other hand, I do cherish the chef's jacket and toque she brought me from the Cordon Bleu after she took classes there. I had no idea she thought my head was that big. Despite my best efforts to wear the toque properly, it kept sliding down, and down, and down—until my face was completely obscured. She thought that was hilarious. When I saw the snapshots I understood why.

I think our friendship, built in large measure on a mutual love of food, also had a foundation in our respective family lives. In their book *Molly Ivins: A Rebel Life*, Austin authors Bill Minutaglio and W. Michael Smith chronicled her reaction to growing up in a wealthy white Houston suburb where people with her background, access, and opportunities were expected to cleave to the haute bourgeois milieu that nurtured them. I was rebellious even though the jam was within my reach too. This was not a good thing for either a middle-class white female growing up in the 1950s or for a middle-class black girl either.

Case in point: Somewhere in or around 1956 I dove off the high board at a swimming pool in the (then) *really* white St. Louis suburb of Webster Groves. As I climbed out of the pool, very pleased with my near-perfect entry, life-guards were closing the pool. Apparently they hadn't noticed me before. I was later told they drained the pool altogether after I left.

It was the same year Frank Blache and I made *Time* magazine for having the unmitigated gall to try to eat at Adcock's, a Jefferson City cafeteria. We were returning from an Episcopal youth camp in southern Missouri. By the time we got to the state capital we were a busload of ravenous teens. Frank and I were the only blacks on the bus. When we were refused service we opted to take our food to go. All of the others did the same, and we sat on the curb in front of the restaurant to eat. When a photographer asked us why we were there, we told him. Next thing we knew, we were enshrined in *Time*. Shortly after the issue came out, the owners of Adcock's saw the future and quietly desegregated its facilities. It was destroyed by fire in 1970. I had nothing to do with it.

Molly once asked me, over a mountain of peach cobbler and vanilla ice cream, why I didn't hate white people, why I wasn't angry—something I also asked myself. The only answer I could come up with was that investing energy in hate is nonproductive. In the end it serves no meaningful purpose other than to corrode whatever vestiges of decency reside within the hater. When I get angry, I write letters. And mail them. Just ask US senator John Cornyn. He had the temerity to think he represents me. By now he knows he doesn't.

The misbegotten behavior of bigots eats away at them even as they fail to recognize the corrosion. Better to invest energy in trying to change the conditions that give rise to such bitterness. Better to sit down and eat together, whenever, wherever, possible.

Another of my favorite movie scenes, after *The Princess Bride* and *Casablanca*, occurs in *The Blind Side*, the movie based on Michael Lewis's beautifully crafted book. It's about a conservative white family's improbable decision to adopt a black teen. In the movie there's a scene where Sandra Bullock's character, the mother, is having lunch with friends. They chide her for her decision. She could have laughed along with their thinly veiled racist barbs, but she didn't. She excused herself, let them know she was done with them and their so-called friendship, and left stunned companions in her wake.

There's a reason power lunches and dinners exist. Discussions over food change the tenor, if not the gravitas, of conversation. The dynamics shift. Food is the foundation on which diners can build a form of communion that has nothing to do with religion.

At this point I'm prepared to let the next generation pick up where mine leaves off and hope they can make it work better than we have.

For all of the gustatory marvels we assembled in the Ivins kitchen, Molly always returned to three favorites: gumbo, that artery-clogging bacon-onion-spaghetti-cheese casserole, and the chicken soup I made when I thought she had bronchitis. On my last Austin visit, a month before she died, I made the soup again. I delivered enough, I thought, to get her through a couple of lunches. Being Molly, she insisted on sharing it with Hope Reyna, Del Garcia, and me, and we promptly consumed it all.

It's a simple soup, made with homemade stock and grated vegetables. It's nourishing, easy to swallow, and easy to digest. I had made it several times during Molly's valiant fight against that demon disease. This time, it would be our last shared meal.

I had promised to make it again when I returned for my birthday in early February. We laughed as she reminded me that I would probably cook it myself as I had done for past birthday parties ostensibly in my honor. This time I knew there would be a difference: she wouldn't be sous chef.

Del Garcia, Hope Reyna, Molly, and I sat in the kitchen that late December day and reminisced about the *Texas Observer* party that had been dedicated to Molly a few weeks earlier. We even managed to extract laughter from that seemingly endless stream of Bush administration bloopers. As weak as she was, she could rattle off names and transgressions—US Representative Tom DeLay's indictment for money laundering; the federal grand jury indictment of Bush fund-raiser Thomas Noe, also for money laundering; Attorney General Alberto Gonzales's knuckleheaded approval of torture at Guantánamo and his less-than-candid testimony before a Congressional committee. Still, for all our levity, I sensed an undisguised air of resignation.

At that moment, Del, who has spent many years working with epidemiological issues around the world and who knew more than she wanted to about the ravages of end-stage cancer, commended Mol on her ability to maintain such good cheer under such chickenshit circumstances. Without missing a beat, Molly replied, "Fuck cheerful. I've sworn off cheer. Cheer is highly overrated."

With that, she threw back her bald head and laughed as hard as her weakened lungs would allow. We laughed with her, fighting back tears. Molly's rejoinder called to mind a wonderful Linda Ellerbee quote: "I have always felt that laughter in the face of reality is probably the finest sound there is and will last until the day when the game is called on account of darkness."

For sure.

Almost everyone I interviewed had an anecdote recalling Molly's sense of humor, a gift that remained throughout her battle with that hateful cancer. One friend, communications consultant Larry Norwood, tells of visiting Molly during one of her end-stage hospitalizations. An adverse reaction to a new medication had provoked a hideous, painful result. As she struggled to find a comfortable position, she looked into Norwood's eyes, smiled, and said, "God, I wish Dick Cheney had these hives."

Although Molly had difficulty swallowing, her love of ice cream was undiminished, and therein lies one of Hightower's more memorable Molly meals, if it can be called that, since it didn't really involve cooking. At some point during her final hospitalization, he got a very late night call. At the other end of the line was a very bored Molly, demanding that he bring ice cream. Right Now.

So he did what Molly friends were ever willing to do: he got out of bed, got dressed, grabbed two spoons, bought the requested ice cream, and headed for St. David's Hospital.

"We stayed up for much of the night in her hospital room, each of us with a spoon, eating ice cream out of the same tub, talking about everything, and solving the world's problems," he recalled. "I don't remember the specific topics, but I do remember the tone, which was very personal and very touching. She knew by then that she would not survive, and I got the impression that she was determined to not waste a minute of her remaining time—she wanted to talk and discuss and listen—and eat a ton of ice cream. The nursing staff was not pleased."

I wasn't there when Molly was discharged to hospice care at her much-loved house in Travis Heights. It became increasingly difficult for her to eat, and food, which had been so important to her for so long, became less and less appealing. Still, friends continued to bring items that might coax her to eat. Johnny Guffey was among them. He brought mashed potatoes, a Molly favorite. Later, Courtney Anderson told Johnny that when Molly learned the mashed potatoes were from Jeffrey's her eyes lit up and she smiled. By then she was so sick it was difficult for her to swallow.

Flash came from Florida. Marg Elliston came from New Mexico. She, like Molly, had a considerable cookbook collection and was a serious Julia Child fan. Molly, Marg, and their friend Marcia Carter had celebrated their sixtieth birthdays together. They dined on the Trio terrace at the Four Seasons Hotel and watched thousands of Mexican free-tailed bats make their nightly exodus from beneath the Congress Avenue Bridge.

"During my Austin visits, I patrolled the kitchen, which was the hub of the house," Elliston said. "Molly had a wonderful array of pots and pans and every gadget you could imagine. I learned about lemon zesters in her kitchen. I was also amazed at her spice collection, not just because of its extent and variety but because the bottles and jars were neatly arrayed on shelves in alphabetical order! Molly assured me that the spice arrangement was not so much indicative of an orderly mind but more of a writer looking for the next inspiration."

The birthday-sharing duo returned to Austin a few days before Molly died to make chili and soup for friends and relatives who were sure to come.

"Marcia and I took up stations in the kitchen, preparing food that could hold, food that the many family and friends who were supporting Molly in her last days could eat without having to think about it," Elliston continued. "From our post in the kitchen, we could also provide advice and support to the various groups who were monitoring phones, trying to make Molly as comfortable as possible and figuring out how in the world to say good-bye."

Recalling that time, when Molly's remaining days were truly dwindling down to a precious few, Jim Hightower took a deep breath and sighed. "It was not too long before she died. Writer Anne Lamotte came from San Francisco; Molly's brother, Andy, Shelia Cheaney, and Betsy Moon were there, too. I had offered my house for Christmas dinner, but Molly said no. There was a Cowboys game on and Molly was feeling okay—not great, but okay. Andy and Betsy Moon did most of the preparation. As we were about to go to the table, she leaned over, touched my arm, and said, 'This has been one helluva ride.'

"We sat down to this huge pasta salad with about nineteen ingredients—well, maybe not that many, but it was a hearty salad. We went on to tell stories from our various trips. The conversation, as always was engaging, entertaining. It was like so many other evenings of shared conversation. It was strange to think that we wouldn't have those conversations again."

Molly couldn't join in the eating, but there was a sense that she was aware of the gathering of friends. The end came late on the afternoon of January 31. Lou Dubose reached me at the *Post* just as I completed edits on a cover piece for the following week's food section. Those closest to her were there—her brother, Andy; his wife, Carla; Courtney Anderson; Sara Speights; Kaye Northcott; Hope Reyna; and Shelia Cheaney. Del Garcia arrived a short time later and helped Hope prepare Molly for transport to the place where, in accordance with her wishes, she was cremated.

Mercedes Peña, herself a cancer survivor, had shepherded Molly through much of her battle with cancer and still finds it impossible to talk about Molly's death. By the time Molly died, Mercy—which is what we all call her—had been wrangling Molly's illness concurrent with that of her longtime partner, Ed Wendler, who died in 2004. Moreover, Mercy has waged a thirty-five-year struggle with her younger son's congenital anomalies. Doctors had said he wouldn't live to be twelve.

In the Philadelphia production of *Red Hot Patriot*, Mercy was one of only three people other than family named in the play—Kaye Northcott, Carlton Carl, and Mercedes. Mercy was credited with persuading Molly to access her emotions, an experience that Molly found thoroughly unenjoyable. She even wrote about the "getting-in-touch" experience for *Time* magazine's February 18, 2002, issue. That too was part of the play. In a column titled "Who Needs Breasts Anyway?" Molly wrote:

I tend to treat my emotions like unpleasant relatives—a long-distance call once or twice or year is more than enough. If I got in touch with them, they might come to stay. My friend Mercedes Peña made me get in touch with my emotions just before I had a breast cut off. Just as I suspected, they were awful. "How do you Latinas do this—all the time be in touch with your emotions?" I asked her. "That's why we take siestas," she replied.

I arrived on my birthday as planned and stayed with Malcolm and Stan. Molly's memorial service, held at the nine-hundred-seat First United Methodist Church in downtown Austin, was standing room only. People came from throughout Texas. The Popes came from New Orleans; Myra MacPherson came from Washington, DC. Eulogies generated tears and laughter. At Carla's request, I read a message of condolence that Nicole Concordet, Molly's goddaughter, sent from France. Linda Lewis cracked wise as only she can, recalling her one birthday "camping" expedition with Molly. Courtney Anderson openly acknowledged her battle with alcohol and praised Molly for her courage in the same war. But it was Marcia Ball who brought home Molly's fiery spirit with her thunderous rendition of a Molly favorite, Jerry Lee Lewis's "Great Balls of Fire." It was not what Marcia originally envisioned.

"I arrived at the church prepared to play something appropriately sedate, not overly religious, but not maudlin," she said. "Then word came down from somebody in authority, I don't even remember who it was, but they said that ["Great Balls of Fire"] was what they wanted."

And that was what they got. With sadness now indelibly hitched to that energetic recessional, the congregation was linked in spirit to the extinguished flame that burned so brightly in Mary Tyler Ivins.

Following the memorial service, Andy and Carla invited selected friends to choose a personal memento from among Molly's belongings. Hannah couldn't come to Texas, so Andy suggested I take something for her, necessitating a quick call to her in Colorado. She asked for the battered copper saucepan, the one she had used to show Molly how to repair a beurre blanc. It now hangs in Hannah's little Aspen kitchen and is periodically removed when she needs to make a butter sauce or heat a bowl of soup. (She refuses to own a microwave.)

I took a small Oaxacan wooden armadillo that, for as long as I can remember, gathered dust on the fireplace mantel of Molly's office, and the Pier 1 salad bowl over which we had many a spirited exchange. I always made too much salad, she said. And you make too little, I said. Too much salad dressing, she said. Too little, I said. Black people are fat because they eat too much, she said. White folks eat *before* they attend dinner parties so they don't leave hungry, I said.

"Sweetsie," she'd say, "anyone ever tell you you're fulla shit?"

"It's 'cause I eat so well," I'd reply.

I miss our juvenile, utterly tasteless exchanges. People who didn't know her would have been appalled at some of the things we said to one another, just as some were shocked at her appearance in *Dildo Diaries*. For those unaware, it was a documentary based on the Texas House of Representatives debate on the illegality of anal sex—or as she defined it, "the law that made it illegal for a prick to touch an asshole." That, she said, made it illegal for half the House to shake hands with one another.

On more than one occasion she let slip one inappropriate comment too many at the dinner table, shocking a guest or two. Detailing the occasion really doesn't matter, but be warned: when tempted to use the word "nigger" in the presence of an Afro-American you don't know, bite your tongue.

And, as Kurt Vonnegut once wrote, so it goes.

One of Molly's frequent interjections was "le plus ça change, plus c'est la meme chose"—the more things change, the more they remain the same.

Since her death a lot has changed.

As she predicted, Barack Obama did get elected president. She chastised me for being an early Edwards supporter; there was something slippery about him, she insisted. 'Nuf said on that score.

The menus at Polvo's are now laminated and the prices have gone up.

Jackie Gaer, a long-haired wisp of a woman, is a Molly fan who bought and renovated her Travis Heights house but took great pains to retain its essence—including a love of cooking good food. "So you think Molly would like it?" Jackie asked earnestly. "Yes," I said, with true honesty. "I think she'd love it."

Local pols continue to amuse—a couple of years ago Governor Rick Perry won a successful bid for publicity by having someone leak the news that he, Governor Goodhair, while jogging, had shot and killed a coyote that threatened his daughter's dog. The weapon of choice was a laser-sighted .385 Ruger with hollow-point bullets—surely something most governors carry on a run. Of course, no one else ever saw the coyote, none of his security people were with him, and no one seems to know what happened to the decedent, but the alleged incident made the *Washington Post*, CNN, Fox News, the *New York Daily News*, and most important of all, all the local papers—a point not lost on voters as the photogenic guv eased up on an election year.

Oh, did I omit the part about the running path being on the property of his 6,300-square-foot rental house (estimated cost: $10,000 monthly) while the governor's mansion—damaged by a yet-to-be-solved episode of arson—underwent repairs? This from the guy who redirected stimulus money from the unemployed to balance the state budget; he who calls for overstretched state agencies to sacrifice.

If only Molly were here to direct some of her formidable energy Perryward, as she did in her response to Florence King, the conservative writer who accused her of plagiarism. Molly publicly acknowledged fault and apologized. But for some reason King couldn't let it go, insisting that Molly never apologized to *her*. So Molly sent a personal letter of apology that concluded with: ". . . boy, you really are a mean bitch, aren't you? Sincerely, Molly Ivins, plagiarist."

How I miss that voice.

As self-deprecating as she could be, as scathing as her commentary could get, she was also plagued by demons. She never resolved her adversarial relationship with her father, yet when he visited she was gracious. Her mother, charming and generally proud of Molly's achievements, never quite understood how Molly could be nominated for a Pulitzer Prize three times and not win one. That inability to grasp what an achievement it was to be so honored saddened Molly. Yet none of this, at least in my mind, detracted from her love of both parents.

For years Molly belabored the notion that she should have been able to do something to prevent her nephew's death. She struggled with considerable psychic pain. It would be a disservice to paint her as larger in death than she was in life, especially since her legacy is sufficiently remarkable and enduring in and of itself. In the end she was human. A truly remarkable writer, but human all the same.

I wrestled with how best to address her eighteen-month victory over drinking, but she was proud of it, so it must be mentioned. As private a person as she was in many ways, I think she would not have wanted me to ignore her final triumph over a battle with alcoholism that she fought most of her life. One Friday evening, about a year before she died, Molly announced that she was turning in at a reasonable hour; she had to be up early for her Saturday morning AA meeting. As she headed to her room, she turned back and said, "You wanna go?"

I felt honored. If I could cook with her, get prescriptions filled, and accompany her to chemo, I could also accompany her to fight another insidious disease. Humanizing her flaws doesn't diminish her legacy. It is yet another measure of what she could do once she committed to a cause. She finally allowed her cause to be herself.

Mercy's admonitions took.

Molly acknowledged her human, vulnerable side. For so many years she fed and nurtured others. In those waning months she understood the importance of nurturing herself. She fought a valiant battle, but once it became personally apparent that even well-fought battles can be lost, she made a decision to die on her terms. As she quietly said in a rare and uncharacteristically confessional moment, "I made the decision that I don't want people to remember me as a drunk."

I said I never thought of her as one; that after her talent and celebrity were stripped away she was, after all, another one of us who, on many an occasion, failed to heed the yellow light that signals caution. And I say shame on anyone who can't understand the toll taken by the pressure she put on herself—not to mention the pressure that comes with formidable talent tethered to celebrity. Had I, like Molly, refused to permanently move away from one of the meanest states in the Union, I'm not sure I wouldn't have sought solace in something beyond green tea and limonadas myself.

The drinking and smoking that unquestionably had a deleterious effect on her health didn't diminish one whit the power with which she wrote about toxic waste, political chicanery, children's rights, bigotry, class prejudice, and corporate greed. In the end she still had a few more things to do. So she conquered smoking. She defeated alcoholism. She had been sober for eighteen months when she died. "Either people will understand or they won't," she said. All I could do was nod and smile.

She will always loom large for me, but as a whole person, not as an idealized luminary. No, as I've said before, I'm sticking with that Native American notion that cherished spirits remain just long enough to guide the living through the pain of loss.

In reflecting on the seed of an idea Bonnie and Gary Moore planted at that 2007 Book Festival, I've concluded that Molly has remained just long enough for that notion to take root. I'll still feel her presence over my shoulder when I make gumbo, insisting that it's okay to include okra *and* file powder. I'll see her smile as I write to yet another congressional bonehead or rail about some new corporate nincompoopery. I'll especially remember her when I forget the grocery list, or snatch up items that were never on it in the first place.

Epilogue

GENTLE CHICKEN SOUP

I've been making this for so long I can't remember where I got the recipe, or who gave it to me, or to what extent I improvised, and added or deleted ingredients. I do know the original called for a stewing hen, but I opted instead for chicken feet, backs, and necks for the best stock. If you're loath to handle chicken feet, use whatever bits and pieces you want, but know that feet, backs, and necks produce a natural gelatin thickening agent and yield the richest flavor. I call this my "gentle chicken soup" because it goes down so smoothly. I don't peel the potatoes because their skins are rich in fiber, vitamins, and other nutrients. The vegetables cook up soft and the flavors are pure. If you have a food processor with a grating disk, making this soup is a breeze. Like most soups, it's best if made the day before it's to be eaten.

INGREDIENTS

2 pounds chicken feet
3 chicken backs
1 pound chicken necks
1 bay leaf
1 tablespoon celery seed
1 teaspoon garlic powder, organic
   preferred
1 tablespoon kosher/sea salt
4 quarts water

1 split chicken breast, bone in
2 large potatoes, scrubbed
3 carrots
2 celery stalks, strings removed
1 large yellow onion
1 teaspoon turmeric
1 cup fresh parsley, chopped fine
   (or ½ cup dried)

DIRECTIONS NEXT PAGE

In a double layer of cheesecloth, securely tie together chicken feet, backs, and necks in a purse-like configuration.

Place cheesecloth bag in a heavy 6-quart stockpot and add bay leaf, celery seed, garlic powder, and salt. Cover with water and bring to a slow boil, then reduce to a simmer for 4 hours. Remove chicken breast from the refrigerator and allow it to come to room temperature.

Add chicken breast to pot and simmer for another 20 minutes. Remove chicken to a colander inside a large bowl to cool. Pour liquid that drains from the cheesecloth sack back into the pot. When chicken is cool enough, pick meat from backs and breast, tear it into small pieces, and place it in a bowl. Cover and refrigerate.

When stock is cool enough, refrigerate for several hours, or at least long enough for fat to solidify. Spoon off most of the fat and slowly warm the stock over a low flame.

While the stock is warming, run potatoes, carrots, celery, and onion through the grating disk of a food processor (or grate them with a hand-held grater, on the side with the biggest holes). Add vegetables to the stock, bring to a boil, then lower heat and simmer, covered, for 30 minutes. Stir in turmeric and parsley, correct seasonings, and serve. Serves 6 to 8.

Photo Album

Kaye Northcott, Sara Speights, and Molly kick up their heels in the New Mexico kitchen of Sara Maley, Molly's sister. Photo by Sandy Richards, courtesy of Kaye Northcott.

At some point in the early 1970s, Molly (third from left) and friends Kaye Northcott, Mike Tolleson, Robert Heard, and his wife decided to have a lesson in bull insemination. Ivins family collection.

Left to right: Linda Anderson, Courtney Anderson, and Molly at Molly's fortieth birthday celebration in 1984.

Shown here in a 1990s photo taken during one of many river-running campouts shared with Dave and Sandy Richards, Molly whips up a pot of stew, nattily attired in her standard oversized shirt, jeans, and boots. Photo courtesy of Sandy Richards.

When Kaye Northcott left the *Texas Observer* in 1994 to become an editor at the *Fort Worth Star-Telegram*, Molly donned a full-tilt boogie tux for her role as mistress of ceremonies. Photo courtesy of Kaye Northcott.

Christmas 1998. Left to right: Linda Lewis,
her son Scott, Shelia Cheaney, and Molly.

This 1998 photograph captures Molly (center) and friends about
to embark on a field trip to Fort Worth to see an exhibit of French
Impressionists at the Kimbell Art Museum. They were leaving
from the house Janet Dewey and her husband, Bob Ozer, owned in
northwest Austin. Prepared to board their rented van were (from
left) Janet, Bob, Austin attorney Malcolm Greenstein, Molly, Texas
state representative Elliott Naishtat, Austin artist Mercedes Peña,
political activist Ed Wendler, and Del Garcia, who is internationally
recognized for her work on behalf of populations with high rates
of infectious diseases. Photo courtesy of Mercedes Peña.

On the porch of Linda Lewis's home in 2003, with
Daryl Slusher, his wife, Adela, and daughter Olivia.

Molly and me at my sixtieth
birthday celebration in 2001.

Index of Recipes

General Index

Page numbers in *italics* indicate photographs.